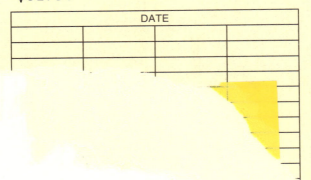

... and the
religion of nature.

$32.50

DATE			

Thomas Paine and the Religion of Nature

Thomas Paine and the Religion of Nature

Jack Fruchtman, Jr.

The Johns Hopkins University Press

BALTIMORE AND LONDON

The Johns Hopkins University Press
2715 North Charles Street
Baltimore, Maryland 21218-4319
The Johns Hopkins University Press Ltd., London

Library of Congress Cataloging-in-Publication Data

Fruchtman, Jack.
Thomas Paine and the religion of nature / Jack Fruchtman, Jr.
        p.   cm.
Includes bibliographical references and index.
ISBN 0-8018-4571-8 (alk. paper)
1. Paine, Thomas, 1737–1809—Views on nature. 2. Nature. I. Title.
JC177.A4F74   1993
320.5′1′092—dc20   92-40586

A catalog record for this book is available from the British Library

To JoAnn, with love and affection

CONTENTS

Preface   ix

1. Introduction: Language, Homiletics, and Audience   1

PART ONE. Nature

2. Natural Man and Common Sense   19

3. Nature and Man's Democratic Calling   38

4. Nature and the Theory of Rights   57

PART TWO. Action

5. The Civil Rights of Man   77

6. National Unity, Revolution, and the Debt   100

PART THREE. Progress

7. Economic Democracy   121

8. Constitutional Invention   139

9. The Vision of the Future   156

10. Conclusion   172

Notes   177
Bibliography   199
Index   209

PREFACE

Thomas Paine defended the most radical ideas of his age, employing a style which, like that of an ardent preacher, formed a stream of secular sermons intended to propagate the faith of democratic republicanism. Powerfully homiletic, this style was never rooted in any particular religious doctrine. It developed as Paine confronted a series of challenges, beginning with personal failures during his first thirty-seven years in England and extending across his career as a tribune for the American and French revolutionary movements.

He was implacable in striving to assert the rightness of his cause. Even toward the end of his life, when faced with severe criticism that he had deserted his original principles, the man who scorned the summer soldier and sunshine patriot excluded doubt from his realm of vision. His disciples, he declared at the age of sixty-nine, will "follow my example in doing good to mankind, [and] they will pass the confines of this world with a happy mind, while the hope of the hypocrite shall perish and delusion sink into despair." From the publication of *Common Sense* onward, his goal remained the same: "to rescue man from tyranny and false systems and false principles of government, and enable him to be free, and establish government for himself."[1]

This study considers Thomas Paine as an eighteenth-century secular preacher in the long tradition of preaching, which is at least as old as the ancient Hebrew prophets. No earth bound religious authority ever officially ordained those prophets, who, like Amos and Hosea, instructed their people on what they should do to save themselves and their nation. These preacher-prophets were certain they had received a divine ordination to speak truth to their people. Jeremiah put it succinctly:

And the Lord put forth His hand, and touched my mouth; and the
Lord said unto me:
> "Behold, I have put My words in thy mouth;
> See, I have this day set thee over the nations and over the
> kingdoms,
> To root out and to pull down,
> And to destroy and to overthrow;
> To build, and to plant." (Jer. 1:9–10)

Like these preacher forebears, Paine communicated to his people the truth
as he saw it developing in the last three decades of the century. His interests
were the same as theirs, namely "to root out and to pull down, and to destroy
and to overthrow" evil tyranny where he saw it and "to build and to plant" the
new seeds of liberty and democracy wherever possible.

In its early modern expression, the tradition of prophet-preaching is
rooted in what Edmund S. Morgan has characterized as the "visible saints"
of seventeenth-century England and America.[2] Church reformers associated
with various sects first attacked the rigidity and liturgy of the Church of
England, then carried their criticism to the political and social problems of
their time. In England, this movement in part contributed to the Puritan
Revolution and the outbreak of civil war in the seventeenth century. The
Puritan preachers whom Perry Miller eloquently described carried on this
tradition in America in the next century.[3] The mantle was later carried by
professional preachers like Ezra Stiles and Jonathan Mayhew, who helped
develop the political or, perhaps more accurately, "civil religion" of American
society.[4] Thomas Paine, though never ordained nor indeed particularly well
educated formally, stepped into this tradition with writing that was, as we
shall see throughout this study, profoundly religious in content and homiletic
in style. At the time of the American Revolution, he articulated the deepest
feelings and longings that Americans shared about their relationship not
only with Britain but with God and freedom. In the words of historian
Winthrop S. Hudson, "It was not only the clergy who interpreted the American Revolution as a cause of God in defense of civil and religious freedom.
Almost every patriot spoke in these terms."[5]

For John F. Berens, the same was true for the French Revolution, when
"a tremendous volume of partisan providential rhetoric" poured from the
pens of writers astounded by the great events in France.[6] This study will
demonstrate that Thomas Paine was one of the most effective writers to use
the tradition of preaching in a homiletic style of writing to convince his
audiences of the righteousness of the cause of liberty and freedom. Through
his powerful style with its rich images and metaphors and his use of the

homiletic tradition with its commanding tone of the preacher, Paine helped transform John Winthrop's religious city on a hill to the secular, republican enterprise of freedom and democracy and thus became one of the most influential writers of his time.

Thomas Paine was certain that he was the keeper of political truth and certain of what was in the best interest of his flock. This certitude permeated his writings. He wrote in *Rights of Man* that he had no small task to undertake for the good of all people. He devoted his life "to conciliate mankind, to render their condition happy, to unite nations that have hitherto been enemies, and to extirpate the horrid practice of war, and break the chains of slavery and oppression."[7] This language was no mere rhetorical flourish. He was positive that he was empowered to bring harmony to the world and unite the nations, to end war and slavery alike. He would do it through his sermons, in the form of preaching on paper, drawing attention to the problems that people could solve if they followed his prescriptions.

Like Jeremiah, he had been ordained by God, he thought, to sound the alarm to awaken people to the many social and political evils threatening them. He cared little for the established beliefs and institutions of his day. He attacked them all. Even less did he heed the consequences of verbally assaulting the institutions he so hated.[8]

One institution, the Church—especially its mythology, biblical scripture—blinded men to the true nature of the world. In matters of religion, his object was "to bring man to a right reason that God has given him; to impress on him the great principles of divine morality, justice, mercy, and a benevolent disposition to all men and to all creatures; and to excite in him a spirit of trust, confidence and consolation in his creator, unshackled by the fable and fiction of books, by whatever invented name they may be called." If he accomplished these tasks, he would have achieved his life's work. "I am happy in the continual contemplation of what I have done, and I thank God that he gave me talents for the purpose and fortitude to do it."[9] These sentiments are a distillation of everything Paine thought he wanted to achieve as a secular preacher.

The present study is designed to elucidate these themes in Paine's remarkable career. The primary objectives here are to contribute to an understanding of Paine's thought, particularly its religious character, and more generally of the politics of the late eighteenth century. Although several descriptions of Paine's thought and many biographies of his life have appeared over the past half century, none have analyzed his social and political thought from the perspective that he was a secular preacher who used a homiletic style to express his message that human destiny was to move forward into the modern age of the democratic republic.

Thomas Paine was not a political or social philosopher, nor did he intend to be. His writings were often disjointed and marred by sarcasm and contradictions. He was a highly iconoclastic thinker whose intellect ranged over every area of politics and society. Paine's approach to each issue was the same: he wanted people to improve their condition for their short time on earth. Nothing was as sacred as the pursuit of truth. In his mission to eradicate the falsehoods, superstitions, and myths that enslaved people, Paine targeted the institutions that for him embodied unfairness, inequity, or evil. He attacked everything that he thought promoted the denial of people's God-given nature.

Paine was a product of his time as much as he was a herald of modernity. His language was often embellished with eighteenth-century flourishes. At other times, he spoke in a vocabulary with a leaner, twentieth-century sound. Like many writers of his era, he consistently used the term man to refer to people or humankind in general. In an eighteenth-century context, the term could easily refer only to persons of the male gender. Paine's usage, however, was almost always universal, including both women and men. If, then, in the course of this study, reference is made to man, it is within Paine's historical and ideological context. His goal was to return all people, men and women alike, to their true selves.

In writing this book, I have drawn encouragement and endorsement from a number of colleagues and associates whom I would like to thank. While I am deeply indebted to each of them, the defects and shortcomings of the study are, of course, my own. Many of my ideas were first critically examined at various conferences, in particular at meetings of the American Society for Eighteenth-Century Studies and the Southern Political Science Association. I want to thank particularly Professors Michael Allen Gillespie of Duke University, Michael Lienesch and William Cody of the University of North Carolina, Alfonso J. Damico of the University of Florida, and James R. Stoner, Jr., of Louisiana State University.

In addition, discussions at the Folger Institute Seminar for the History of British Political Thought conducted in the spring of 1987 by Professor J.G.A. Pocock were invaluable for me. I benefited not only from Professor Pocock's insightful comments but from those offered by Professors Jack R. Pole of Oxford University, Gordon Schochet of Rutgers University, Vincent Carretta and R. K. Webb of the University of Maryland, Anthony La Vopa of North Carolina State University, Robert Ginsberg of Penn State University, and Rhys Isaac. I would also like to thank Professors Benjamin Barber and Wilson Carey McWilliams of Rutgers and Isaac Kramnick of Cornell University for their penetrating understanding of the eighteenth century and

Henry Y. K. Tom, executive editor of the Johns Hopkins University Press, for his generous support of this project. I especially appreciate the superb and sympathetic work of my manuscript editor at the Press, Terry Schutz, who straightaway understood the nature of this study.

Stephens Broening, a master of prose style, was always an invaluable, accessible critic and a splendid inspiration. Ann Stiller was helpful in far too many ways to list here. Finally, my colleagues at Towson State University, especially our interdisciplinary eighteenth-century discussion group, the Redoubtable Dons, led by Professor H. George Hahn, II, offered a unique opportunity to try out new concepts in the lovely, congenial setting of Auburn House.

Parts of chapter 2 first appeared as "Nature and Revolution in Paine's *Common Sense,*" *History of Political Thought* 10 (Autumn 1989): 421–38 and parts of chapter 9 first appeared as "The Revolutionary Millennialism of Thomas Paine," in *Studies in Eighteenth-Century Culture* 13, edited by O. M. Brack (Madison: University of Wisconsin Press, 1984). For the former, I would particularly like to thank Professor Iain Hampsher-Monk of the University of Essex for his keen insights and suggestions.

Finally, to my wife, JoAnn, who understands me better than anyone, I dedicate this volume with all my love and affection.

Thomas Paine
and the Religion
of Nature

❧ I ❧

Introduction: Language, Homiletics, and Audience

Vilified by his contemporaries as an atheist, Thomas Paine, one of the most advanced political thinkers of the eighteenth century, was nevertheless a profoundly religious thinker. He operated within a religious context largely of his own thinking and professed his peculiar faith dramatically in his writing. His religion was the religion of nature, and the form of argumentation was homiletic. He preached the gospel that a new era was at hand, that the world was entering the modern age through progressive changes everyone could participate in, and that his role was to advance the cause of liberty for all people everywhere.

It is virtually impossible to gauge how consciously Paine expounded a religion of nature or chose homiletic modalities. Through investigating his major and minor writings and correspondence, however, we may see that despite anti-Christian and anticlerical opinions, which he never tired of expressing, he often used religious themes and imagery. We will also see that he expressed these themes and imagery in a number of the available languages of his time, ranging from the language of classical republicanism to that of the pastoral, from the language of political economy to that of millennialism.

On different occasions for specific purposes, we find him choosing the language he thought most appropriate to his subject matter. At times, for example, he spoke the Old Whig or Country language of virtue and corruption and at other times used Lockean themes of the social contract and its accompanying rights, liberties, and obligations that every citizen possessed. Still at other times, we find him using the vocabulary and imagery of the

Georgic, the pastoral, to convince his readers of the importance of living in accordance with their nature. Moreover, he articulated Madisonian themes when he argued the case for a constitution, first for America in 1776, then for France in the 1790s, and throughout all this time for his former British homeland.

He also spoke the languages of political economy and secular millennialism, two major and important vocabularies of the late eighteenth century, which he used to appeal to a lower- and middle-class audience of Americans and British citizens, even though he himself never believed in the doctrine of political economy because it largely consisted of conservative economic principles or in millennialism because he thought the second coming of Christ not only implausible but absurd. Through an analysis of his use of all of these languages, we will see how he sought to appeal to the lower and middle classes of America and England, all the time employing a homiletic style of argumentation. We will, in short, determine his intent in using the various languages he chose and their impact on the audiences at which he aimed his words.

Paine's Religion of Nature

Paine preached throughout his writings, but not as a priest who would spread the myths and superstitions of the Bible or the Church. Priests were students of theology, which, "as it stands in Christian churches, is the study of nothing; it is founded on nothing; it rests on no principles; it proceeds by no authorities; it has no data; it can demonstrate nothing; and it admits of no conclusion" (*Age of Reason, CW* 1:601).[1] Preaching a theology, especially Christianity, defeats the purpose of religion, which, so far as Paine was concerned, was a simple, straightforward matter; he made the point twice in *Rights of Man:* "Every religion is good that teaches man to be good" (*RM:* 260, 270). Thus, "if man must preach, let him preach something that is edifying." (*Age of Reason,* 604). Let him preach the religion of nature, of God's creation as we can know it, and the "repugnance we feel in ourselves to bad actions, and the disposition to do good ones" (596).

Paine's religion of nature comprises two main themes. There is, of course, nature itself, a theme which he never developed into a coherent theory. His discussion of nature was at times contradictory and confused. At other times, it was a model of lucidity. In general, he distinguished those things which God had created from those which resulted from human invention. Things natural were on a higher plane, evidence of the cosmic divinity which permeated the universe, part of God's creative power. Things in nature were therefore good: the world and its universe; man and his inherent capabilities to improve his world; the rights of man. These were all creations of God, natural creations as part of his original handiwork.

But it was not enough to say that all nature was good, including man's inventions, which were, however, less good, though Paine clearly divorced the natural from the unnatural. Probing this strain in Paine's social and political thought demonstrates its complexity and depth. As we will see, he often compromised his own view of the natural by asserting that things he did not like were simply unnatural. One example was kings and lords, whose humanity we may not question but who Paine would argue were inhuman creatures, a clear contradiction. He knew full well that if he believed God had made the world and all that was in it, then God also created those of royal and noble rank (though not the ranks themselves). Paine's rambling ideas about nature hardly fit together to form a strong conceptual theory: a person cannot simultaneously be both natural and unnatural.

Linked to nature was a second theme, nature's God, a concept with which, yet again, Paine's writings were seriously ambiguous and muddled.[2] He consistently claimed, for example, that he was a deist. To his eighteenth-century readers, deism meant the belief that after God created the universe and everything in it, he reserved to man the responsibility to improve it without removing the freedom to destroy it. Man became his own agent, a creature with free will to do good (or godly things) or evil (ungodly things). But Paine often wrote that after God had created the universe, he did not step back to allow men to do what they would with it. On the contrary, he often either hinted or asserted that God literally permeated the universe. His was a constant divine presence, a being whose personality was immanent in all of nature. Such thinking gives Paine's ideas an ironic, indeed a logically impossible, twist: he reveals himself as both a deist and a pantheist simultaneously, a philosophically (and probably theologically) incoherent position.

Reconciling these disparate, contradictory views is a difficult task, if it is at all possible. One thing is certain: consistency and systematic thinking were never among Paine's virtues. Paine's thinking was, however, never sufficiently sophisticated to consider these philosophical issues in any detail. Nor did he seem to be fully aware of them. His interests lay in setting forth his views of politics and society in a bright, vivid language designed to convince his readers that he was right to condemn tyranny and praise democracy. He was not a learned philosopher and never claimed the status of one. As it is, he did in fact confound his deism with a pantheistic vision of the universe, confounding the deity's initial creative moment with an eternal presence. In the midst of this muddle, Paine developed a highly personal notion of nature's God, a concept which once again he barely developed into a satisfactory philosophical construct, though it served as the foundation for his understanding of the world.

Nature was part of God's original invention of the universe, and nowhere did God reflect his own creative capabilities more than when he created human beings. God imparted to them a vestige of his own inventive power. People who lived according to their natural qualities could create a world of justice, equality, and democracy. This belief, too, reflected sloppy Painite logic. If a nation was debased by the opposite of these qualities—that is, by tyranny, injustice, and inequality—then the people's natural potential would be snuffed out. Thus, some people acted against those natural capabilities that God had given them and forced others to do the will of a minority. One thing was certain: even in Paine's eyes, God never personally intervened, nor had he ever intervened, in history. Whatever progress or regression the world had experienced was due to people's conduct alone, not to God, whose cosmic goodness should have inspired all people to improve their condition on earth.

Paine thus took personal responsibility quite seriously. He believed that he himself possessed the duty to bring the message of progress and truth to the lower and middle classes of England and America through his writing. This belief gave Paine's writing a religious sensibility, which he reflected in his political and social thought and often expressed in homiletic terms.

Paine's Audience and His Homiletic Style

Thomas Paine's homiletics were directly linked to the various audiences he appealed to throughout the last decades of the eighteenth century. Every historian who has studied his life and works agrees that he ranks as one of the most significant and influential writers of the late eighteenth century. Part of the reason for this influence has to do with his style of writing, which, as many commentators have observed, was simple, direct, and designed to appeal to a wide readership. Thus, part of his significance and influence was due to his explicit appeal to a lower- and middle-class audience, primarily in America and Britain.

He accomplished this end chiefly by using biblical language and allusions, which were popular in Paine's day. He used them all quite often, with great effect and relish, knowing full well they would help convince his audiences of his political principles. Biblical language, which Paine used in his secular preaching in his writing, was familiar and comforting to his British and American lower- and middle-class readers.[3]

His major writings, often offered in cheap editions to make them available to the lower classes, sold literally in the hundreds of thousands: *Common Sense,* for example, sold well over one hundred thousand copies in its first year of publication at the relatively cheap price of a shilling per copy.[4] The same was true for his other major work, *Rights of Man,* the sales of which may have reached a half million. Part 1 sold for what was then regarded as a trifling three shillings per copy. It was therefore widely available to the lower and middle classes, from the working poor to the artisan and mechanic to the manufacturer and financier.

The present study inquires into what accounted for Thomas Paine's popularity and his significance and why he appealed to the kinds of people in America and England that he specifically addressed. To answer these questions, the study looks principally at Paine's homiletic style: in particular how he consciously or unconsciously appealed to the audiences he addressed in the last three decades of the eighteenth century, using the language and tone of voice of a secular preacher teaching his flock that a new political day had begun and that the people themselves had the duty to ensure that freedom, justice, and harmony would prevail. For Nathan O. Hatch, Americans in particular were susceptible to this style of communication. "American Christians reveled in freedom of expression, refused to bow to tradition or hierarchy, jumped at opportunities for innovative communication, and propounded popular theologies tied to modern notions of historical development. No less than Tom Paine or Thomas Jefferson, populist Christians of the early republic sought to start the world over again."[5]

Beginning with *Common Sense, The American Crisis* series, and on through the 1780s, Paine's audience was principally American. Writing in a typically straightforward style filled with graphic illustrations, metaphors, and images, his intention was to rivet the Americans' attention to his call for separation from Britain and to convince them that he was right. He wanted as many Americans as possible to read these works (or to hear his words read aloud if they could not read).

First and foremost, he sought to draw in those who believed as he did that a revolutionary age was impending and that men had to act if they were to create a new, constitutional order of democratic government. In these works, we often find that he taught his readers what he thought they needed to know and then told them unequivocally what to do: "'Tis time to part," he exclaimed in *Common Sense,* or "Let the assemblies be annual" and, "Ye that dare to oppose, not only the tyranny, but the tyrant, stand forth!"[6] During these years in America, Paine aimed his appeal at the manufacturers, financiers, and industrialists as well as the artisans, tradesmen, and craftsmen, who were most susceptible to his plain, open style of writing.[7]

Second, and from a historical perspective perhaps more important, was the audience he sought to cultivate in the years during and immediately following the French Revolution. No longer did he attempt to convince one group of people (the Americans) to separate from another (the British), to rally the people to this cause during the war, or to find the basis for stability in government, politics, and economics after war's end. Those had been his goals in the 1770s and 1780s before his 1787 departure for England. After the French Revolution, he truly believed that political transformation would now take place everywhere in Europe with France leading the way to the downfall of all the old regimes. The next country to end tyranny, he dearly hoped, would be his own former homeland, Britain itself.

His desire for a continental audience, however, never met with the success that he wished, although his *Rights of Man*, like *Common Sense* and the *American Crisis*, were widely distributed, widely read, and widely discussed and debated. In the former work, he often abandoned the didacticism of his early years as his homiletics generally (though not always) took on a more exhortatory style. He more carefully used historical examples to set forth his position, which he often declared by stating his own wishes and desires. In *Rights of Man*, he gave a long explanation of how man originally came upon his rights in history, bringing his discussion up to the present by reprinting the entire "Declaration of Rights of Man and of Citizen."[8] More circumspect in his thinking in the 1790s, Paine was no less powerful in advocating political transformation.

All this was due to his intention to rally many people to the causes he advocated: from American independence to the success of the new nation in the war against Britain, from the creation of a sound constitutional and democratic order to the establishment of a stable and fair economic and commercial system, from the regeneration of politics in Europe to revolution and democracy in Britain. In undertaking this task, which he was convinced was his alone, he accommodated his individual style to these intentions.

The study is organized according to three distinct themes in Paine's writing: nature, action, and progress. Part 1 concentrates on the theory underlying Paine's political thought: his conception of nature, specifically his vision of natural man and natural rights. Inquiry is made into his use of rich imagery and metaphor as he applied these to the natural world and natural man as well as in his blistering critique of monarchical government and aristocratic privilege. Part 2 focuses on specific civil rights of man, such as his intellectual and voting rights, as well as his social duties as an independent, autonomous being who makes the best use of his natural rights in a democratic republic. These rights and duties empower man to design the best (hence, the most natural) forms of social and political organization and inform his consciousness so that he naturally seeks to aid his less fortunate brethren.

Finally, part 3 examines Paine's vision of the democratic republic and economic democracy. We see that he often used apocalyptic language to explain his belief in a future earthly paradise of democratic virtue. Paine was no millennialist, but as in, for example, *Common Sense* and *Rights of Man*, which expressed religious themes, he was never loathe to make use of an available vocabulary to state his most fervent case. Taken together, these themes provide us with the foundation of Paine's religion of nature, the subject of his homiletics.

Painite Homiletics and the Religion of Nature

Although Thomas Paine spent his adult life almost exclusively in urban settings, the physical natural world, in its multitudinous variety, deeply fascinated him. Images of nature permeated his work because nature reflected God's creation (and presence). He perceived the world as the invention of a Creator who bequeathed it to the ingenuity of his greatest creation, people, who reflected God's creative power by their own inventive talent.

Nature provided Paine with a context for his writings. He was convinced that she (nature always had a female character for Paine) possessed special qualities that no person could ever duplicate, qualities that people recognized only when they lived according to the natural principles by which God had first created them. People could rediscover those principles once they learned that they had departed from them—usually, though not exclusively, because one man (a king) or several men (nobles, for example) sought to enslave and control them. To return to natural principles was to behave naturally.

To follow nature as he understood it (as a creation of God and a vessel of God's immanence) was itself a religion, which Thomas Paine, the secular preacher, taught to all those who would listen, or at least read his work. This religion possessed its own set of principles, which Paine himself had devised, ranging from the entreaty to live according to one's natural self (that is, the way God created people) to the exhortation to recognize those rights which God had naturally given and which no man could confiscate. Paine preached these themes, in his own peculiar homiletic style and developed a loose, secular ministry to those who read his works in America and England.

Like his idiosyncratic lifestyle, Paine's preaching was unstructured; it was his way to disseminate his message to as wide a public as possible.[9] He preached a religion of nature, to be sure, but one which must be distinguished from the more formal eighteenth-century inquiries, such as Joseph Priestley's *Institutes of Natural and Revealed Religion,* David Hume's *Dialogues Concerning Natural Religion,* or William Wollaston's *The Religion of Nature Delineated.* These works, and others like them, were ubiquitous throughout the century. Their authors applied a technical meaning to *revealed* and *natural* religion, a meaning which had gained wide acceptance in eighteenth-century theological circles. Their intention was to investigate the knowable differences and relative merits of those principles God had made known to mankind through divine revelation, as opposed to those which man could know through the rational power of his mind.

Paine never formally considered the differences between revealed and natural religion. He once wrote that so far as he was concerned both of them were absurd. "The words 'revealed religion' and 'natural religion' . . . are both invented terms, contrived by the Church for the support of priestcraft," which Paine thought contributed only to the ongoing superstitions of Christianity. Revealed religion had no place in the world. "With respect to the first, there is no evidence of any such thing. . . . The sun shines an equal quantity of light all over the world—and mankind in all ages and countries are endued with reason, and blessed with sight, to read the visible works of God in the creation." As for natural religion, "it is upon the face of it, the opposite of artificial religion."[10]

Paine's religiosity centered on the natural content of the world and the human beings in it, how they might best live naturally in accordance with how God had created them. If man made use of his abilities, his moral sense, he would always be developing an increasingly freer world. As progress spread, two things would follow: he would never enslave his fellows, and he would achieve his highest potential.

In Paine's own way, he undertook a lifelong study of nature in all its manifestations, to wit, the physical world and its splendor, the nature of man as a reflection of God's creation, man's rights in both their natural and civic forms, and finally the divine, which he adulates. The last of these is the most difficult to clarify because of Paine's highly idiosyncratic religion. He believed in nature's God as Creator. But he also knew, or thought he knew, that God had "called" him (Thomas Paine) to undertake a secular ministry to preach the gospel as Paine knew it to be "True." In Paine's intellectual universe, the gospel was not a standard religious message of last days, salvation, and redemption. It was, on the contrary, a highly charged political message, revolutionary and radical at times, more conservative in later life, which summoned his fellow human beings to return to their true selves, to live their lives as God had originally intended, as a reflection of divine cosmic goodness.

Paine shared this fascination with nature with other eighteenth-century writers whose intellectual maturity was powerfully shaped by Newtonian science. To appreciate Paine's social and political ideas from the 1770s to his death in 1809, we need to understand his appreciation and use of nature and nature themes throughout his work. In this way, we may gain a better grasp of his method and style in the rapidly changing, at times revolutionary, world of the late eighteenth century.

Nature's splendor, while apparent to many British and continental thinkers, was even more obvious in the New World, which provided a veritable laboratory for people to investigate the mysteries and the order of the universe. There, they could inquire into the very qualities that fascinated Paine, qualities like a natural longing for liberty and a desire to live in a free community with their fellows, to determine whether they had universal application. A new people (the American Indians) and new plant and animal life were objects of wonder for many settlers and visitors to these shores.

According to Wilson Carey McWilliams, "America was the redemptive land which had escaped European corruptions and recovered the *liberty of nature*."[11] Myra Jehlen goes farther by suggesting that "America was an avatar of the world prior to feudalism and, in the sense that it still awaited its primal molding, it was anterior to the old world's divisions. Responding only to nature (as it had no history), American civilization remained at one with it and embodied nature's laws organically, as the adult embodies the child.[12]

Appreciation of the physical world of America and Europe spilled over into literature and art and, for Paine, into politics as well. That nature was no longer the preserve of the naturalist, the natural philosopher, or the nature reporter was a development that had begun in seventeenth-century England. The Royal Society of London, created in 1660, formalized and broadened the study of nature to include the non-scientific writer. In the New World, Benjamin Franklin established the American Philosophical Society "for promoting useful knowledge." (The society rejected Paine's membership application in 1781 but elected him four years later.)[13]

Although Paine was neither a nature reporter nor a natural philosopher, nature figured forcefully in his work as a secular preacher. Images and metaphors of nature abound throughout his writings. On one level, his vision of nature was the outdoors, the physical landscape, and the heavens. Often, like Rousseau, he was nostalgic about nature. His adulation of nature, his infatuation with it, was the basis of his religious faith. His was a secular, natural love of God's handiwork. He once spoke, for example, of retiring to his New Rochelle farm, had he only the financial means, to enjoy a restful, peaceful existence in the full splendor of nature for the rest of his life. Moreover, metaphors and images of physical nature run throughout his commentary, his correspondence, and his poetry. He speaks of the "winter" of political oppression (*CS* 89), of the renewal of a political "spring" (*RM* 272–73), and of "the cypress of disappointment."[14]

On another level, Paine believed in nature's cosmic qualities. As I have indicated, even as a deist Paine believed that God's divine presence permeated nature and linked all of human history in a single line from creation to Paine's own time. His use of nature's cosmic attributes is most evident in his writings on religion, such as *The Age of Reason*, which, though viewed by some as the atheistic product of the Devil, was a veritable celebration of God, nature, and mankind. Nature contained the essence of life. Through it, God's intention was made immanent: from the physical world to human nature to the natural rights of man.

Although Paine made abundant use of natural images and metaphors, he nowhere presented a systematic theory of nature or nature's God. And yet, when all his writings are taken as a whole, they demonstrate his strong belief in the unity and harmony of all human beings and the natural world through God's initial act of creation. God created the world as a gift to enable human beings to reach their greatest potential. They possessed a nature or essence that made them as natural as all animal and plant life. Their natural sociability and common sense, he thought, distinguished them from these lower forms of life.

For Paine, nature's God was the Creator of the universe and all that was in it. Never a deity whom one could successfully petition on a personal level (God did not answer a man's prayers), God had created man in his image by giving him an intellect not only to explore the mysteries of the world, but to improve his lot on earth. Man was, in effect, on his own to promote progress toward modernity (which for Paine meant the spread of democratic republics and economic democracy everywhere) or, conversely, to halt that progress. Indeed, as he explained throughout his work, some people might even destroy that progress.

As manifestations of God's creation, all people were obliged to work for the betterment of everyone else. God himself served as a model. Here we encounter an ancillary theme in Paine's religion of nature. His arguments about nature demonstrate his belief in a tension between things natural and unnatural: between natural and unnatural man, between natural and civil (man-made) rights, between the republic (the most natural form of government) and revolution (a human invention).

In the image of God, man was *homo faber*, a maker, an inventor. But while God could, if he chose, create natural perfection, man was a maker of artificial, not natural, creations. He could never recreate the earth or the heavens. Man was, however, a creator at his own level. If no one impeded his creative ability, man could concoct the most wonderful articles and inventions to benefit his fellows: from better bridges and candles to a sounder economy and a better political constitution. Indeed, Paine participated in developing each of these. Man's inventions would not be perfect creations. In time, however, they might well approach perfection as man improved on his past efforts. On the other hand, men could also create terrible, unnatural things of destruction, such as war, poverty, and slavery.

Paine was certain that with every step forward, with each new inventive modification, progress in government, in the economy, and in society in general was inevitable. Follow nature, he said, as well as you can when you create. And where you are unable to duplicate her, allow for modifications as time moves forward and progress takes shape. Write a constitution, for example, but include a mechanism for changing it, specifically an amending process, so that future generations may perfect it. He preached effectively in this manner for more than thirty-five years.

As I have stated, any inquiry into Paine's social and political thought has its own inherent problems. Paine was more unsystematic than any writer of the eighteenth century, with the possible exception of Jean-Jacques Rousseau.[15] This characteristic may have been due to the breadth of his interests, which ranged from politics and economics to science, theology, engineering, and even poetry. Some analysts have handled this problem by focusing on particular areas of his thought, such as democracy, constitutionalism, economics, revolution. This approach, however, artificially isolates portions of his work and deprives us of the rich tapestry that Paine has woven.[16]

By investigating Paine's ideas through his use of a homiletic style (outlined below), we can better see how he presented his arguments to a wide array of people in differing contexts and times, and we can understand Paine's thought in ways that are at once more comprehensive and more analytical than previous scholarship has uncovered. For this reason, this study does not follow a strictly chronological course but instead attempts to judge Paine as he appealed and preached to shifting audiences in the last decades of the century.

No modern scholar has attempted to deal with Paine in these terms, although modern scholarship on his work has taken many forms. The most considerable Paine scholar has been Alfred Owen Aldridge, who first began to describe Paine's ideas almost forty years ago.[17] More than anyone else, Aldridge has both studied Paine's work and undertaken an assiduous search for his previously unpublished letters and manuscripts. Studies paralleling Aldridge's descriptive approach include the several biographies which have appeared over the past three-quarters of a century. One early biography, that of Moncure D. Conway, stood for eighty years as the standard work. David Freeman Hawke's has now largely superseded it.[18] None of these studies approach the sophistication of Eric Foner's analysis of Paine's ideas. In investigating the sociology of Paine's ideas, Foner places Paine's radicalism in the crises and events of Philadelphia society during the 1770s and 1780s. He shows how the social and political events of this period influenced both Paine's style and his thought. Foner's goal is "to trace a special set of processes: the relationships between a particular brand of radical ideology and the social and political theory of revolutionary America."[19]

The present study is designed to complement Foner's work and to move beyond it along the lines discussed in this chapter. It subscribes to the methodological approach which suggests that historical inquiry may be made into the structure of a political argument through a recovery of the languages available to a writer, his intentions as we may know them, and the modes of discourse through which he chooses to express himself.[20] Paine used a variety of languages throughout his career, ranging from the older Country language of virtue and corruption to the new science of political economy, from the natural vocabulary of the pastoral to the religious expressions of millennialism. Moreover, we can determine his intentions by examining which mode of discourse he chose to express his social and political principles.

This approach to the study of political and social thought has led to new assessments and productive conclusions about such historical figures as Machiavelli, Harrington, Locke, and Burke.[21] It has also become controversial over the past decade as poststructuralist critics have begun to question the historian's ability to recreate contexts and to inquire into the languages available to a writer and into a writer's intentions.[22] The present inquiry into Paine's social and political ideas is designed to uncover "an author's language no less than . . . his intentions."[23]

In this study, I take Paine as he presented himself through his work. I do not attempt to exceed the bounds he set for himself and his writings. I allow Paine to speak for himself and bring to bear on his words the meaning that arises from his own vocabulary and stated intention. My purpose is not to answer Paine. He had plenty of enemies during (and indeed after) his lifetime. I do, however, examine deficiencies and inconsistencies in his argument as they appear. My particular focus throughout is his homiletic style and his attempt to appeal to a lower- and middle-class audience of Americans and Britons.

Assessing Paine's Radicalism

Paine was a political radical in only some respects, in eighteenth-century terms, especially in his social welfare proposals of the 1790s and in his desire for people to take charge of their lives and to engage, when necessary, in transforming or revolutionary activity. His responses to the events that he witnessed relate to his, and not our, time. The present study seeks to determine whether there are concealed meanings to his claimed discovery of certain universal principles of politics and society.

One of the most puzzling difficulties in Paine's thought is whether it fits into any of the eighteenth-century political categories. Was Paine a Whig, a classical republican, a democrat? Was he a radical Jacobin or a bourgeois radical? Indeed, does it matter? Surely he was no Whig. He consistently denied the Norman myth and the Ancient Constitution. He rejected the idea that government should consist of a balance between the one, the few, and the many. He found such ideas simplistic, even laughable. On the other hand, he often spoke of the republic, the *res publica*, but when he did he had in mind not the commonwealth but the democratic republic. If anything, Paine was a wide-ranging writer with roots in republican theory as well as social welfare statism. He offers us a link between late Enlightenment thinking and nineteenth-century liberalism.

For Paine, a true republic would never have a king. It must have a representative system of government based on a constitution so that all the people, without regard to property qualifications, were guaranteed participation in decision making. Because all men were sovereign citizens, the political structure must offer them the right to participate in government by voting for their representatives.

Moreover, Paine was not necessarily a bourgeois radical, either.[24] He may have at times advocated middle-class values, such as talent, merit, frugality, persistence, and industriousness, and he may even have thought of the bridge he invented and tried to sell in England and France as a money-making enterprise. But his vision was broader than that. The bridge was a paradigm of social progress and modernity.

Paine, of course, spoke the language of virtue. Then again, just about everybody else in the century did, too, including Edmund Burke, who argued that the aristocracy alone possessed the requisite virtue to rule. Paine rejected Burke's position, just as he rejected all Burkean arguments from historical prescription. While he spoke favorably of virtue, he did not think that it was a quality all men had once possessed and now had to recapture, or that it was something only some people possessed, as the Whig spokesmen argued.[25] For Paine, people would achieve virtue only in the future, when they moved the processes of history and progress forward. To accomplish this task, they would have to "turn the world upside down."[26]

To use this phrase is not to suggest that the proper context for Paine was that of the seventeenth-century Ranters and Seekers. It is simply to say that he was subjected to many influences throughout his career. As an autodidact, he was highly susceptible to the ideas of many writers and to the events of his day. Any attempt to determine who most influenced Paine is terribly difficult, if not impossible, and unconvincing because many people influenced him.[27] Despite the loss of Paine's library due to two fires, Caroline Robbins has found that it is still possible to delineate the literature he probably read or with which he was at least familiar.[28] We may speculate that Paine read a great deal more than he let on, that he did not necessarily tell us the truth when he said that he read very little because reading interfered with his thinking.[29] Moreover, we know that he was well attuned to the major issues of his time; he read the newspapers and talked and debated with whomever he could.[30]

In reality, we know very little about Paine's ideological development. By the time he arrived in America, he had already passed thirty-seven extraordinarily difficult years in England. His three very different careers had all ended in failure: staymaking, excise tax collecting, and retailing. His two marriages had also failed. At some point, he may have developed an inordinate hatred for his native country, perhaps due to the failures. Perhaps, too, it was a result of his later experiences in America. One thing is certain. America was always precious to him. Even while abroad for fifteen years, he always planned to return to his adopted home. America, he said in 1802, when he returned to the United States, "is the country of my heart, and the place of my political and literary birth."[31]

On his arrival here in 1774, he almost immediately joined a circle of Philadelphia political activists who stimulated his thinking about America's continued relationship with Britain. He concluded that separation was the only solution if America were to be free and if her citizens were to live natural lives. He articulated what many Americans were probably already thinking. *Common Sense*, published in January of 1776, "was consciously and enthusiastically seized upon by statesmen and politicians, indeed by public opinion in the widest sense of the word, as a complete guide to action; not just as an analysis of reality by an acute mind, containing wise reflections and stimulating ideas, the way in which a political pamphlet would have been treated in the past." These words of Jacob Talmon speak of the 1789 pamphlet by the Abbé Sieyès, but they could just as easily apply to *Common Sense* in 1776.[32]

In 1787, without second thoughts, Paine returned to his British homeland, thinking himself fully American. How he could have returned to a land he loathed is not knowable. One might speculate, however, that he was disillusioned with the United States because he felt insufficiently compensated, materially and otherwise, for his efforts on behalf of American independence. He appealed to Congress on several occasions for remuneration, fearing his indebtedness might send him into poverty. Moreover, he was associated with the Silas Deane affair, and he may have feared becoming directly implicated in Deane's war profiteering. Perhaps he thought the time was right to return to England to sell the bridge he had invented. From a purely financial perspective, all of this sounds plausible enough. From an ideological point of view, however, it makes little sense. Not knowing that his return to England would foment revolution there—an effect he did not desire—he went back probably as much to leave America as to return home. In the end, he wrote that he wanted to see his old parents at least one more time.[33]

These issues aside, one problem all interpreters of Paine's work confront is the contradictions in his writings. How could a person who called himself a Quaker advocate war with Britain and support the French Revolution, the European war that followed it, and also Napoleon's imperial ambition? How was it possible for a man to believe in nature and at the same time advocate economic progress and materialist growth and development? How was it that a radical democratic republican writer could associate with wealthy Philadelphia merchants like Robert Morris and promote their cause, the Bank of North America? This study does not ignore these questions so much as it simply incorporates them into an analysis of Paine's ideas. Paine spoke to Americans and Europeans, and as he did, these issues arose never to be fully resolved but, in the end, they all contributed to the set of ideas that made Thomas Paine a wandering homiletic writer.

PART ONE

Nature

❧ 2 ❧

Natural Man and
Common Sense

When Thomas Paine pondered what political and social institutions were most appropriate to man, he asked what human qualities made man a natural creature. The theme of human nature runs throughout his work, but nowhere did he present it with such drive and clarity as in *Common Sense,* his first major pamphlet, which became one of the most wildly popular publications of the eighteenth century. And yet, while *Common Sense* contained a great deal about human nature, Paine's other writings added to the picture in ways we simply cannot ignore. In them he drew on the earlier lessons from *Common Sense* to depict natural man in deep conflict with those who would enslave him.

Man's nature originated in God's creation of the physical world. As it was the nature of a tree to grow to a great oak from a small seed (a popular eighteenth-century literary and political image), so human nature prescribed man's development into adulthood and eventual possession of what was naturally his, namely his reason and passions, his rights and liberty. God created man as a complete being who at first needed neither government nor society to aid in his maturation.[1] As man collectively matured, he passed into new eras, and eventually into modernity. His possession of natural qualities meant that he had a "natural love of liberty."[2] No one could permanently destroy this love. Under certain political conditions, such as monarchy, however, the people could be lulled into the unwitting slumber of slavery. At that point, they no longer consciously desired freedom, because kings and nobles deadened their natural abilities to think and feel. When that happened, their rulers totally controlled them.

How could this happen if freedom was truly "personal property," prop-

erty of which no person could deprive others without violating nature?[3]
Paine's answer was that historically man always desired freedom, even when
that desire lay dormant. At some future moment, someone like himself
might reawaken that desire, and the people would again strike out to secure
liberty. Of course, Paine had no way to present demonstrative proof that this
was the case. He simply asserted its truth. In any case, so far as he was
concerned, the problem was how to reawaken man's desire for freedom.

Paine's solution was to investigate the potential which he found in the
revolutionary activity at the end of the century. People possessed certain
powers, the greatest of which were embodied in Paine's most famous phrases
in *Common Sense:* "We have it in our power to begin the world over again"
(82), and "Now is the seed-time of continental union, faith, and honor" (120).
One such people, the Americans in 1776, had reached the necessary stage of
consciousness to renew the struggle for freedom. These words, which went
beyond mere encouragement, were designed to awaken the Americans to
move immediately to throw off the chains that the British ministry had
placed on them. After all, the Americans lived in "an age of Revolutions, in
which every thing may be looked for" (*RM* 146).

Paine was aware of the homiletic role he played in awakening the Americans from their sleep. We must remember that Paine claimed to address
what he thought was a wide audience of Americans who were themselves on
the verge of accepting separation. Only they were not quite yet ready to take
the final step, war against Britain. His Philadelphia compatriots, men like
David Rittenhouse, Charles Willson Peale, and Timothy Matlock (artisans
all) and Robert Morris (a financier), were open to the dangerous ideas that
Paine expressed in *Common Sense.* He had only to convince them that the
king and his cohorts had distorted the American subjects' nature, their very
essence. In a secular sermon, Paine designed what he thought was an irrefutable argument. He depicted kings (and indeed their courts) as historically
denatured, inhuman creatures, totally alienated from humanity. They enslaved people who in their unconscious selves still retained a will to resist. In
extraordinary times, a people would reawaken to resist tyranny and then
form the government which best provided for their natural well-being. His
language was strong and direct. His intention was clear: to move America
forward toward independence, now. More often than not, he thought, it
took a great man, one like Thomas Paine, to stimulate people to act. Once
they were reawakened, they exercised "common sense" (*RM* 176–81).[4]

Common sense was one of Paine's most powerfully charged phrases.
Some commentators have defined *common sense* as a person's intuitive or
moral powers.[5] This interpretation, though essentially correct, is incomplete. Common sense was part of human affections, the innate moral

sensibilities. But common sense also included man's ability to reason. Now, Paine was no epistemologist. He never set forth a lucid, cogent explanation, like Locke's or Hume's, of how the mind operated or how man knew anything at all. But he did have strong opinions about how people knew how to conduct their lives. They knew through both their affections and their reason.

Paine was not the first writer to use *common sense* as a term for the faculty for understanding, nor was he the first to consider this faculty a corollary to human moral sensibilities. Lord Shaftesbury, though clearly an elitist, had so used the term, as had the Scottish Common Sense philosophers such as Thomas Reid. Although these philosophers' works were available to him, Paine probably never read Shaftesbury's *Characteristicks* (1711) or Reid's *Inquiry* (1764). Even so, common sense as a sensory faculty, a sixth sense, encapsulated his idea of what natural man was and ought to be.[6] The term was well known and obviously in broad usage at the end of the eighteenth century, including in America.

For Shaftesbury, Reid, and Paine, common sense was an all-encompassing faculty of mind and feeling that gave people the power of immediate discernment.[7] The Scottish philosopher Thomas Reid observed that common sense forced him "to take my own existence, and the existence of other things upon trust," and to believe that snow was cold and honey sweet.[8] These things were knowable spontaneously when people first encountered them. For the skeptic to deny this phenomenon undermined the true basis of human knowledge.

But how did common sense operate? Although his epistemology is vague, Paine used the term to express both reason and sensibility.[9] Common sense was the means by which the mind understood the way the heart felt about reality. It had nothing to do with abstract reasoning or metaphysical concepts. It was wholly empirical because it was based only on sensory perceptions. The Americans did not need abstract ideas of freedom to convince them that the British oppressed them. They needed only listen to the dictates of their common sense. As Paine noted, "Common sense will tell us" (*CS* 105). It will tell us because the powers of the mind and the heart are like lightning bolts of spontaneous discernment. The mind knew and the heart felt that "however our eyes may be dazzled with snow, or our ears deceived by sound; however prejudice may warp our wills, or interest darken our understanding, the simple voice of nature and our reason will say, it is right" (*CS* 68).[10] To see how this works, it is imperative to analyze the linguistic and epistemological roots of the expression *common sense*.

First, common sense by necessity included reason. As Paine said in *The Age of Reason*, "the most formidable weapon against errors of every kind is reason. I have never used any other, and I trust I never shall" (*CW* 1:463)."[11] As for America's relationship to England prior to 1776, "it is repugnant to *reason* . . . to suppose that this continent can longer remain subject to any external power" (*CS* 89, emphasis added). Indeed, he once declared that the new era of politics in which he lived was "the age of reason" (*RM* 268), which was also, of course, the title of one of his major writings. Common sense was clearly a function of man's rational capabilities, his ability to reason.

But common sense included affection as well. The relationship with Britain did not feel right to men because it violated their moral sensibilities. All one needed to do to gauge whether the colonies ought to remain linked to Britain was to judge the relationship by "those *feelings* and *affections* which nature justifies. . . . Examine the passions and feelings of mankind," and judge that relationship by the standards that nature supplied (*RM* 268).[12] During the war with Britain, as the military situation deteriorated, "what we have to do," said Paine, "is as *clear as light,* and the way to do it as straight as a line."[13] This light—this clarity—was what common sense provided to people. Such clarity, for those who followed their true nature, gave directions.

First, they could achieve positive political and social changes. They would know by both reason and affection what was right and what wrong in society and government. Second, common sense was the vehicle for the people's inventiveness. As common sense informed them when and how to make or invent revolutions, by extension it was also the creative spark that moved them to enhance progress. Human inventions improved life for everyone. When Paine was struggling with the design of his iron bridge, he realized he had to moderate his "ambition with a little 'common sense'" in order to make the necessary modifications.[14] It was a powerful turn of phrase which Paine undoubtedly knew would deeply impress his wide American audience.

Every person, he taught, possessed common sense. The problem was that it became impaired when brute force enslaved the people, when kings and lords, or ruffians and banditti, made others do their will. They deprived their subjects or victims of the freedom to choose and destroyed or badly compromised their sense of self. When that happened, common sense was distorted. People no longer thought straight (as a line), and nothing was clear (as light). Such force had a numbing effect on their minds and hearts. They might never even feel the pain of that force and might never be aware of it.

This state of affairs violated man's nature as a creature with the God-given ability to reason. "Men," said Paine, "have a right to reason for themselves."[15] When kings and their cohorts stole this right from their subjects, the subjects were no longer whole persons. They were slaves, the puppets of others, who used them as they saw fit. They lost their sense of self and became objects—indeed, the property—of others. For Paine, human beings universally shared this same nature. How then did he explain that some men were indeed different?

Here Paine used his natural versus unnatural theme in a rhetorically powerful way, convincing his artisan and financier readers, though with an argument less certain to persuade those more philosophically inclined. He defined the characteristics of these thieves of common sense and human freedom by virtually defining them out of humanity itself. These denatured creatures were usurpers—these kings, these aristocrats, their followers, and later the Federalists, too. They were unable to use their natural powers of common sense as God had meant people to use them. Their desire for dominance and violence prevented them from living a life of reason and moral affection. "A mind habituated to actions of meanness and injustice, commits them without reflection, or with a very partial one."[16] They responded only to their basest instincts, not common sense, to seek power over others. Thus, base instinct (in this case, seeking power and dominion) opposed common sense (reason and sensibility).

The British government, especially George III (whom he never specifically named in *Common Sense* because his target was kingship generally and not individual kings), was such a creature. He once noted in regard to the king's cabinet that a universal human characteristic was the inability to change once intellectual patterns and habits were firmly set. "Once the mind loses the sense of its own dignity it loses, likewise, the ability of judging it in another."[17] Several years later, while in France, Paine modified his view and advocated that Louis XVI's life be spared. But in 1776, the Americans had no choice. Separation was their only alternative, and for them, separation was a symbolic execution of the king.[18]

The British government had failed to use its collective common sense to deal fairly with the Americans. Such a failure meant that Britain distorted America's well-being because it viewed the Americans as being like the British. "The American war has thrown Britain into such a variety of absurd situations, that, in arguing from herself she sees not in what conduct national dignity consists in other countries." For the same reason, since the consummation of the treaty between America and France, the British had been seizing Dutch vessels in the belief that they might be carrying French supplies to America. Thinking the United Provinces would never resist them, the English ministry continued to "plunder [their ships] as they pleased."[19] But British common sense was defective. The Dutch in 1780 entered into an alliance with Catherine the Great of Russia to protect supplies shipped in neutral vessels. England, finding herself at war with the United Provinces, had to send a substantial naval force to the North Sea. Once a nation no longer used common sense, no matter what that nation did, its actions were illogical, wrong, and immoral. They defied, in short, its natural inclination to do good. This was both affectively and rationally true.

Common sense was in part rooted in a person's affective nature because God had implanted in him "unextinguishable feelings" to do good. These feelings were the guardians of God's image in the human heart. "They distinguish us from the herd of common animals," he said. "Otherwise, the social compact would dissolve, and justice be extirpated from the earth, or have only a casual existence" (*CS* 99–100). Man's affections drove him into the social realm in the first place. This was a result of common sense. He lived with his fellows in a cooperative arrangement for the benefit of all.

A social contract existed among men outside the realm of the sovereign and his lords. "There necessarily was a time when government did not exist, and consequently there could exist no governors to form such a compact with" (*CS* 92). Although Paine did not identify Locke explicitly, his language describing the social contract was Lockean, and he was never loathe to give a Lockean lesson.[20] "The fact therefore must be, that the individuals themselves, each in his own personal and sovereign right, entered into a compact with each other to produce a government: and this is the only mode in which governments have a right to arise, and the only principle on which they have a right to exist" (*CS* 92). Man was fully conscious of the self in this decision making, so that he consciously came together with his fellows to form society for reasons having to do with his natural affections toward others.

As he wrote of these "unextinguishable feelings" and the historic ideal of the social contract, he fully believed that George III and his ministry did not possess such feelings and never would, nor would they ever fully understand the implications of the contract. They felt no sense of justice because they were in fact different. Common sense informed the Americans that a continued relationship with Britain was doomed. "To talk of friendship with those in whom our reason forbids us to have faith . . . is *madness and folly*"; that is, it was against reason and sensibility. (*CS* 99, emphasis added). The people themselves must use their common sense to assert their right to participate in governmental decision making.

Monarchical government in England had distorted the proper relationship between the people and their government. This distortion arose because common sense was lacking. Kings and lords and people like them were inhuman. He avoided having to reconcile their inhumanity with his belief that human nature was universal by literally reading them out of the human race. It was a powerful argument, even if it was logically bewildering to read of a human being who lacked human nature. Then again, Paine was not addressing an audience of philosophers but rather of lower- and middle-class Americans who, he thought, would be convinced by this rhetoric to support America's separation from Britain.

Natural Man, Inhuman Creatures

Kings, lords, and all those who sought to dominate others were "apostate[s] from the order of manhood" (*CS* 114). This telling phrase requires some analysis to understand the full power of Paine's exposing the unnatural aspects of monarchy and aristocracy. In writing kings and lords out of humanity, he used rhetorical flourishes like a fiery preacher holding forth from the pulpit: he fulminated against those creatures who were inferior even to the most brutish beasts. His intention was to show that they were creatures who could not use the natural and human quality of common sense. Although cooperation was a human characteristic, these beings lived cooperatively with no one. In making this argument, Paine held that the people's struggle was on a plane higher than they knew. This made the "killing of the king," as Winthrop Jordan has shown, a less painful experience for those who were unconvinced or who were squeamish about such matters.[21]

Paine's argument here was particularly powerful for two reasons. First, his language was easy to understand: because many of Paine's American readers were artisans, tradesmen, and craftsmen he presented awful images of inhuman people who controlled their daily lives. Second, the argument appealed to those who already thought as Paine did: men like Charles Willson Peale and David Rittenhouse agreed that the relationship with Britain must end, but now Paine's powerful argument gave them a stronger rationale for ending it.

Monarchs and such never understood that people naturally loved freedom. Rulers wanted to deprive people of their God-given rights and sought to destroy the natural equality that existed among them. In reality, kings and lords were murderers, a term Paine specifically used in his poem, "An Address to Lord Howe," when he compared George III to the biblical Cain:

> From flight to flight the mental path appears,
> Worn with the steps of near six thousand years,
> And fill'd throughout with every scene of pain,
> From George the *murderer* down to murderous Cain
> Alike in cruelty, alike in hate,
> In guilt alike, but more alike in fate,
> Cursed supremely for the blood they drew,
> Each from the rising world, while each was new.
>
> (*CW* 2:1093)[22]

In *Common Sense*, Paine indicted the entire English nation for its complicity in the blood it had caused to flow. "The last cord is now broken, the people of England are presenting addresses against us. There are injuries which nature cannot forgive; she would cease to be nature if she did" (*CS* 99). The British, under the leadership of their inhuman (and unnatural) king, had once again violated nature.

This step was unforgivable, but the people of England were not to blame because they, too, were subjects of an evil lord. Hence, mitigating circumstances surrounded their complicity. The oppressors of their country, those inhuman creatures, had forced them into aiding them to subdue the Americans. Thus, although he probably should have, Paine was reluctant to indict his former compatriots fully for being in collusion with the king. Most of them were guilty of allowing the Crown to oppress the colonies. They did not interfere. He attributed their acquiescence to ignorance, to a lack of common sense. Like the Americans themselves, the English people had been blinded to the true nature of the events in America.

> When information is withheld, ignorance becomes a reasonable excuse; and one would charitably hope that the people of England do not encourage cruelty from choice but from mistake. . . . They see not, therefore they feel not. They tell the tale that is told them and believe it, and accustomed to no other news than their own, they receive it, stripped of its horrors and prepared for the palate of the nation.[23]

These are, indeed, powerful words, sufficiently powerful, he thought, to move the small American nation to take action against a hopelessly evil and corrupt sovereign.

Paine wished that there were no kings in the world. In using a clearly homiletic style, he tried at times to appear prayerful, although he always denied the use of prayer: "No man more heartily wishes than myself to see them all in the happy and honorable state of private individuals," he told the Abbé Sieyès.[24] But as long as kings existed, Paine was intent on analyzing them in the two ways he knew best. First, he used a syllogistic, though faulty, logic to prove that kings were not human at all. Human nature was universal, and God had never created people who lacked common sense. But kings did lack common sense. Thus, kings were inhuman. Second, men themselves under some extraordinary influence must have introduced kingship into the world. He surmised that they must have done so at a very early stage of human history in a period before common sense had fully developed.

As for the first, kingship was not the work of God. "It was the most prosperous invention *the Devil* ever set on foot for the promotion of idolatry" (*CS* 72, emphasis added). Kings were a denial of nature herself: "as nature knows them *not,* they know *not her*" (*CS* 113–14). They denied a person's essence as a creature whose very being reflected, however imperfectly, the goodness and virtue of nature herself. "To be a king, requires only the *animal* figure of a man—a sort of breathing automaton" (*RM* 174, emphasis added).[25] They might look like men because they were clothed and in the shape of men, but they were not men at all. Of course, Paine did not believe that kingship was literally the creation of the devil but rather of the devil in man, that is, the worst aspects of human creativity.

What, then, were kings really? In one of Paine's more extreme metaphors in *Common Sense,* he likened the king to a worm, the lowliest of creatures. Paine's image of kings suggests both the devil-serpent (the seducer in Genesis) in particular and sexual licentiousness in general. Satan himself, evil and sin personified with an infinite sexual appetite, could have figuratively been responsible for kings. "How impious is the title of *sacred majesty* applied to a worm, who in the midst of his splendor is crumbling into dust!" (*CS* 72).

This image constituted a severe indictment of kingship: the serpent, dried up and dead like the winter fungus but still resplendent in his purple satins and crown jewels. Later Paine included not only kings, but those who revered them as well: "Here is idolatry even without a mask: And he who can calmly hear, and digest such doctrine, hath forfeited his claim to rationality—an apostate from the order of manhood; and ought to be considered—as one, who hath, not only given up the proper dignity of a man, but sunk himself beneath the rank of animals, and contemptibly crawl through the world like a worm" (*CS* 114). He echoed this theme sixteen years later when he announced, "Kings are monsters in the natural order, and what can we expect from monsters but miseries and crimes?"[26] This was what Locke had meant when he spoke of prepolitical man, who lay outside the law of nature and was not a rational creature.

Paine's portrait of kings' inhuman, base characteristics was devastating in light of his suggestion that, like worms, they were lower than animals. America, he said, was a refuge for those who wished to go far from "the cruelty of the *monster*" (*CS* 84). The monster that Paine was referring to was, as Ronald Paulson has indicated, "Saturn devouring his children," a popular image in eighteenth-century art and culture.[27] Paine noted that kings were lower than the animals because while animals did not consume their young, kings did. The father-monster king, with "the pretended title of Father of his People," contrasted with the "infant state of the colonies," colonies which were in their "youth," their "non-age." "Even brutes," he declared, "do not devour their young, nor savages make war upon their families" (*CS* 107–8).

Paine used this image in two other instances. In 1775, he wrote that "the portrait of a parent red with the blood of her children is a picture fit only for the galleries of the infernals," in a reference once again to the king of England. Thus, "the reign of Satan is not ended; neither are we to expect to be defended by miracles."[28] Almost twenty years later, he turned this image around somewhat; in a moment of despair over the beginning of the Reign of Terror, he reportedly told Danton that "Vergniaud had been right when he said that the French Revolution was like Saturn devouring its own children."[29]

Paine matched his contempt of kings with a profound hatred for aristocrats. They were the kings' "parasites" (bloodsucking vermin) who participated in his monstrous acts. In Paine's assault on English primogeniture, he wrote that "aristocracy has never more than *one* child. The rest are begotten to be devoured. They are thrown to the *cannibal* for prey, and the natural parent prepares the unnatural repast" (*RM* 82).[30] The result was as satanic as it was unnatural. The king and his "worthless adherents . . . hath wickedly broken through every moral and human obligation, trampled nature and conscience beneath his feet" (*CS* 114). The ancients had deified their dead monarchs. Moderns, whom he described as Christians to distinguish them from ancient pagans, "improved on the plan by doing the same to their living ones" (*CS* 72).[31] This was devil worship, as ungodly as it was unnatural. Such worship was therefore unscriptural.[32]

Paine's syllogism contained its own, inherent fallacy:

> God creates only natural beings.
> Kings and lords are unnatural.
> God did not create kings and lords.

Paine never understood the weakness of this argument. If kings and lords were inhuman, and God had not created them, how could they be accounted for? Paine refused to see them as the product of the devil and was satisfied to conclude in his own mind that other men, in a debased form of the creativity that God had given them, had created the institutions of kingship and aristocracy. Once situated in these offices, men somehow lost their natural powers of goodness and became evil and unrestrained in their desire to control others. In this way, Paine's argument, while shifting away from the syllogism, remains consistent in terms of his emphasis on the natural aspects of God's creation.

What is intriguing is Paine's use of scripture as authority to prove the legitimacy of his argument. Although part of his didactic approach to convince his readers, it was an uncertain strategy in light of his later book, *The Age of Reason*. In that work, he argued that no rational person ought ever to rely on the Bible because it consisted only of fable and superstition. Examined carefully, scripture was obviously false: "These books beginning with Genesis and ending with Revelation (which, by the bye, is a book of riddles that requires a revelation to explain it), are, we are told, the Word of God. It is, therefore, proper for us to know who told us so, that we may know what credit to give the report. The answer to this question is that nobody can tell us, except that we tell one another so" (*CW* 1:472). These sentiments about the Bible were nowhere evident in his earlier attack on kings and lords, in which he comfortably cited scriptural authority to prove that kings were not part of God's creation but were the work of the Devil, who used some inhuman creatures in the form of men as his agents. The Bible was clearly acceptable to a vast number of his audience, and he used it because it

> expressly disapproves of government by kings. All anti-monarchial parts of scripture have been smoothly glossed over in monarchial governments, but they undoubtedly merit the attention of countries which have their governments yet to form. *"Render unto Caesar the things which are Caesar's"* is the scriptural doctrine of courts, yet it is no support of monarchial government, for the Jews at that time were without a king, and in a state of vassalage to the Romans. (*CS* 73)

He used scripture as a rhetorical device to preach the truth that monarchy was unacceptable to God and even to the ancient Hebrews until they, from hubris and conformity, demanded a king for themselves. The Bible so strongly opposed monarchy that it was "ranked in scripture as one of the sins of the Jews, for which a curse in reserve is denounced against them" (*CS* 73).[33] It ranked, in fact, as a sin on a level with the murder of the Messiah, since both were the work of Satan. Man, in this case the Jews, turned against God to establish the monarchical principle. "It is a form of government, which the word of God bears testimony against, and blood will attend it" (*CS* 80).[34] In this argument lay Paine's distinction between natural man and monsters, between those who followed God and those who followed the Devil, between kings (and their agents) and citizens. No human being with true common sense behaved the way kings and aristocrats did.

Paine's hatred of monarchy did not mean he wished all monarchs dead. In his 1793 plea for the life of Louis XVI, he argued that monarchy as an institution, not the king himself, was evil: "I am inclined to believe that if Louis Capet had been born in obscure condition, had he lived within the circle of an amiable and respectable neighborhood, at liberty to practise the duties of domestic life, had he been thus situated, I cannot believe he would have shown himself destitute of social virtues" (*CW* 2:552). It was the institution of kingship that made kings inhuman. Besides, Paine recalled Louis's assistance to the Americans during the Revolution. Louis had the ability to behave as a man but suffered the misfortune of becoming king.

Nature and Sociability

In the meantime, he taught, human beings were naturally social creatures, something Paine would have agreed with Shaftesbury about, had he ever read his works.[35] Human sociability was one of the most consistent themes in Paine's long career. It was an idea that he preached first in 1776 in America, then in his 1792–93 writings about the French Revolution, and finally again on his return to the United States in 1802. He promoted society over government, which was at best a necessary evil. Society would always be good because it was natural. Government could be made tolerable, but ultimately it existed because of man's frailties, not his strengths, that is, the very things that made society possible. Society was an outgrowth of what God wanted of man; hence, man knew early on through his common sense to enter society. Government was a device designed to control men when their common sense failed them, something which sometimes happened. In essence, Paine was certain that "man is so naturally a creature of society that it is almost impossible to put him out of it" (*RM* 164).

When "nature created him for social life, she fitted him for the station she intended. In all cases she made his natural wants greater than his individual powers. No one man is capable, without the aid of society, of supplying his own wants; and those wants, acting upon every individual, impel the whole of them into society, as naturally as gravitation to a centre" (*RM* 163). Once again, we find Thomas Paine preaching a powerful theme of sensibility and community to distinguish the people from unnatural kings and noblemen. His intention here, to undermine kings and lords, was designed to stimulate his readership in England and France to distance itself from monarchy and to establish a sound constitutional framework. After 1789, the French were on the road to doing just that, and now it was up to the virtuous English citizenry to follow.

Like Locke, then, Paine distinguished between government and society.[36] In fact, Paine's arguments directly paralleled those of John Locke, and he used an explicitly Lockean language to prove his point, hoping that this language would be understood by even his lower-class readers. In his *Second Treatise of Civil Government*, Locke had argued that in the state of nature, before people agreed to form governments, they lived in a kind of natural community where every individual was bound by "the law of nature," which "teaches all mankind, who will but consult it, that being all *equal and independent,* no one ought to harm another in his life, health, liberty, or possessions" (9).

This law of nature cautioned them "to *preserve the rest of mankind*" and "the liberty, health, limb, [and] goods of" all people (9). Government for Locke came about because some people, unwilling to abide by the law of nature, took advantage of their fellows and deprived some of them of their life, liberty, or possessions. "I easily grant, that *civil government* is the proper remedy for the inconveniencies of the state of nature, which must certainly be great, where men may be the judges in their own case" (12). Locke went on to say that "though men, when they enter into political society, give up the equality, liberty, and executive power they had in the state of nature, into the hands of the society, to be so far disposed of by the legislative, as the good of the society shall require; yet it being only with an intention in every one the better to preserve himself, his liberty and property" (68). Government arose mainly for negative reasons, to protect men's possessions and at the same time to remove from people the obligation to be police, judge, jury, and executioner in all cases regarding violations of the law of nature (66).[37]

As Locke had implied, Paine, too, using Lockean language, believed that society "encourages intercourse" for a person's collective well-being (*CS* 65). Society was as natural to mankind as government was an unnatural, artificial creation. Society was providential, an idea that was common to Paine, the Dissenters, and even Burke, although for quite different reasons.[38]

Government was, even in its best state, "a necessary evil" and "in its worst state an intolerable one." Although the people had the potential for doing good, government was necessary because they were not always virtuous. They created government to provide a system of rewards and punishments in as painless a way as possible. "Government, like dress," he said in an oft-quoted remark, "is the badge of lost innocence; the palaces of kings are built on the ruins of the bowers of paradise" (*CS* 65). The people wore government as they wore their clothes, to cover their shortcomings, or as Paine said, "to supply the defect of moral virtue" (*CS* 66). Although they possessed a conscience, a Godlike inner voice that automatically told them how and when to distinguish good from evil, their conscience was not always "clear, uniform, and irresistibly obeyed" (*CS* 66).[39] Even if their moral defects were limited to "the few cases to which society and civilization are not conveniently competent" (*RM* 164), in this very narrow area government was not only possible but necessary.

Even so, human beings were essentially social, not political, creatures. This is an important distinction.[40] The less people had to do with government, the less they were caught up in the factional, divisive issues and debates of the day, the more natural they would be. This seems paradoxical, given

Paine's love of debate. (Could he have found political debate to be a necessary evil, though an enjoyable one?) Like Locke, he posited a time past when
government did not exist, when people lived in a natural condition in which
they enjoyed unlimited natural freedom. Separated at first from one another,
early people lived a solitary life in nature. There, "society will be their first
thought," because they were not born to be hermits, their "mind[s] so unfit-
ted for perpetual solitude" (*CS* 66).

His intention was to argue that although people were originally separate
and alienated, God had always meant them to be social creatures. He did not
create society for them. That was the result of a collective and common-
sense decision. After God created the first people, he left it to them to make
the conscious decision to form society. This was a logical and natural choice.
Just-born man, "unconnected with the rest . . . is soon obliged to seek assistance and relief of another, who in his turn requires the same" (*CS* 66).
The decision to "enter into society" was a consequence of "the mutual depen-
dence and reciprocal interest which man has upon man, and all parts of the
civilized community upon each other," he explained (*RM* 163).

After this initial decision, society became a permanent feature of a person's existence. He needed to live in association with his fellows for mutual
self-help, to overcome the inconveniences of the state of nature, and to
ensure the protection of life, liberty, and property. This was the case even if
he lived without "the mere imposition" of government (*RM* 164). Thus,
society existed even when government did not exist. If government ended,
society would remain intact. Without government, a person's natural inclinations would cause him to seek "common security" with his fellows
through social interaction (*RM* 164). And yet, in what ways could Paine
explain in the years of American and French revolutionary upheaval how
people's sociability displayed itself?

A person's temperament was a key factor in his social consciousness.
Temperament had more to do with affections, passions, than with intellectual capabilities. It had more to do with the sensibility of common sense than
with its intellectual or rational side. When a person's temper was poor or
when he was angered or saddened, his ability to reason properly would be
impaired. Consequently, he would be unable to make good (i.e., right or
virtuous) decisions. A person would be vulnerable to all sorts of grief, including slavery, because he would acquiesce to sovereign commands, including
those which were not in his interest. His temper was, then, a crucial part of
his nature. "Men of good temper," as Paine called them, would always desire
to live among their fellows.

Paine saw how this worked in real life in 1778, in terms of a collective
temperament, when a group of Anticonstitutionalists wanted to overturn the

radical 1776 Pennsylvania Constitution. These events gave Paine an opportunity to convince his audience. Paine suggested that the Anticonstitutional-
ist faction ought to allow the constitution more time before it was changed or
eliminated. To live well together, he said, the people must have a "good
temper. . . . As a great part of happiness of any people depends on their *good
temper* with each other, so whatever tends to consolidate their minds, remove
any misconceived prejudice, or illustrate any controverted point, will have a
tendency to establish or restore that happiness." This good temper was a
natural attribute which could become twisted into a bad, passive, or prejudi-
cial temper, given the wrong environment or set of circumstances, such as
those developing in 1778 in the debate over the constitution.

Paine claimed that he himself was a man of good temper, a model for
others, for Americans especially, to emulate. He said he was cool headed and
he used "fair reasonings" always without the arguments of factional and party
politics. This was more modesty that was usual for Paine. Even so, he
claimed that he possessed "no interests, connection with, or personal dislike"
for either side (the Constitutionalists or Anticonstitutionalists), although he
was sensitive to criticism about his relationship to the Philadelphia financiers and to the charge that he was their hired pen.[41]

Still, the people could achieve a good temper, if they wanted it, if they
set their hearts to it. Such people lacked prejudice, for prejudice, "if un-
disturbed, will fill [the mind] with cobwebs, and live, like the spider, where
there seems nothing to live on. If the one prepares her food by poisoning it to
her palate and her use, the other does the same; and as several of our passions
are strongly characterized by the animal world, prejudice may be denominated the spider of the mind."[42] People must strive to be different from
spiders. They must be more like natural man, so that their decision making
would become, like that of Thomas Paine, cool and calculating, based on
good temper.

Paine knew that this was an ideal which few men (other than himself)
could achieve. But he was conveying an important idea. People who were
unprejudiced, that is, people of good temper, best displayed their natural
sociability. Although he denounced prejudice and ill temper, Paine was one
of the most biased men of the eighteenth century. He never let good temper
stand in the way of his own opinion if something irritated him. And yet,
there is no particular reason to believe that he was not serious here about his
desire that all people possess a good temper.

The natural desire to live together without prejudice reflected a more
complicated motivation than Locke suggested—the need to secure life, liberty, and property. Paine did not use Locke's negative argument that the
origins of government lay only in man's desire to protect his goods. Al-

though man entered society for these reasons, he did so also because nature "has implanted in him a system of social affections, which, though not necessary to his existence, are essential to his happiness." Like good temper and the absence of prejudice, social affection (his natural love of his fellows) was a function of human happiness. "There is no period in life when this love of society ceases to act. It begins and ends with our being" (*RM* 163). Man had entered society because "society in every state is a blessing, a patron," which "promotes our happiness positively by uniting our affections" (*CS* 65).[43]

In contrast, the British caused the Americans to lose whatever social affections they might have had for Britain. Americans could no longer keep society with Britain. "She wore out their temper" so that "the most unoffending humility was tortured into rage."[44] Pamphlets like *Common Sense* made Americans aware of the reasons why they must seek separation. Revolution by itself was not necessarily a natural act; after all, the people's enslavement had numbed their common sense. After suffering British tyranny, Americans could no longer associate with British society.

This conclusion was not simply the result of either modern, enlightened thinking or a natural desire for freedom. All earlier revolutions pitting faction against faction were "little more than the history of their quarrels." Now, for the first time, the natural, social inclinations of people of good temper, without prejudice, were endangered. The war with Britain was a war that would be different because it was the consequence of "the sullenness and intractableness of the temper."[45] The British were the cause of this sullenness because of their intransigence. This opportunity was totally new. In this sense, Paine announced that "the birth-day of a new world" was at hand, and it would begin in America (*CS* 120).

If America did not seek immediate separation from England, the alternative would be the transformation of the Americans' good temper into what he called "passive temper" (*CS* 88). This was the affliction of those people who believed that reconciliation with Britain was still possible. Actually, Paine admitted that he himself had once believed this when he first came to America.[46] By 1776, he knew reconciliation was absurd, given the unnatural relationship between Britain and the colonies and the inhuman nature of kings and their followers. "Men of passive tempers," he wrote, might "still hope for the best" and try to renew America's historic bond with Britain. "But," he demanded in America in 1776, "examine the passions and feelings of mankind." (He did not say examine the *facts*.) "Bring the doctrine of reconciliation to the touchstone of nature, and then tell men, whether you can hereafter love, honour, and faithfully serve the power that hath carried fire and sword into your land" (*CS* 88).

People of such passive tempers lost their affections, their sensibilities. Others easily took advantage of their passivity and manipulated them. Numbed and unfeeling, these people failed to see that any future relationship with Britain would "be forced and unnatural." To advocate separation in such extreme terms "is not inflaming or exaggerating matters, but trying them by those feelings and affections which nature justifies, and without which, we should be incapable of discharging the social duties of life, or enjoying the felicities of it" (*CS* 89).

In joining together here what he thought was natural (or what people possessed by nature) to social affections, Paine preached that the result could only be people of good, not passive, temper. Should the relationship with Britain continue much longer, Americans would inevitably lose their humanity, a powerful argument for Americans to hear. Alongside the obvious political reasons for separation was an even greater reason for American independence. The British were literally undermining Americans' natural inclinations. Paine saw that his task was "to awaken us from fatal and unmanly slumbers" (*CS* 89).

He did not intend the word "unmanly" to serve as the opposite of the classical-republican notion of "virtue" or "manliness."[47] If "unmanly" is examined in the context of his reference to "men of passive tempers," his goal was to alert the Americans to the deterioration of their very nature. The British government was dehumanizing America. It was turning its people into unfeeling, unthinking creatures. It opposed common sense; it was a government that was "repugnant to reason" (*CS* 89). Paine wanted to awaken Americans' collective sensibilities to these dangers because "nature justifies" it.

Repeating this argument consistently nearly fifteen years later, Paine wrote in the vastly different context of the French Revolution that society was in danger. In a society where the government allowed the people to be fully human, a society where they could use their common sense, in that type of society, Paine encouraged, "the human faculties act with boldness, and acquire . . . a gigantic manliness" (*RM* 140). His use of overstatement reflected his shift away from the simple didactic language of the American revolutionary years to the more imperative tone he used during the turbulent years of upheaval in France. The citizens of France in 1789 experienced an even worse threat than the Americans had encountered in 1776. His hope was that people everywhere would heed his preaching, become conscious of what they must do to restore their humanity, and respond positively to his exhortation.

Under the circumstances, they had recourse only to revolution if they were to begin the process of renewing their nature. For the Americans and the French (and the British as well) to be fully human, they must participate in revolution because revolutions allowed for "a renovation of the natural order of things, a system of principles as universal as truth and the existence of man, and combining moral with political happiness and national prosperity" (*RM* 144). Revolutions set aright things that those denatured creatures who possessed political power had hoped to destroy: human nature. The lesson Paine preached here was how the Americans had once listened to him and had successfully defeated England, "condemning the viciousness of its government" (*RM* 159). With America as their model, other nations of the world could now learn that their enslavement placed them in a state of horrid dissonance with their true nature.

Paine's pamphlet was, then, not only a call to arms for revolution. It was a call for all people to return to their nature and to separate from denatured creatures like kings and such. This return promised "a new era to the human race" (*RM* 162). If man dared to describe human nature on the basis of "kings, courts, and cabinets," he would never have a portrait of genuine humanity. He would have only a portrait of a creature "that reflection would shudder at and humanity disown. . . . Man, naturally as he is, with all his faults, is not up to the character" (*RM* 169).[48]

Paine's duty, as a secular preacher, was to advocate strongly the people's return to their true nature as God originally designed it. Surely, people were imperfect beings. God never intended to make a perfect human being. That would have been tantamount to God recreating himself. A person must therefore remake himself in the image God had intended. Paine thus told the Americans what it was they must do if they were to succeed in returning to their true nature. The imperative voice rang throughout the conclusion of *Common Sense,* as he thundered:

> 'Tis time to part. . . . Let their [the Americans'] business be to frame a Continental Charter. . . . Let a day be solemnly set apart for proclaiming the charter; let it be brought forth placed on the divine law, the word of God, let a crown be placed thereon, by which the world may know, that so far as we approve of monarchy, that in America, the Law is King. For as in absolute governments the King is law, so in free countries the law *ought* to be King; and there ought to be no other. But lest any ill use should afterwards arise, let the crown at the conclusion of the ceremony be demolished, and scattered among the people whose right it is. (*CS* 87, 97–98)

Although human beings were fallible, they also possessed the capacity to improve the world through common sense. Paine said of the French Revolution, despite his disillusionment with it after 1793, that its principles were sound. Its ruin was brought about not by those who tried to see it fulfilled but by those who by the mid-1790s were clearly as inhuman as kings and their ministers, or at least it seemed to Paine that they were made so by the foreign invaders, who were infected and cruel creatures. They lacked common sense: "With respect to the French Revolution, it was begun by good men and on good principles, and I have always believed it would have gone on so had not the provocative interference of foreign powers, of which Pitt was the principal and vindictive agent, distracted it into madness and sown jealousies among the leaders."[49]

The double meaning here of "foreign powers" is evident. They were foreign because the nations of Europe invaded France, but they were also alien to humanity. Pitt, the Devil himself incarnate in the guise of the king's minister, was the agent. The war that France fought against the world's monarchies was a war that made world history. The ultimate goal was the recovery of the people's true nature, a doctrine that Paine by 1795 was certain he had conveyed through his preaching. This was the lesson he taught in the late 1790s as he had as early as 1776, when he first discovered the promise of man's powerful and revolutionary common sense.

❧ 3 ❧

Nature and Man's
Democratic Calling

Human nature was one dimension of nature in Paine's ministry. Another was the physical world: the landscape and the heavens as God had created them. In the act of creation, God gave his people the trees, the sea, and the sky as well as human freedom and the rights of man. Human beings possessed freedom and rights as naturally as trees produced leaves or the ocean swelled into waves. The idea that human nature was directly joined to freedom and rights provided Paine with still another powerful argument to attack the government of kings, lords, and their supporters. By showing that this form of government conflicted with human nature, hence with God's physical creation, Paine also showed that it was necessarily evil and satanic.

In turning to the natural world, one mode of discourse Paine drew on, consciously or not, was the pastoral, which from the Greek poet Theocritus and the Roman Virgil to Paine's own time focused on the bucolic ideal of peace and serenity. No evidence shows definitively whether Paine used this tradition merely to embellish his style or whether he truly believed the physical world was godly. Elements of the bucolic clearly appear in his writings, especially in *The Age of Reason*. Throughout this and other works, he demonstrated his fascination with nature, which he made into a veritable religion. Through a series of secular sermons, he was certain he could convince Americans and Europeans that the moment for political transformation had arrived.

According to one literary historian, "the bucolic ideal stands at the opposite pole from the Christian one, even if it believes with the latter that the lowly will be exalted and that only bad shepherds are shepherds of men."[1] Paine's ideas mirrored this description. He denounced Christianity as a religion which institutionalized myth and fable. More significantly, the lowly, those enslaved by royalty and aristocracy, would someday conquer their masters. Although he never saw himself as a literary shepherd who left the corrupt cities for quiet musings in the countryside, he shared with pastoral writers the belief in the importance of the world of sight and sound, where lies and superstitions had no place.

The pastoral tradition focused on the plight of the dispossessed as a critical social problem in ways that the gospels could never effectively do. Paine worried about the condition of the poor and outlined social programs for them in *Rights of Man* and *Agrarian Justice*. In these works, he expressed his desire that poverty be ended and commercial prosperity achieved. He preached that all people had a duty to aid the lowly.

Two problems immediately arise here: who were the lowly and who were the "people" he expected to help them? Paine never defined the "lowly" only as disadvantaged people at the lowest rung of society. The lowly also included all those below what he called the "exalted" status of king, lord, or priest. As for the people to whom Paine preached this message, in the second part of *Rights of Man* especially, we can see that he was appealing to the same kind of people whom he wanted to read *Common Sense:* an audience who understood his direct language, sometimes saturated with phrases they themselves might use. Thus, his appeal was to the lower orders, the artisans and tradesmen, and the middle classes, the merchants and financiers. He asserted that Burke's language was so sophisticated and learned that it was incomprehensible, and he offered to translate it. "As the wondering audience, whom Mr. Burke supposes himself talking to, may not understand all this learned jargon, I will undertake to be its interpreter." Burke's logic was as silly as his language: "What a stroke Mr. Burke has now made! To use a sailor's phrase, he has swabbed the deck" (*RM* 117).

At any rate, the trappings of royalty or nobility did not complicate the physical landscape, which was simple and ordered, pure and virtuous. It was, in short, in the tradition of the bucolic. To engage in invention we must look to "a principle in nature, which no art can overturn, viz. that the more simple anything is, the less liable it is to be disordered" (*CS* 68).[2]

Richard Price, friend of Paine's and a leading Dissenter and minister of Newington Green, once advised the same thing: that men would be better off if they lived according to nature. "Let us then value more the simplicity and innocence of life agreeable to nature; and learn to consider nothing as savageness but malevolence, ignorance, and wickedness. The order of nature is wise and kind. In a conformity to it consists health and long life; grace, honour, virtue, and joy. But nature turned out of its way will always punish."[3] In a passage in *Rights of Man* that echoed these themes, Paine urged his readers to observe the good things that nature in America, the New World, had to offer:

> The scene which that country presents to the eye of a spectator, has something in it which generates and encourages great ideas. Nature appears to him in magnitude. The mighty objects he beholds, act upon his mind by enlarging it, and he partakes of the greatness he contemplates.—Its first settlers were emigrants from different European nations, and of diversified professions of religion, retiring from the governmental persecutions of the old world, and meeting in the new, not as enemies, but as brothers. The wants which necessarily accompany the cultivation of a wilderness produced among them a state of society, which countries, long harassed by the quarrels and intrigues of governments, had neglected to cherish. In such a situation man becomes what he ought. He sees his species, not with the inhuman idea of a natural enemy, but as kindred; and the example shows to the artificial world, that man must go back to Nature for information. (*RM* 159–60)[4]

This passage suggests Paine's desire that those in the "artificial world" return to nature but not to an original state of mankind. The possibility that America presented to the world of invention was that of a natural environment where all people might learn (he said seek "information") from the example that nature offered.

This passage contains an explicit statement about the relationship among nature, humanity's needs, and political organization. From ancient times to the present, human beings had made great material progress in the world. But moral failure accompanied this material progress. Duping and tricking into kingship was immoral. For a few men to control the lives of many was immoral. Common sense, the very attribute that made man different from the lower animals, had failed when this happened. It was obviously a fallible faculty. Man could no longer enjoy the rights, freedom, and equality that God had given him. Paine seemed certain that his explanations would enable the common people who read his work to understand his message, whereas they could not comprehend the rich phrases of an Edmund Burke.

Paine was thus often preoccupied with natural phenomena and the physical landscape in his French revolutionary writings. This was due, in part, to his new environment, which he found particularly striking. He wrote Franklin his impressions in the summer of 1787. "The country from Havre to Rouen is the richest I ever saw. The crops are abundant, and the cultivation is nice and beautiful order. Everything appeared to be in fulness; the people are very stout, the women excessively fair, and the horses of a vast size and very fat" (*CW* 2:1262).

His preoccupation with the physical environment in the 1790s was also due, in part, to two Parisian encounters. First, there was his association with the Theophilanthropists and their worship of the sun as both a symbol and a reflection of God's illumination in man's mind and soul. Second, and perhaps more tellingly, there was his close relationship with Nicholas de Bonneville, whom he met in 1791, and *le Cercle Social,* whose principles included a curious combination of continental Illuminism and French Masonry.[5] Moreover, he knew Rousseau's work, often used it in his own writings, and was inspired by the Swiss author's emphasis on and use of nature.[6]

These two influences aroused in Paine the desire to preach that average men, his lower- and middle-class readers, could now reawaken their common sense and, in effect, as he said in *Rights of Man,* "go back to Nature for information." Had American independence alone come about, this reawakening could not have taken place. But independence was "accompanied by a revolution in the principles and practices of government" on a continental scale (*RM* 159). This revolution provided an environment to which people could revive common sense and return to nature. Then they could determine their true needs and legitimate desires in a genuinely democratic society. On this basis, they would then fashion a political order that they themselves legitimized.

If the Old World was to experience the same revolution America had, it would need to look to nature. This evocation of the natural world as a symbol of a person's return to his senses, so to speak, was Paine's way of longing for a new Age of God, a new Arcadian world of perfect justice. At times, he focused on this vision, especially in his rhetorical flourishes, which sang of the common people's power to begin the world over again.

But though Paine often used utopian language (see chapter 9), he never espoused a thoroughly utopian vision. He was too much the realist for that. A return to nature never entailed departing from urban areas for the primitive or rural reaches of the countryside, where he would go unclothed without modern facilities and pursue a natural condition of life. Neither Locke nor Rousseau advocated such a return either, though Rousseau did believe that man was best when he was fresh out of the state of nature and society had not yet corrupted him.

Paine never went that far. Nature for him exemplified simplicity, innocence, and order. The natural environment taught lessons in moral dignity. Nature told people what to do. Paine often personified her and gave her a distinctive personality. "Nature justifies," said Paine, or, "Nature cannot figure." Or "he who takes nature for his guide" or "the simple voice of nature says." Physical nature's moral grandeur included those rights which a person possessed as a part of his physical existence. The outdoors and democracy were united in such a way that, like Rousseau, Paine "turned the pastoral vision into a vehicle for the democratic idea."[7] If people were to progress, they must learn God's purposes from nature.[8]

The Prize of Nature

Paine, like Rousseau and other eighteenth-century writers concerned with nature, had no desire to go beyond the frontier, to return, in effect, to the state of nature.[9] He was essentially the product of an urban environment, although he had his early experience of the outdoors in small English Midlands towns. He spent the first nineteen years of his life in the small country town of Thetford. According to Conway, Paine's first serious biographer, the town "conveys the pleasant impression of a fairly composite picture of its eras and generations. There is a continuity between the old Grammar School, occupying the site of the ancient cathedral, and the new Guildhall, with its Mechanics' Institute. The old churches summon their flocks from eccentric streets suggestive of literal sheep-paths."[10] A more recent assessment noted that the area "was rich in wildlife and flowers, river and grassland. The young Paine could have plucked the tall-stalked, blue-flowered Viper's Bugloss, the musk thistle and wild mignonette, and watched the flight of innumerable birds, including the Great Bustard who long ago left our shores." These sights and experiences undoubtedly impressed the young Thomas Paine. During the Seven Years' War, his experiences at sea on the *King of Prussia* must also have had a profound effect. Audrey Williamson notes that he could, "on starry nights, have dreamed his dreams by the ship's sail, and had a vision of those inhabited worlds in space which so prophetically intrude into his book of deistic dissent, *The Age of Reason*."[11] The boundlessness of space and an apparently infinite sea surely impressed the young sailor. After the war, he pursued his interest in the outdoors purchasing globes and a telescope in England from the famous astronomer Dr. John Bevis of the Royal Society. "The natural bent of my mind was to science," he reported in *The Age of Reason* (*CW* 1:496).

His adventures at sea might account for his myriad uses of nautical metaphor and his particular interest in navies and gunboats.[12] Moreover, his interest in astronomy might directly relate to his theory that "the probability . . . is that each of those fixed stars is also a sun, round which another set of worlds or planets, though too remote for us to discover, performs its revolutions, as our system of worlds does round our central sun" (*Age of Reason, CW* 1:502). His projection of "a plurality of worlds" and "a multiple creation" might have resulted from stargazing in Thetford and at sea. Even his excise work provided "a healthy, open air life and Paine probably enjoyed it."[13] There can be no doubt that early experiences provided him with the grist for his religion of nature.

While Paine was a wanderer, he was no pioneer, like some rude and gruff fellow. He was satisfied with the scientific and cultural atmosphere of modern, urbane Philadelphia, London, and Paris. As he wrote to the Abbé Raynal in 1782, civilized man was no longer a "barbarian. . . . Man finds a thousand things to do now which before he did not. Instead of placing his ideas of greatness in the rude achievements of the savage, he studies arts, sciences, agriculture and commerce, the refinements of the gentleman, the principles of society, and the knowledge of the philosopher" (*CW* 2:241). These activities were all good, and Paine busied himself with many of them. One, of course, was writing. He had a natural facility for writing, and he used it powerfully.[14]

Although he was awed "by the immensity of space," the study of nature included all of God's works, including the microscopic world beyond perception. "Every tree, every plant, every leaf serves not only as a habitation but as a world to some numerous race, till animal existence becomes so exceedingly refined that the effluvia of a blade of grass would be food for thousands" (*Age of Reason, CW* 1:499–500).[15] From the vastness of the heavens to the secret, quiet world beyond man's sight, nature was a great reflection of God's creative genius.

And yet nature, in its primitive and wilderness form, was not a habitable place for Paine though he thought it possessed a part of God's divinity. God was the foundation of all life in the universe. A Quaker by upbringing, Paine noted that, while he agreed with the morality of the Friends, "if the taste of a Quaker could have been consulted at the Creation what a silent and drab-colored Creation it would have been! Not a flower would have blossomed its gayeties, nor a bird been permitted to sing" (*Age of Reason, CW* 1:498). The loss to him of these natural wonders, which he loved so much, would have been immeasurable.

Nature, Invention, and the Bastille

Like many eighteenth-century writers, Paine distinguished nature from invention—those things which had come into being through natural (or divine) causes from those things which exist because of man's creativity. This distinction focused first on things natural, which a person's common sense identified as good. Opposed to these were human inventions which, depending on the purposes for which they were used, might either be good or bad.[16]

To Paine, man's most evil institutions were monarchy, aristocracy, and the priesthood (and, later, political factions such as the Federalists). All of these worked against the dictates of common sense. The people could create good government only if they went "back to Nature for information." This hearkening back to nature was a constant knell sounded in his French revolutionary writings. He used it to argue that the revolution possessed a historical dimension so profound that it had a cosmic meaning. The very future of the world was at stake. In using images from nature during the 1790s, Paine expresses his desire about the future.

His intention was to show that the alternative to monarchy and aristocracy was what nature herself justified. What was a "natural" political association for mankind? The democratic republic was comparable to an organic, hence natural, being. "Like the nation itself, it possesses a perpetual stamina, as well of body as of mind, and presents itself on the open theatre of the world in a fair and manly manner" (*RM* 182). Indeed, "the representative system is always parallel with the order and immutable laws of nature" (*RM* 183). Monarchy, on the contrary, was "a mode of government that counteracts nature" (*RM* 182).

If all men were makers, Paine found it unthinkable that some men were barred from political decision making. He failed to understand, much less be convinced by, Burke's argument that the propertied class born to wealth should govern society. For Burke, any other class's claim to govern was foolish and wrongheaded and against nature.

> As ability is a vigorous and active principle, and as property is sluggish, inert, and timid, it never can be safe from the invasions of ability, unless it be, out of all proportion, predominant in the representation. It must be represented too in great masses of accumulation, or it is not rightly protected. The characteristic essence of property, formed out of the combined principles of its acquisition and conservation, is to be *unequal.* The great masses therefore which excite envy, and tempt rapacity, must be put out of the possibility of danger.[17]

Paine's response was that anything that compromised "things natural" (such as Burke's myth of the gentry) was unnatural or, in the case of Christianity, supernatural. People like Burke compromised nature to obtain political control for their own insidious purposes. Indeed, they misused language to convince their audiences of what (to Paine, at least) was wrong, misleading, and confusing.

Paine desired a return not to nature herself but to nature's calling. He argued that through common sense man knew what was natural. By studying God's creation, people could learn to use common sense wisely. There was a direct connection between the power of one's mind and heart and the natural physical world. Through individualization and self-realization, the self develops to its greatest potential. But first it is necessary to learn from nature. Two of Paine's best-known passages, both from his French revolutionary writings, reflect his use of physical nature to draw lessons from. The first occurs at the end of the second part of *Rights of Man* and focuses on the arrival of spring, the budding revolutionary era that had started in America and was now flowing into France in 1789 and from there throughout the world. The renewal of the earth symbolically represents the coming regeneration of continental government. This kind of symbolism is also part of Paine's homiletic style.

> It is now towards the middle of February. Were I to take a turn into the country, the trees would present a leafless winterly appearance. As people are apt to pluck twigs as they walk along, I perhaps might do the same, and by chance observe, that a single bud on that twig had begun to swell. I should reason very unnaturally, or rather not reason at all, to suppose this was the only bud in England which had this appearance. Instead of deciding thus, I should instantly conclude, that the same appearance was beginning, or about to begin, everywhere; and though the vegetable sleep will continue longer on some trees and plants than on others, and though some of them may not blossom for two or three years, all will be in leaf in the summer, except those which are rotten. What pace the political summer may keep with the natural, no human foresight can determine. It is, however, not difficult to perceive that the spring is begun.[18] (*RM* 272–73)

In this famous passage, Paine drew together several elements of his political ideology with natural imagery to make a powerful argument.[19] First, of course, was nature herself. Walking in the country in midwinter the observer might be tempted to conclude that all was yet dormant. But common sense told him this was not the case. The natural transformation that the change of seasons brings has already begun to happen, as has the transvaluation of human political principles. The springtime of political renewal was just beginning. This springtime was different from all other springs. It was to last forever, and the people would never return to "the present winter," something the Americans also had experienced before their revolution (*CS* 89).

The new spring was inevitable, just as it was the fate of the worm to become a butterfly, an image he used in *The Age of Reason*. The worm in this image is different from the worms he used to represent kings. Like the spring, the transformation of the worm parallels the transvaluation of politics.

> The most beautiful parts of the creation to our eye are the winged insects, and they are not so originally. They acquire that form and that inimitable brillancy by progressive changes. The slow and sleeping caterpillar-worm of today passes in a few days to a torpid figure and a state resembling death; and in the next change comes forth in all the miniature magnificence of life, a splendid butterfly. (*CW* 1:592)

The lowliest of creatures, the worm, once emblematic of the king, has now been transformed into a new being. A transvaluation of kingship to democracy has taken place with the transformation of worm to butterfly. First, the worm appeared to enter a deathlike state, but not death itself. It was rather "a state resembling death." From this state, the new creature emerged. Like the passage from winter to spring, this change was quite natural. And as the new springtime was permanent, worms would never again be like kings. Now only butterflies and springtime abound. From cold, dark slavery and tyranny, man entered into a new era of light, freedom, and democracy.

   In this connection, the storming and subsequent destruction of the Bastille in 1789 became a powerful metaphor for revolutionary action.[20] Its fall, like the transformation of the king-worm into the butterfly, eliminated an unnatural creation. Here Paine's homiletics reached a heightened sense of immediacy: his tone was full of anxiety and fear. As we will soon see, for Paine, it was a battle in extremis. The Bastille, a physical extension of monarchy, had to be destroyed. On its site, Parisians erected nature herself: a statue of great fertility, where on 10 August 1793, a celebration took place, a celebration that the great revolutionary artist, Jacques-Louis David himself, arranged:[21]

> The gathering will take place on the site of the Bastile [*sic*]. In the midst of its ruins will be erected the fountain of Regeneration representing nature. From her fertile breasts (which she will press with her hands) will spurt an abundance of pure and healthful water of which shall drink, each in his turn, eighty-six commissioners, sent by the primary assemblies—one, namely from each department, seniority being given the preference.
>
>   A single cup shall serve for all. After the president of the National Convention shall have watered the soil of liberty by a sort of libation, he shall be the first to drink; he shall then pass the cup in succession to

the commissioners of the primary assemblies. They shall be summoned alphabetically to the sound of the drum, a salvo of artillery shall announce the consummation of this act of fraternity.[22]

Paine pronounced the Bastille "the high altar and castle of despotism" (*RM* 56). Even the conservative Horace Walpole called it "a curious sample of ancient castellar dungeons, which the good fools the founders took for palaces—yet I always hated to drive by it, knowing the miseries it contained."[23]

David described what would happen as the great August procession continued through the streets of Paris:

> At [Liberty's] feet will be an enormous pyre, reached by steps from on all sides: there in profoundest silence shall be offered in expiatory sacrifice the impostured attributes of royalty. There, in the presence of the beloved goddess of the French, eighty-six commissioners, each with a torch in his hand, shall vie with each other in applying the flame; there the memory of the tyrant shall be devoted to public execration and then immediately thousands of birds restored to liberty and bearing on their necks light bands on which shall be written some articles of the declaration of the rights of man, shall take their rapid flight through the air and carry to heaven the testimony of liberty restored to earth.[24]

David here combined the elements that Paine, too, believed were united into a single whole: nature in all her glory, the new light that emanated from Liberty, the rights of man, and eternal freedom. David's report of this celebration, this *fête révolutionnaire*, was very Rousseauistic. Rousseau had presaged just such a *fête* in *Emile* (474) when he wrote of the festivals that Emile and Sophie might bring to the countryside. For the French after 1789, their newly won freedom became a cause for celebration in a natural setting. Indeed, as early as 1758, Rousseau noted, in his *Letter to d'Alembert*, that "we already have many of these public festivals; let us have even more. . . . It is in the open air, under the sky, that you ought to gather and give yourselves to the sweet sentiment of your happiness. . . . Plant a stake crowned with flowers in the middle of a square; gather the people together there, and you will have a festival."[25] The French celebrated such open-air festivals in Paris in just the way David described the transformation of the Bastille into "a ballroom beneath the trees" and the symbolic transformation of the Champ de Mars from a field of military assembly to "a natural earthen arena" to commemorate the first anniversary of the revolution.[26] Thereafter, the revolution was dedicated to nature, especially the sun, the symbol of the great illumination that had taken place in 1789. It was "pure fire, eternal eye,

Burke rejected the claim of British noisemakers, rabble like Richard Price, that they themselves represented a majority in English society. "No such thing," he thundered, "I assure you."

> Because a half a dozen grasshoppers under a fern make the field ring with their importunate chink, whilst thousands of great cattle, reposed beneath the shadow of the British oak, chew the cud and are silent, pray do not imagine, that those who make the noise are the only inhabitants of the field, that of course, they are many in number; or that, after all, they are other than the little shrivelled, meagre, hopping, though loud and troublesome insects of the hour."[33]

The "shadow of the British oak" extended far. It stultified the annoying bugs that made all the commotion beneath its great branches.

Paine would have none of it. The British oak must come down, or it would rot. So must the French oak. For Paine, the tree directly contrasted with the castle prison of the Bastille. In 1791, speaking at the Thatched House Tavern in London, Paine congratulated the French people "for having laid the axe to the root of tyranny, and for erecting government on the sacred *hereditary rights of man*."[34] In its place, in the place of the aristocratic oak of Edmund Burke, free men could now plant a liberty tree.

Rousseau used this same natural imagery when he described "bands of peasants . . . regulating their affairs of state under an oak tree, and always acting wisely."[35] Echoing this, Paine early on had cited the precedent that men long ago had gathered to form their first government "at some convenient tree" to "afford them a State House, under the branches of which, the whole colony may assemble to deliberate on public matters" (*CS* 67).[36] This tree, Paine's version of the oak, was emblematic not only of their association, but of men's free choice to join together. In the shade of this tree, they found comfort and solace, which was quite different from what the English found under "the shadow of the British oak." Here, they found that they could naturally use their innate capabilities without outside interference. It was not by accident that they chose a tree to do it under. Like the earth, the tree united the community to nature.

They gathered there to deliberate the great issues of the day. The tree was not left to those sleepy-eyed, cud-chewing cows in the pasture lying in a somnolent state under its rotten branches. For Paine, the grasshoppers (in Burke's imagery) now abounded. They were not merely noisemakers, that is, they were different from the ungainly mobs of the Gordon riots, "who committed the burnings and devastations in London" (*RM* 58). Those engaged in revolution were, for the most part, now behaving naturally. "The Almighty hath implanted in us these unextinguishable feelings for good and wise purposes. They are the guardians of his image in our hearts" (*CS* 99–100). This was true of all people. No matter what anyone, including Burke, said, this could not be changed. After all, said Paine, "whatever appertains to the nature of man, cannot be annihilated by man" (*RM* 44). Man in his person reflected the justice of God. No person could ever destroy this phenomenon.

Addressed to the Americans in 1775, Paine's poem, "Liberty Tree," allowed the poet to sing of the arrival of "the Goddess Liberty" in "a chariot of light." She brought with her a gift: a plant, which was "a pledge of her love." She called the plant "Liberty Tree."

> The celestial exotic stuck deep in the ground,
>   Like a native it flourished and bore;
> The fame of its fruit drew the nations around,
>   To seek out this peaceable shore.
> Unmindful of names or distinctions they came,
>   For freemen like brothers agree;
> With one spirit endued, they one friendship pursued,
>   And their temple was Liberty Tree.

These "freemen" thrived beneath its boughs. But England, which he mentioned by name, showed

> How all the tyrannical powers,
> Kings, Commons, and Lords, are uniting amain
>   To cut down this guardian of ours.

For the poet, the tree would survive this assault and grow to full fruition for all people everywhere, because they would "unite with a cheer, / In defense of our Liberty Tree."[37]

No barriers, then, separated the American people from nature, or from God. Nor, in fact, did they separate any people anywhere from God. "Before any institution of government was known in the world, there existed, if I may so express it, a compact between God and Man, from the beginning of time; and that as the relation and condition which man in his *individual person* stands in towards his Maker, cannot be changed" (*RM* 113).

Burke would have wanted intermediaries (kings, lords, and priests) to stand between the people and God, on the one hand, and between the people and nature, on the other. Not so Paine: For the first time, a person could become truly conscious of his status in the natural world. He could learn what nature meant him to be and what nature had imparted to him. It was a powerful argument, expressed clearly and homiletically, and especially frightening for the British establishment, which feared the spread of revolu-

tionary ideas and actions to their island nation. Paine's case was so forcefully
made that *Rights of Man* (like *The Age of Reason* within a few years) was
banned in England, and Paine outlawed.

God, Nature, and Light

In considering this permanent bond among the people, God, and nature, we should wonder how far Paine was willing to take it. In a 1797
pamphlet, written as a letter to Thomas Erskine, in which Paine defended
The Age of Reason, he contended that he had a right to deny the truth of the
Bible. He then set out to argue why it was "a duty which every man owes
himself, and reverentially to his Maker, to ascertain by every possible inquiry
whether there be a sufficient evidence to believe [the scriptures] or not." In
the course of his analysis, Paine suddenly broke off, as he was wont to do, and
wondered why it was necessary for anyone to have to explain contradictory
and miraculous stories. Having concluded that such contradictions should
cause any reasonably intelligent person "to suspect that it is not the word of
God," he continued:

> What! does not the Creator of the universe, the Fountain of all wis-
> dom, the Origin of all science, the Author of all knowledge, the God of
> order and harmony, know how to write? When we contemplate the
> vast economy of the creation, when we behold the unerring regularity
> of the visible solar system, the perfection with which all its several parts
> revolve, and by corresponding assemblage form a whole; —when we
> launch our eye into the boundless ocean of space, and see ourselves
> surrounded by innumerable words, not one of which varies from its
> appointed place—when we trace the power of a creator, from a mite to
> an elephant, from an atom to a universe—can we suppose that the
> mind that could conceive such a design and the power that executed it
> with incomparable perfection, cannot write without inconsistence, or
> that a book so written can be the work of such a power?[38]

On the simplest level, this passage reflected Paine's deism. He presented
God, nature's God, as a creator, a first cause, who brought order and harmony to the universe and who was the author of human reason. And yet,
something deeper, more mystical, was going on here. The bond that he saw
between the people, God, and nature placed him in the company of those
whom Margaret C. Jacob has termed members of "the Radical Enlightenment:" the freemasons and pantheists who, like Paine, were mystical,
democratic thinkers at the end of the eighteenth century.

There are indications that Paine's version of the bond among God, the people, and nature tended to mimic in language the radical Enlightenment, which included pantheistic elements, a curious notion for a deist. Even so, the essentials of this tendency included the idea that God was more than the creator, more than the force that ordered the universe. He resided in that very order itself. He was "the Grand Architect," whose spirit dwelled within every living creature in the natural world.[39] This spirit empowered people to rule themselves without the intervention of kings, lords, and priests. Nature and man were linked in a way that had mystical, almost magical, connotations. It was the convergence of these three elements—God, the people, and nature—which gave substance to Paine's religion of nature, the way in which he expressed his worship of God's manifest creation in his own peculiar way (largely through his writings).

Paine's evocation of an orderly and well-regulated universe in his letter to Erskine went beyond a Newtonian vocabulary. God was more than a watchmaker. He was a divine immanence in the world. His power was traceable throughout all creation: from the lowliest, tiny mite to the gigantic elephant; from the atom, the smallest known element, to the entire universe itself. God not only created but continued to create the universe. His spirit and power were eternally present in time and space as a continual creation. Paine said in *The Age of Reason* that "the Creation speaks a universal language. . . . It is an *ever-existing* original, which every person can read" (*CS* 1:483). Do we want to know what God is? We will find God only in what we are, what we see, what we feel. God was in our very being. A person reflected God's nature, and a person's common sense, through its combination of reason and sensibility, reflected God's wisdom. Follow the dictates of your heart and mind, and your "moral life will follow," said Paine, adding an "of course" to the end of this sentence (*CS* 1:485). Through the medium of the natural world, through nature herself, "God speaketh universally to man." Study nature, Paine advised, and you will not only find "the works of God" but will soon discover that the power of God dwells in all living things (*CW* 1:487).

Shortly before writing to Erskine, Paine helped form an association in Paris whose purpose was to underscore the bond of the people, God, and nature. This association was the Society of the Theophilanthropists, the "adorers of God and friends of man."[40] While it remains debatable that Paine was ever a member of a Freemasonry lodge, he was definitely an early member of the society. Its records show that he addressed its membership at its gatherings, and he probably had a hand in drafting its bylaws.[41] Attached to the Erskine letter was a history of the Theophilanthropists, which Paine himself wrote.

The term *theophilanthropist* embodied the spiritual linkage that Paine thought existed among God, the people, and nature. Paine's history of the society made clear that worship of God was a matter of individual faith and belief. Not only were interventions by priests and appeals to superstition unnecessary; they were beyond the bounds of belief. God-in-his-natural-creation was the only subject of the theophilanthropists' adoration. The ethical traditions recounted in their "festivals," as Paine called their worship (echoing perhaps the celebrations and *fêtes révolutionnaires* in the 1790s), were not foreign to Paine. After all, "the wise precepts that have been transmitted by writers of all countries and in all ages" provided the foundation for these ethical traditions. Theirs was a universal understanding of God-in-nature, and their ideas were the same ones he incorporated into *The Age of Reason*.[42]

Paine's linkage of the people, God, and nature was even more pronounced in his discussion of Freemasonry. He often used the contrast between dark and light to emphasize the transvaluation of life in the new revolutionary age. While darkness might be as much a part of nature as light, blackness embodied evil and slavery. In *Rights of Man,* he preached that "what we have to do is clear as light" and that the rights of man emanated as "illuminating and divine principles." A person could know this immediately and automatically, for "the sun needs no inscription to distinguish him from darkness" (*RM* 159). Paine's understanding of Freemasonry and its origins fitted into this scheme. It originated with the ancient druids, whose primary focus was sun worship. Their beliefs, pure and virtuous, were grounded in a simple, innocent piety that served as a model for those who claimed to be in the community of the faithful.

The druids' sun worship greatly inspired Paine. In the course of his discussion, independent even of his history of Freemasonry, he remarked that the sun was "this great luminary." In "Origins of Freemasonry" he called it "the great visible agent" of God.[43] He evidently admired the centrality of nature in the druids' lives. They possessed "that wise, elegant, philosophical religion," which he took for the exact "opposite to the faith of the gloomy Christian Church" (*CS* 2:835). Those who founded their practices and who formulated their beliefs were obviously "a wise, learned, and moral class of men," everything that Paine hoped he could be (*CW* 2:837). Through them, all people could learn true moral duty and acquire a love of nature that worked its way directly and inevitably to the divine itself.

Paine worshiped the sun as a reflection of the luminescence of God's creation. It is difficult to pinpoint exactly how Paine arrived at a religion of nature. His experiences in Thetford and the English countryside in early life were important influences on his love of and appreciation for the physical landscape. They may explain the place of nature in his work of the 1770s and

1780s. But his later writings led in an alternative direction toward his French experiences, in particular to his long association with one of the most interesting and curious journalists of the time, the romantic Nicholas de Bonneville.

Paine met Bonneville perhaps as early as 1791 and visited him often from 1797 until his return to America in 1802.[44] Bonneville's wife, Marguerite, with her three sons (one of whom was Paine's godson and namesake, Thomas Paine Bonneville), followed Paine to America the next year and at various times lived on his farms in Bordentown and New Rochelle. Paine provided for them in his will to ensure their financial stability. In the meantime, he took it upon himself to look after two of her sons (the eldest in 1804 returned to his father) and saw to their education.[45] Paine and Nicholas de Bonneville, twenty-three years his junior, were intimate friends. After 1802, in correspondence, Paine continually urged Bonneville to come to America, but it appears that he was unable to emigrate under the Napoleonic regime. He finally arrived after Paine's death.[46]

Bonneville was the founder of a revolutionary organization called "*le Cercle Social,*" of which Paine was probably a member.[47] As a journalist, he edited several newspapers, some of which printed Paine's writings. For James H. Billington, the Social Circle "combined the Masonic ideal of a purified inner *circle* with the Rousseauist ideal of a *social,* and not merely a political contract."[48] Bonneville was an early follower of Illuminism (which, because he spoke German, he helped bring to France from Germany). Illuminism paralleled existing French Masonic ideas of peace and brotherhood, light and brilliance. These were things that Paine was interested in as well. From the Social Circle, Bonneville declared, there would "emanate a *circle of light* which will uncover for us that which is hidden in the symbolic chaos of masonic innovations."[49]

The Social Circle was a small, secret, Masonic-like organization whose members adopted assumed names and carried secret identity cards. To support it, Bonneville organized a larger mass association, "the Universal Confederation of the Friends of Truth," the "servant of the Social Circle" and "of all the circles 'of free brothers affiliated with it.'"[50] Bonneville envisioned it producing yet another new society for the new breed of men: the new Illuminati, the men of vision. "The Circle of Free People [will] pour forth with a sure hand thy luminous rays into the dark climates."[51] The French newspaper *Mercure* reported that Bonneville addressed these remarks to the sun with the words, "Eclairé, le monde sera éclairé!"[52]

It is difficult, if not impossible, to know with certainty whether long association with Bonneville and his Illuminist ideals directly or indirectly stimulated Paine's religion of nature. His ideas were certainly suggestive.

Because fire destroyed much of Paine's work after his death, the difficulty is compounded. And yet, the pattern that Paine established in his writing does, however circumstantially, point to Bonneville and his followers.

The brilliant spirit and power of God penetrated the natural world. The people reflected this spirit and power through their inventive capabilities, particularly their power to transform the world, if they wished. The Freemasons, the Theophilanthropists, the Illuminati all focused on nature's link to God and the people. In so doing, they provided a means, indeed an entire language, for Paine to attack those who, in his opinion, denied the people what was theirs by nature, and hence by God. By using common sense, people could know that the natural world, from the landscape to the rights of man, was authentic, virtuous, and ultimately sacred.

Natural rights were inherent qualities of all mankind to a greater extent than anyone before had suspected. A person had a natural right, in effect, to these rights because they were part of nature with its indwelling presence of God and his power. More important, the people possessed a divine right to them, because God from the beginning of time itself, from eternity, had ordained it. This was the lesson Paine preached in the 1790s to his audience of common people, principally in America and England, but also in France. He hoped this message would soon spread to Britain and eventually throughout the continent to induce all Europeans to restore the rights of man.

❧ 4 ❦

Nature and the Theory
of Rights

Like the physical landscape, rights were part of the natural world. The people's struggle to exercise them was more than a struggle for freedom. It was also a struggle to regain what God intended for them. When he created the earth, hence nature, God simultaneously created the rights of man. They were a gift to all people, not a select few. No individual could deprive anyone of God's gift of "the divine right of man to freedom."[1] Natural rights were also the basis of inherent equality. All people possessed an equal share of rights. Usurpers might claim that they ruled by some authority other than nature: by the authority of divine right, hereditary tradition, or even bald political power. In reality, however, they were merely usurpers, and their arguments were as shallow as they were false.

Thomas Paine used a "language of human rights." Richard Tuck has wondered whether such language signified anything more than the assertion that someone is "the beneficiary of someone else's duty." If talk about rights is looked at historically, then it becomes a more complex phenomenon: it is tied directly to the political theory of any given thinker. As a result, "we have to be sure about what role the term played in the various theories about politics which engage our attention."[2] Paine's position was that a person should acknowledge as divine those rights inherent to the life of man, those that make him a free and equal creature. To speak properly of hereditary succession, a person should speak only of the passage of natural rights from generation to generation to everyone and not merely to the few. The people must constantly struggle against those who seek to gain sufficient power to compromise the rights of man.

When addressing one man's desire to dominate another, Paine used

natural rights language as it had developed principally in Lockean theory.
Paine preached the historical roots of rights and the measures the people
must take to assure the security of these rights. His most developed ideas of
rights are found in *Rights of Man*, which he wrote in the aftermath of the
revolution in France. Here, he used Lockean themes of natural rights but
spiced his discussion with powerful images and metaphors that would appeal
to his primarily British audience of middle- and lower-class people. As part
of God's gift, indeed as part of nature herself, man's rights (like his nature)
were synonymous with man's life and character. Nature, from the natural
world and human nature to the rights of man, was indivisible. Natural rights
were the core, the centerpiece, of a person's life as a political animal, just as
they were the essence of his humanity. They gave him his most powerful
weapon against governmental encroachments on his person and on his freedom, especially his conscience and intellect.

Natural rights bridged the gap between man as individual and as citizen.
Paine always knew that government, though he disliked it, existed to bring
order to a fundamentally disordered world. Its system of rewards and punishments helped "to supply the defect of moral virtue," to keep the people's
passionate tendencies under control (*CS* 66). Even as he entered into political society and took the step beyond natural, social relations to civic or
political relations and as he exchanged certain natural rights for civil rights,
man always retained natural rights of the mind and soul independent of
government or society. They were his alone.

Entry into civil society did not destroy these rights, or as Paine called
them, this class of rights. They were fundamental. God had decreed that a
human being always possessed them, no matter what. Even if some external
force like government prevented a person from exercising them, these rights
remained part of his being.

If God gave these rights as a gift, that gift signified God's immanence in
time and history. Bonneville's mysticism may shed some light on Paine's
notion of God's spirit dwelling in nature, but Bonneville may not be Paine's
only link to pantheistic ideas. The philosopher Benedict de Spinoza also
informed Paine's thoughts about the divine origins of human rights. An
investigation into the similarities between Paine and Spinoza offers more
than a comparative study in ideas.

Paine and Spinoza

Like Spinoza, with whose works he was familiar, Paine conceived of an
immanent divine presence in history. The political and philosophical paral-

lels between the two writers clarify Paine's position in regard to divine immanence and indicate one of the foundations of his homiletic style. Paine's belief in God's immanence throughout history gave his preaching a force and power which it may not have otherwise had.

Although Spinoza and Paine were separated by one hundred years, they shared several ideas about life, nature, and politics. Paine specifically noted Spinoza's influence in his later works, especially *The Age of Reason,* in which he cited Spinoza as an authority to attack the Bible's infallibility. (*CW* 1:547).[3] Although Spinoza's works were available in English translation at the end of the eighteenth century, Caroline Robbins and R. R. Palmer suggest that Paine probably read only the *Tractatus Theologico-Politicus.*[4] More interesting are the similarities in their political views and personal styles. They both believed in the separation of church and state and strongly adhered to the principle of religious freedom.[5] Moreover, Spinoza and Paine were strong advocates of the principle of free expression. Paine's writings were his lifeblood. He wrote passionately in order to instruct, indeed to preach. No theme was out of the question. Spinoza, like Paine an artisan (he was a lens grinder), preferred a private intellectual life. Although he rarely showed his writings to anyone, the ideals of intellectual freedom permeate his work. "Spinoza was the first political philosopher of modern times to avow himself a democrat."[6] These parallels indicate a superficial similarity in the two writers' ideas. After all, to believe in religious and intellectual freedom in the late eighteenth century was to fall into the mainstream of liberal thinking of the time. More striking is that their ideas of nature were astonishingly parallel.

For Paine, divine immanence enlivened nature; life on earth, the product of God's creation, was a holy affirmation of a man's success, and his passage through time amounted to ineluctable progress toward human perfectibility and oneness with God and nature. Paine was not simply espousing an Enlightenment ideal of perfectibility. The presence of God, through God's creation, inspired him. Because nature contained the divine, it was incalculably more special to Paine. Its divinity made it qualitatively different from the inventions that man had forged on his own. Those inventions, like government, were but a pale reflection of God's works. As man aspired through his own creative impulse to achieve the divine, to achieve perfection in this life, all that he could hope for was to live well (and increasingly better) in a God-centered world containing God's indwelling spirit.

Paine's religion of nature sounds quite Spinozistic. God is in nature, said Spinoza, although God and nature are not one and the same because they consist of two distinct substances.

I hold an opinion about God and Nature very different from that which Modern Christians are wont to defend. For I maintain that God is, as they say, the immanent cause of all things, but not the transeunt [*sic*] cause. Like Paul, and perhaps also like all ancient philosophers, though in another way, I assert that all things live and move in God; and I would dare to say that I agree also with all the ancient Hebrews as far as it is possible to surmise from their traditions, even if these have become corrupt in many ways.[7]

Spinoza's view, like Paine's, was incipiently liberal and democratic in its implied equality. God's presence, never reserved for an elect few, was manifested in all people, equally and uniformly.

Lewis Feuer has noticed a parallel between the ideas of Spinoza and Quakerism (of which Paine was a member from early life), a connection that may best explain the parallels between Paine and Spinoza. Spinoza at one point met William Ames, an English Quaker, who was trying to persuade the Dutch Mennonites to combine with the Friends. "They shared the same ideas on the inner light of reason, and they both rejected the interpretation of Scripture by authority."[8] For Spinoza and Paine, for the Quakers and even the Levellers of Spinoza's time, the democratic character of this universal endowment was clear: "the highest good of those who follow virtue is common to all, and all may equally enjoy it."[9] Equality overcame the aristocratic predominance inherent in Calvinism and the hereditary succession of the Elect, which logically followed.

Spinoza lived for a time in Rijnsburg with a group of Dutch Collegiants, spiritual descendants of the Anabaptists, whom Feuer calls "religious communist revolutionaries."[10] Although their views were similar to those of the Quakers, Paine never mentioned them. The sixteenth-century Anabaptists, however, drew their support, as Paine was to do two hundred fifty years later, mainly from the lower classes: the urban craftsmen and mechanics, such as tailors, bakers, carpenters, and other artisans and tradesmen.

By the seventeenth century, the Anabaptists' theology had passed to the Mennonites, who renounced violence as a means to induce social change. The Mennonites retained Anabaptists' influence over the skilled Dutch artisans. According to Margaret Jacob, Mennonite communism was a peaceful affair. Even so their insistence on common ownership angered Grotius, who thought their communism would lead, says Jacob, to "nothing but discontent and dissension." The Collegiants, whom Spinoza joined, were Mennonites who met in "collegia," not churches, to avoid the government's harsh persecution. They maintained close ties to the English Quakers.[11]

A natural link connected democratic values and God's immanence in nature, on the one hand, and Paine's Quaker background, on the other. To suggest that he was a spiritualist or animist misses the point. And he was not merely a radical democrat or a follower of Spinoza. The element of pantheism must, however, be included, but on Paine's terms. If God were in nature, including all men, then certainly those who attacked nature were not in nature. Paine here moved beyond Quakerism, beyond the inner light philosophy inherent in the Society of Friends, because he knew that the immanence of God in his creations was a matter of faith.

Paine's emphasis on the inner light which naturally shines within all human beings was a leitmotif of his homiletics, especially as he condemned those whose inner light he thought had been extinguished. They in fact denied this inner light and were consequently the enemies of nature and the enemies of men, and thus of God himself. In effect, their lives were spent contrary to the light of nature, a theme Paine used in his condemnation of slavery and the slave trade.

It is impossible to say with certainty where Paine picked up on this theme, but he used it throughout his work, especially in the 1790s. It was clearly a concept in widespread use in the latter part of the century, when images of the light of reason, the Enlightenment, and such abounded. Paine, however, may have been influenced by his Quaker background in this, although he himself never linked his usage of it to the Quakers. What is important is that he felt that people who denied the light of nature were the enemies of democracy. To deny people freedom, an inherent part of their life, reduced them to creatures less than human. This was the lot of the slave, who was worse treated than the lowliest of creatures.

Slavery: Black and White, Indian and Female

Paine first indicated his belief in inherent equality in his 1775 writings in America. He was convinced that he could teach his newly adopted American brethren that the white man's enslavement of blacks was morally equivalent to British dominance of America. With typical passion and force, he condemned both slavery and the slave trade that accompanied it. He did not limit his views about slavery to the horrible conditions of blacks in America. As bad as these conditions were, they were typical, at times allegorical, of all Americans (white and black), who were slaves to Britain, to that "royal savage," the king, as Paine told Cato in the second Forester letter.[12]

In his essay, "African Slavery in America," Paine preached against the unnaturalness of slavery. He wondered how people could identify themselves as Christians and at the same time participate in the slave trade and own other human beings. The root of his sentiment lay once again in Paine's vision of nature. Freedom was a natural condition, whereas slavery was an outright denial of what God had manifestly given people. Within a month of the piece's publication, he joined an abolitionist society.[13]

Explicitly using the inner light theme, Paine claimed that slavery in any form was "contrary to the light of nature" and "contrary to the plain dictates of natural light, and conscience."[14] People, he said, were born with rights, and though they might not have the opportunity to exercise them (because of an oppressive regime), they did not lose their humanity. They always retained their rights, no matter how horrible the oppression was. Thus, slaves deserved freedom. So long as the British pursued slavery in America and the slave trade, all Americans (white and black) endured a "wicked and inhuman" practice (*CW* 2:16).

American black slaves were not criminals. No court of justice had convicted them of crimes with the penalty of forfeiture of freedom and rights. Slavery was an extreme action. Any case brought against them which led to a sentence requiring them to remain slaves was immoral. "As these people are not convicted of forfeiting freedom, they have still a natural, perfect right to it." To favor slavery is akin to acclaiming "murder, robbery, lewdness, and barbarity" (*CW* 2:18)—all evil activities which Christian teaching condemned. He carefully instructed his American audience that if they held freedom and democracy dear, then slavery and the slave trade must end. For as long as the black African in America was enslaved, white America was, too.[15]

This was the underlying meaning of his statement in the third Forester letter (1776) that "a republican form of government is pointed out by nature—kingly governments by an unequality of power. In republican governments, the leaders of the people, if improper, are removable by vote; kings only by arms: an unsuccessful vote in the first case, leaves the voter safe; but an unsuccessful attempt in the latter, is death." (*CW* 2:78–79). God's intention was not for men to be the slaves of others, white over white or white over black. "To live beneath the authority of those whom we cannot love, is misery, slavery, or what name you please. Security will be a thing unknown, because a treacherous friend in power is the most dangerous of enemies." Such a "friend" was dangerous because he made men into slaves. Americans must choose and choose now to throw off the monarchical bonds and opt for the republic. "She hath a blank sheet to write upon. Put it not off too long," he declared. And in a footnote, Paine abjured his readers to "forget not the hapless African" (*CW* 2:82).

For his American audience, Paine neatly tied the freedom and independence of America to the emancipation of the slaves. Both peoples were slaves, black and white. Some people, like Cato and others who wrote against *Common Sense,* did not perceive this connection. Just four years later, Paine drafted the 1780 preamble to a Pennsylvania legislative act which was the first measure to emancipate slaves in America. Despite America's enslavement by Britain and the war that was in progress, the preamble ran, "We are unavoidably led to a serious and grateful sense of the manifold blessings which we have undeservedly received from the hand of that Being, from whom every good and perfect gift cometh" (*CW* 2:21). [16]

Paine argued that men possessed a duty to release their slaves

> from the state of thralldom, to which we ourselves were tyrannically doomed, and from which we have now every prospect of being delivered. It is not for us to inquire why, in the creation of mankind, the inhabitants of the several parts of the earth were distinguished by a difference in feature or complection [*sic*]. It is sufficient to know that all are the work of the Almighty Hand. We find in the distribution of the human species, that the most fertile as well as the most barren parts of the earth are inhabited by men of complexions different from ours, and from each other; from whence we may reasonably as well as religiously infer, that He, who placed them in their various situations, has extended equally His care and protection to all, and that it becomes not us to counteract His mercies. (*CW* 2:21–22)

America alone had both the power and the will to return to these people, "denominated Negro and mulatto slaves," the "common blessings that they were by nature entitled to." These statements echoed the sentiment articulated four years earlier in the third Forester letter, that "all men are republicans by nature, and royalists only by fashion." He taught, therefore, that slavery was as unnatural as monarchy. It was immoral. It deprived some people of the opportunity to exercise their natural rights, and for that reason, everyone should condemn it. America's liberation from Britain and the liberation of America's black slaves were thus inextricably connected.

These forms of slavery were not the only manifestations of the denial of human rights. Paine's sentiments were the same, for example, when he reflected on British misrule in India. In his 1775 reverie about Lord Clive, Paine envisioned him murderously governing India with a corrupt administration that brought him great wealth and high position. At the end of Clive's life, Paine had him recanting his inhuman deeds. If "some sacred power [could] convey me back to youth and innocence," Paine's Clive said, "'I'd keep within the value of humble life.'"[17] Knowing the misfortunes he caused hundreds of Indians, Clive wished he had offered them peace and justice instead. No foreign troops misbehaved worse than the British troops under Clive in India, Paine later wrote in the third Forester letter. "The tying men to the mouths of cannon and 'blowing them away' was never acted by any but an

English General or approved by any but a British court." Then in a footnote, filled with the biting irony he was famous for, Paine noted that "Lord Clive, the chief of Eastern plunderers, received the thanks of Parliament for his 'honorable conduct in the East Indies" (*CW* 2:77).

This same tone pervaded Paine's writings concerning women, which coincided with those expressing abhorrence of slavery. Paine emphasized and reemphasized the unnatural relationship between slave and servant. In an early piece in 1775, Paine argued that "women more than share all our miseries, and are besides subjected to ills which are peculiarly their own."[18] He placed women's liberation in the same category as liberation of African slaves.

In line with the conventions of his time, he described nature as having a feminine gender. But his reference to Providence as a woman has no tradition in England or America in the eighteenth century. For Paine, Providence was a kind of composite of God (as creator, and a male image in most of his work) and Nature (always female). Providence as clearly a woman and not androgynous was a concept that may well have been peculiar to Paine. In the sixth number of the *American Crisis* (1778), he called on "the interposition of Providence, and *her* blessings on our endeavors" in the American effort against Britain (*CW* 1:131).[19] And two years later, in a letter to General Nathanael Greene, for whom he served as aide-de-camp during the war, Paine commented on the Benedict Arnold affair with the words, "Why, if Providence had the management of the whole, did *she* let Arnold escape: Perhaps to be hung afterwards by the Enemy for some act of traitorship against them."[20]

On his return to America in 1802, he continued this theme. Sobered by the revolutionary Terror, he accused the Federalists of being as evil as Robespierre and speculated why "they have not yet accused Providence of Infidelity," since they had accused Paine of treason. He continued:

> Yet according to their outrageous piety, *she* must be as bad as Thomas Paine; *she* has protected him in all his dangers, patronized him in all his undertaking, encouraged him in all his ways, and rewarded him at last by bringing him in safety and in health to the Promised Land. This is more than *she* did by the Jews, the chosen people, that they tell us *she* brought out of the land of Egypt, and out of the house of bondage; for they all died in the wilderness, and Moses too.[21]

Womanhood had power. Paine's sentiments were for the immediate liberation of women just as he argued for the liberation of slaves everywhere: black or white, male or female, Indian or even British.[22]

And yet, although Paine condemned the mistreatment of women by men, of blacks by whites, and of the Americans and Indians by the British, he never once placed all men, all British, or all whites in the category he reserved for kings and nobles, priests and Federalists. The latter were unregenerative creatures who deserved no sympathy. Some white men, some British for that matter, and some males had redeeming characteristics. Men like Thomas Paine, for example, taught them how to reform their ways. Ultimately, they could contribute to the improvements and progress that the majority of society experienced in a world undergoing revolution.

Burke's Challenge

Paine faced the challenge of his life in the arguments of Edmund Burke against human rights.[23] In *Rights of Man*, Paine sharpened his focus on rights largely because of Burke's response to Richard Price's famous sermon, the *Discourse on the Love of Our Country* (1790). Here Paine developed his most penetrating theory of human rights, engaging his audience in a historical review of the immediate developments of the French Revolution, the nature and origins of human rights, and the direction in which the people must go if they were to succeed in creating a good and just constitution. He tried to convince his readers of the need for revolution throughout Europe to end all examples of the ancien régime.

Burke's *Reflections on the Revolution in France* (1790) defined the doctrine of prescription, his hallmark of political conservatism, which set forth the principle that historical longevity confirmed the worth of political and social institutions. The rights of man as Price had articulated them, fumed Burke, amounted to a spurious concept not rooted in history and experience. Price and radicals like him founded rights by appealing to abstract reason. This was wrong, for prescription and historical precedent, tradition and the hereditary principle were what made the English constitution work, not the ahistorical, metaphysical, or rational faculty or some "theory" mortal men conjured up, a theory that bore no relationship to historical development. "They have," said Burke, "'the rights of men.'"

Having set the tone, he continued:

Against these there can be no prescription; against these no agreement is binding: these admit no temperament, and no compromise: any thing withheld from their full demand is so much of fraud and injustice. Against these their rights of men let no government look for security in the length of its continuance, or in the justice and lenity of its administration. The objections of these speculatists, if its forms do not quadrate with their theories, are as valid against such an old and

beneficent government as against the most violent tyranny, or the
greenest usurpation. They are always at issue with governments, not on
a question of abuse, but a question of competency, and a question of
title. I have nothing to say to the clumsy subtilty [*sic*] of their political
metaphysics. (148–49)

For a true understanding of the "science of government," one had to be
"practical." Government was "a matter which requires experience, and even
more experience than any person can gain in his whole life, however
sagacious and observing he may be." A man must use "infinite caution"
before thinking of "pulling down an edifice which has answered in any
tolerable degree for ages the common purposes of society, or on building it
up again, without having models and patterns of approved utility before his
eyes" (152). Otherwise, we are left solely with metaphysical rights, which
deny the complexities of politics and government. "When I hear the simplicity of contrivance aimed at and boasted of in any new political constitutions, I am at no loss to decide that the artificers are grossly ignorant of their
trade, or totally negligent of their duty"(153).

These artificers, whom he also called "speculators" and "metaphysicians," "sophists" and "confiscators," were all misguided. They thought that
they could bring liberty into reality just by calling it so, whereas this was not
the case. "Is it because liberty in the abstract," he asked, "may be classed
amongst the blessings of mankind, that I am seriously to felicitate a mad-
man, who has escaped from the protecting restraint and wholesome darkness
of his cell, on his restoration to the enjoyment of light and liberty?"(90).

The language of his answer was as hilarious as it was serious: "The wild
gas [a reference either to Joseph Priestley or flatulence, it is not clear], the
fixed air is plainly broke loose: but we ought to suspend our judgment until
the first effervescence is a little subsided." If government is to work effectively for the good of society, men must learn to combine it with liberty—
"with public force; with the discipline and obedience of armies; with the
collection of an effective and well-distributed revenue; with morality and
religion; with the solidity of property; with peace and order; with civil and
social manners." Without these things, liberty "is not likely to continue long"
(90–91) In other words, historical usage prescribed the continuance of established institutions.

But longevity was not the sole standard for Burke. Men must maintain
the institutions of government that they had, not only because they had
lasted, but because they produced positive results. These institutions "are the
instruments of wisdom," he said. "Wisdom cannot create materials; they are
the gifts of nature or of chance; her pride is in the use" (267).

Therefore, "old establishments are tried by their effects. If the people are happy, united, wealthy, and powerful, we presume the rest. We conclude that to be good from whence good is derived" (285). Elsewhere, he wrote, "a prescriptive government, such as ours, never was the work of any legislator, never was made upon any foregone theory."[24] The speculators and the metaphysicians, the projectors and the sophists were all responsible for the revolutionary destruction plaguing France and endangering Britain. The only outcome would be the reestablishment of order by a dictator, who would command the army and become "the master of your whole republic" (*Reflections*, 342).

Burke emphasized historical experience and convention, prescription and presumption. Paine thought he neglected the most important element concerning man's character, namely his origins as a natural and social being.[25] If Burke wished to argue from historical precedent, Paine suggested that he would inexorably and logically be led to human origins, hence to what God had intended to pass onto his creation. To argue from the perspective of history demanded a historical consciousness, which, Paine said, Burke ironically lacked.

Paine consequently provided a powerful argument, with yet a paradoxical twist, in Burke's own prescriptive terms. The ideals that Paine advocated (rights and freedom, equality and justice) were not metaphysical abstractions, as Burke had claimed. They were founded in history, deeply rooted in the human past, indeed in mankind's very creation. They were, in short, rooted in prescription, not convention. How Paine did this marked not only a clever, but a brilliant tour de force over Burke

Paine's Mythicization of History

Paine basically turned the tables on Burke's argument by mythicizing history.[26] He began with the claim that historical facts demonstrated conclusively what he said about the origins of mankind. Even so, he knew full well that he could not possibly prove his argument with any data. In reality, Paine played a mean trick on Burke, whose starting point for all social and political institutions was human history. He took Burke's argument from prescription and presumption and turned it on its head. Look to history, to experience, to usage, but do not stop at the words of some arbitrary, dead monarch like Elizabeth or William. Seek the roots of what a person is through his inheritance by examining his ultimate origins at the moment of creation. What happened afterward was often the result of accident and error, naked power and artful manipulation.[27]

Paine's fullest development of this argument came in *Rights of Man*, his lengthy consideration of Burke's prescriptive doctrine. There, he asked, "Does Mr. Burke mean to deny that *man* has any rights?"(*RM* 65).[28] If this were Burke's real meaning, Paine wanted to know whether Burke had included himself as well. But Burke, in *Reflections on the Revolution in France,* had said that man's sole right was the right of heredity, a principle that had lasted in time and had worked well in the British political system. "Men have a right," Burke bellowed, "to live by that rule," the right to obey.

> They have a right to the fruits of their industry; and to the means of making their industry fruitful. They have a right to the acquisitions of their parents; to the nourishment and improvement of their offspring; to instruction in life, and to consolation in death. Whatever each man can separately do, without trespassing upon others, he has a right to do for himself. . . . In this partnership all men have equal rights, but not to equal things. . . . As to the share of power, authority, and direction which each individual ought to have in the management of the state, that I must deny to be amongst the direct original rights of man in civil society; for I have in my contemplation the civil social man, and no other. It is a thing to be settled by convention.(149)

Man's only right was, in short, the right of inheritance: from his parents, from his own hands, to his children, nothing more. Thus, any appeal to natural right would by necessity destroy the rights that men have gained by convention. After all, Burke proclaimed, "government is not made in virtue of natural rights," but by "a contrivance of human wisdom"(150–51). For Burke, convention was a decisive improvement on natural right.

Paine was not interested in the argument that man's rights resulted from inheritance and convention, which included the obligation to obey men of higher social position and economic status. His purpose was to prove, using Burke's own argument, that man's rights were as natural and as original as his very creation. He thus appealed to the divine origins of these rights, which gave them a firmer foundation than Burke would ever have granted.

Rights were part of the human baggage that God had given to men from the beginning. He argued that "the error of those who reason by precedents drawn from antiquity, respecting the rights of man, is, that they do not go far enough into antiquity." And because they do not go the whole way, they are illogical. "This is no authority at all" (*RM* 65).[29]

Burke had said that one generation could bind those that followed it with prescriptions that were "an entailed inheritance derived from our forefathers, and to be transmitted to our posterity" (*Reflections,* 119). He rooted the idea of binding in his distrust of human reason, which he said, caused men like Thomas Paine, Richard Price, and Joseph Priestley to consider abstractions like rights to be valid. Reason was an abstraction, and from this abstraction others, such as human rights, were formulated. "The pretended rights of these theorists are all extremes; and in proportion as they are metaphysically true, they are morally and politically false. . . . Political reason is a computing principle; adding, subtracting, multiplying, and dividing, morally and not metaphysically or mathematically, true moral denominations" (153).

The idea that one generation bound all future ones was as repugnant to Paine as it was to Thomas Jefferson.[30] For Burke, it fitted into his prescriptive view that changes only occurred over very long stretches of time. "I would not exclude alteration neither," Burke wrote toward the end of the *Reflections*, "but even when I changed, it should be to preserve. . . . In what I did, I should follow the example of our ancestors. I would make the reparation as nearly as possible in the style of the building. . . . Let us add, if we please, but let us preserve what they have left" (375–76).

Paine did not wholly disagree with this. He asked only why Burke did not go to the source instead of to some intermediate stage of "hundreds" or even "thousands" of years back in time. Generations do not by right bind posterity. God alone does. Men of wisdom

> revolt at the idea of consigning their children, and their children's children, to the domination of persons here after to be born, who might, for anything they could foresee, turn out to be knaves or fools; and they would finally discover, that the project of hereditary governors and legislators *was a treasonable usurpation over the rights of posterity.* Not only the calm dictates of reason, and the force of natural affection, but the integrity of manly pride, would impel men to spurn such proposals.[31]

If generations did not, indeed could not, legally bind future ones, what were the best uses of the past? What precedents could the people consider legitimate? Precedents that passed from one generation to the next and onward to the future were arbitrary and were usually linked to a specific past moment and a specific set of circumstances. Time and space bound them. It was ridiculous to conceive that in a hundred or a thousand years from his time a future generation could "take us for a precedent" (*RM* 65).

What then was to be done? In a central passage in *Rights of Man*, Paine rather astonishingly suggested that we must look to "the divine origins of the rights of man at the creation" (*RM* 66). This was the sole resting place for the debate on prescription. By returning to creation, Paine explicitly used Burkean arguments of historical continuity, but for reasons quite different from Burke's. In his made-up historical argument, Paine argued from the perspective of eternity, a totally untenable and factually undemonstrable position. But he carried on: if we traced the genealogy of Christ to Adam, it was perfectly logical to "trace the rights of man to the creation of man." What was it that we would find? His answer was that we would find "the illuminating and divine principle of the equal rights of man." God had not given this principle only to the first generation of men, but "to generations of men succeeding one another. Every generation is equal in rights to the generations which preceded it, by the same rule that every individual is born equal in rights with his contemporary" (*RM* 66).

This did not mean that physical or intellectual differences among people did not exist. Paine's point was that other differences, namely class distinctions, were essentially the result of social artifice, that is, what people had created as social barriers. Some men were wealthy, others poor because of social usages and designs. These distinctions were not natural. In fact, they were beyond nature. They were not part of God's creation. At the same time, they did not vitiate a person's natural equality or his natural rights. Every succeeding generation, therefore, must consider itself as having the same rights as the very first generation. As Paine put it, "Every child born into the world must be considered as deriving its existence from God. The world is as new to him as it was to the first man that existed, and his natural right in it is of the same kind" (*RM* 66). Not only had the Judaeo-Christian tradition long maintained the principle of human equality, but all religions of the world subscribed to "the *unity of man,* as being of one degree"(*RM* 67).

Despite his utter distaste for scripture, Paine used it when it served his homiletic purposes. He turned to the Bible to demonstrate that the Mosaic account of creation, fully accepted in Christian doctrine but totally false to Paine, described God as creating man in his own image with "the only distinction between male and female: no other distinction is even implied." (*RM* 67).

In mythicizing man's past, Paine undoubtedly knew he was playing a mean trick on Burke. And he knew that Burke would not question the historical authority of scripture. Scripture was to Burke and many others an authentic historical source, and Paine employed it with great relish for his own purposes, even if he did not believe it. He argued that it showed that "the equality of man, so far from being a modern doctrine, is the oldest upon record." With the one exception of male and female, all other distinctions among people were man-made. God had created man with equal rights, and after that man alone erected governments which broke down that natural equality. Government separated man from his fellows. Though necessary, it was evil, and it was made more so by the hereditary principle. "When [man] forgets his origin, or, to use a more fashionable phrase, his *birth and family* . . . he becomes dissolute" (*RM* 67). His origin was, of course, at creation, and his family, the family of man.

The result was social differentiation. Hence, England had three classes: royalty, nobility, and commons. Social differentiation masked two of man's most important duties, neither of which had anything to do with governing. His first duty was to love God and appreciate God's creation, a duty that he naturally knew. It was one that "every man must feel," that he knew through his senses, through passion and feeling, naturally, and ultimately through his common sense (*RM* 67).

His second duty, no less important, man owed not to God but to his fellows. It took effect only after the creation of government. It was incorporated in the Biblical injunction "to do as he would be done by" (*RM* 67). Magistrates possessed this duty because their responsibility was to treat citizens as they wished citizens to treat them. This notion presumed an elected magistracy, one to whom the citizenry specially delegated authority. This magistracy consisted of those whom the people themselves had chosen and who would behave properly because they were electorally accountable. Any magistrate who acted otherwise was a usurper.

Paine specifically excluded kings and nobles, "those to whom no power is delegated" (*RM* 67–68). They had seized power, stolen it, to enforce their sovereignty. They had denied the people's natural equality. Hence, they also denied God's original creation. They were beyond reason, a godly quality that human beings shared, but in their case, "the rational world can know nothing of them" (*RM* 68). Natural equality, logically, meant a democratic order. Other forms of government not only denied natural equality but also denied God's will, which had determined man to be a free and equal creature.

In the context of duties and natural equality, the people made use of their natural and civil rights. Paine particularly had in mind those rights that stemmed from the rational faculty, their "intellectual rights," or what he called "the rights of the mind" (*RM* 68).[32] These rights included what Americans enumerated as first-amendment rights the same year as the publication of the first part of *Rights of Man*.

Moreover, natural rights encompassed those rights that allowed an individual to secure his comfort and happiness as long as his actions did not interfere with the rights of others. Paine accepted the Lockean doctrine that natural rights gradually evolved into civil rights.[33] When man made the transition from the natural condition of life to civil society, he did not decide to enter society "to become *worse* than he was before" but to secure those rights that he already possessed (*RM* 68). As he entered into the social contract, the responsibility to protect the citizenry now fell to the government in exchange for the citizens' obligation to obey the civil laws of the state.[34]

In relationship to his fellows, a person had a public, or civic, personality. Because the individual alone lacked the power to enforce his natural rights in civil society, "the common stock of society" must do it for him. This did not mean that he surrendered any rights. It only meant that government now had the duty to protect natural rights. Paine concluded that natural rights were human attributes inhering in man as a result of God's creation. From these rights grew the people's civil rights and thus their civil or political progress. Government's minimal responsibility was to notice the divine origins of natural rights and consequently to protect its citizens in ways that the individual alone could not protect himself. Wanton attacks of whites on blacks, British on Americans, men on women were all aberrant behavior. Paine knew that human beings were not perfect. Because government had to supply the defect of moral virtue in man, government's responsibility was to ensure that the people would continue to possess and allow them to exercise their natural rights. In joining together in government, therefore, each individual's power to secure his rights was theoretically enhanced. At the very least, he should not suspect that his rights were more secure before government existed.

But suppose a government acted without responsibility, as had the British government? What if it sought to enslave, not protect, its people? Paine noted that the individual's power to protect his rights was weaker when he was alone. But when he erected a government, when he joined with his fellows, his power increased. This power protected his rights. It did not do the opposite, that is, "it cannot be applied to invade the natural rights which are retained in the individual, and in which the power to execute is as perfect as the right itself" (*RM* 69). If it did, such a government destroyed its only reason for existence. Paine's logic and language here were clear: human beings as a collective entity always retained the right to reform their government. When government worked to destroy either their natural or civil rights, the people needed no longer obey that government. Such a government denied the very reason for its existence. Hence, "the right to reform is in the nation in its original character" (*RM* 73.[35]

Paine preached, therefore, the most basic (and in many respects, the simplest) justification for revolutionary or constitutional change in any part of the world. He based his justification on his own mythical view of the nature and origins of natural rights. He forced the Burkean argument from history and experience, prescription and presumption, to return to the divine origins of man's rights. These arguments display Paine's language and style at its homiletic best. His intentions were clearly to convince his English and

American brethren that Burke was wrong and, conversely, that he (Paine) was right. God had, after all, designed people to be different from the lower animals. People naturally possessed the rights God had granted them. This argument, Paine thought, was far more appealing than the dead, historical, prescriptive argument that Burke offered.

PART TWO

Action

❧ 5 ❧

The Civil Rights of Man

Thomas Paine's investigation into the origins and nature of human rights was largely theoretical and hypothetical. But his arguments often went beyond the theoretical and hypothetical. He set forth several concrete rights which people possessed when they displayed their civic personality. The difficulty with sorting out these rights is that Paine's writings, especially on philosophical subjects, were frequently imprecise. This was most apparent when he discussed how natural rights became transformed into civil rights.

Writing in the 1790s with Condorcet, for example, he combined natural, civil, and political rights into a confusing composite.

> The aim of men gathered together in society being the maintenance of their natural, civil, and political rights, these rights are the basis of the social compact, and their recognition and their declaration should precede the constitution which assures their guarantee. The natural, civil, and political rights of man are liberty, equality, security, property, social guarantees, and resistance to oppression.[1]

Although Paine's distinction between natural rights, on the one hand, and civil and political rights, on the other, was vague, his ideas of specific rights may be culled from his French revolutionary writings. In *Rights of Man*, he argued that with this new era of revolution, freedom, justice, and peace would spread everywhere as political and economic democracy became the order of the day. He virtually pleaded with his British audience to join in the marvels of the new day.

In *Rights of Man*, Paine was primarily preaching to a British audience of the middle and lower classes, the people of the same socioeconomic level

Common Sense had addressed in America. With the success of the Americans over the British and in the shade of the French Revolution, he believed that Britain was now ripe for a radical transformation of its political system. It would be a revolution, he hoped, which would parallel the events in France in the years 1789–91. His arguments, which were leveled against Edmund Burke, could not, however, be limited to the position he took in America in the 1770s and 1780s. Quite obviously, it was not a question of separation but one of ending monarchy and aristocracy. Thus he demonstrated the desirable outcome of the revolution, and his focus was always on what the people would gain from revolutionary activity: their rights.

Paine held that human beings always retained their natural rights even as they exercised their civil rights in a political context. He wrote Jefferson in 1789 that "the more perfect of those imperfect natural rights or rights of imperfect power we . . . thus exchange, the more security we possess" (*CW* 2:1299). People possessed two classes of natural rights. First were the rights of personal competency, which included the rights of speaking and believing, thinking and forming and stating opinions. These no one could surrender. They were as much a part of a person as his very being. Second were those rights of defective power, which were rights a person exchanged for greater security. These latter were the rights of personal protection and the acquisition and possession of property.

On entering civil society, people did not simply surrender all of their natural rights for greater security. Instead, a transfer of rights of the second type took place. To explain this Paine used the model of a marketplace, something that his middle-class readers could immediately grasp. Now instead of a marketplace of goods, it was a marketplace of rights, where a vendor (natural man) offered a buyer (the community) a commodity (that defective set of natural rights) in exchange for other products (protection and security). The citizen (no longer natural man) gave up these rights only as he received a new right, a civil right, in return.

By Paine's definition, rights of personal competency could never be surrendered to any authority under any condition. A person possessed them as divine gifts. Civil rights, that is defective rights, included security, property, and social guarantees. Finally, political rights, the product of the exchange, included the rights to resist oppression, to stand for and vote in elections, and to form a new government, through peaceful change or through revolutionary action.

A person, then, continued to possess those rights which God had originally given him. By definition, civil rights had no meaning in nature because a civil order did not exist there. Natural rights were inherent in man at creation, whereas civil rights were man's invention. The latter were imperfect because they were human, not divine, and thus manufactured by imperfect men through trial and error. Civil (and political) rights could thus change, but natural rights of personal competency were immutable. People best secured their lives and property and protected their liberty by carefully designing and often revising the law, depending on the political circumstances of the moment. Civil rights, unlike natural rights, did not have a timeless quality. In designing government, clearly an artificial construct, the people simultaneously created a new set of rights which could not have originated at creation. Some governments might not grant civil or political rights, but the individual always retained his natural rights of personal freedom.

To Paine, God was not a personal deity whom one could petition. If someone wanted civil rights, he had to create them. Such things did not come from God. Only in a democratic republic, depending on its written constitution (a necessary prerequisite), did civil rights pervade all levels of society. Under the democratic republic, man's person, including his liberty and material goods, was more secure than under any other system of government. Under either monarchy or a republic, the people always retained the rights of personal competency as long as they lived. Monarchical and other forms of repressive government only limited their freedom to exercise these rights but could never destroy them. Their divine origin (Paine's historical myth making) prevented it.

Paine acknowledged only one legitimate limitation on a person's free exercise of his rights. It came in his argument from harm. As John Stuart Mill later stated, "the only purpose for which power can be rightfully exercised over any member of a civilized community, against his will, is to prevent harm to others,"[2] so Paine said that "liberty is the power to do everything that does not interfere with the rights of others: thus, the exercise of the natural rights of every individual has no limits save those that assure to other members of society the enjoyment of the same rights."[3] In this way, Paine intended to identify what natural rights were and how man created a new set of rights as he passed into civil society.

Rights of Personal Competency and Collective Security

The model was, naturally, the events which had transpired so recently in France. When the French overthrew their monarchy, they sought to regain the freedom the regime had unjustly stolen from them. They wanted to destroy a power, political in form and military in substance, that had grossly limited and in some cases annihilated the free exercise of their rights as citizens. Using the French model, Paine explained to his British readers that natural rights were at once inherent, equal, hereditary, and eternal.[4] The most basic of all civil rights was the right of the people to establish a government of their own choosing. Surely all governments were inventions because all were man-made. But some forms fitted man's natural character, others did not.

Monarchy, for example, "reverses the wholesome order of nature. It occasionally puts children over men, and the conceits of nonage over wisdom and experience. In short, we cannot conceive a more ridiculous figure of government, than hereditary succession, in all its cases, presents" (*RM* 173). On the other hand, the democratic republic parallels man's nature. "The representative system . . . is always parallel with the order and immutable laws of nature, and meets the reason of man in every part" (*RM* 182–83). This meant that if people needed to have government, which they surely did, then if left alone to devise a government of their own choosing, they would naturally seek a representative system.

Unlike Rousseau, who rejected representative democracy, Paine held that it was the best that man could hope for. Moreover, the citizens could, if they wished, change this government, just as they possessed the natural right to form a government of their own choosing. "A Nation has at all times an inherent indefeasible right to abolish any form of Government it finds inconvenient, and establish such as accords with its interest, disposition, and happiness" (*RM* 142). The terms *inherent* and *indefeasible* were precisely the words he used to describe natural rights. People did not suddenly give up the right to change or even abolish unnatural government when they entered civil society or when they formed government for the first time. The nation retained this right because the people were always sovereign. "The right of the Nation is an original right, as universal as taxation. The Nation is the paymaster of everything, and everything must conform to its general will" (*RM* 120). This appeal, with its distinctly Rousseauistic reference to a general will, demonstrated that popular sovereignty ensured that natural forms of government were superior to unnatural ones. This was hardly a lesson lost on Paine's British audience, who were already buying *Rights of Man* in droves. Nor was it lost on the public authorities who would eventually prosecute Paine for his seditious opinions.

In the early 1790s, then, we find Preacher Paine advocating the power of the people's will, expressing his desire for them to exercise that will through revolutionary action. Revolution, a mechanism for renovation, was a vehicle to restore lost rights in the same way that the Old Whigs or Country ideologues demanded the return to first principles as a restoration of their lost rights. Paine regretted the license he preached in *Rights of Man* after his persecution during the Terror (see chapter 8). Even so, in 1791, he advocated revolution on demand as a way to regain stolen or lost rights. Arguing that the formation, change, and abolition of government were all rights inherent to a person's being, Paine in the early nineties thought that each of these was prior to civil rights. They were all part of the same class of rights. Men in association formed or changed government as if they resided in a natural, or prepolitical, condition. This was true even if civilization had advanced beyond the state of nature. Because political change and reform were fundamental to all people, they were, by definition, natural. And yet, the right to form or change government hardly fit into a class of rights of personal competency because no one person possessed the exclusive right (or power) to create or change government on his own. But if such a right were inherent and indefeasible, how could it not be a personal right?

Actually Paine allowed this right to be in the first class of rights. Even though it did not reside within the single, solitary individual; it was a consequence of a person's social nature. To form and change government, man must act in association with his fellows. Change was a function of the community as a whole, or what Paine called the nation. Here Paine approached the Madisonian precept of the "aggregate interests," a concept which he no doubt felt some British readers recognized. In arguing for the rectitude of the new Constitution, Madison had said in *Federalist No. 10* that "the Federal Constitution forms a happy combination in this respect; the great and aggregate interests being referred to the national, the local and particular, to the state legislatures."[5] It is a mark of the extreme individualism of Paine's political ideas that this natural right was the only one that was collective. The others were personal and immediate. They primarily consisted of the rights of the mind and the conscience, the intellectual and religious rights. Other rights, such as the right to safety of life and property, remained with the individual, but only as long as he possessed the power to ensure his own safety and protection.

Whenever a man confronted another human being or a group of human beings, he had no guarantee or hope that God would intervene to save him. He was responsible to act on his own, and his fellows', behalf. On this point, Paine had once used a Lockean image of how human beings used their rights to establish government. He had instructed Jefferson to picture twenty people coming together in a heretofore uninhabited land (not necessarily a state of nature). These twenty individually and equally possessed a will which made each of them sovereign in his own right. Although they retained the right to rule their own persons, they were more secure together than when they resided in total isolation. But nineteen of them could unite against one. "Each might be exposed, not only to each other, but to the other nineteen. It would then occur to them that their condition would be much improved, if a way could be devised to exchange that quantity of danger into so much protection; so that each individual should possess the strength of the whole number."[6]

The key element here is Paine's notion of an "exchange." It had nothing to do with the surrender of certain natural for civil rights. That would have meant a diminution in natural rights, which went against nature, against God's gift of these rights. Hence, it was not a question of giving up certain rights but rather of exchanging danger for security. This exchange, or arbitrage, occurred when the people decided to guarantee collective protection. By not yielding on the question of surrendering rights, Paine's argument took on a more radical tinge, which appealed to his British middle- and lower-class audience. Now they could understand directly how the king and his lords had stolen what was naturally their birthright, their natural rights.

Paine made this clear in the following way. "Their rights in the first case are natural rights, and the exercise of those rights [is] supported only by their own natural individual power."[7] Because natural rights existed within the individual, they remained part of him as long as he lived. Exercising them (that is, outwardly expressing them) became much more difficult when he enforced the physical power of others. A man might exercise his natural rights to a certain extent by virtue of retaining within himself the ability to speak and think. On the other hand, an oppressive government might prohibit him from speaking or praying in public or from writing as he wished. The full exercise of natural rights required the protection of society, and if these rights were usurped, revolutionary action was necessary. The point is that the individual always retained natural rights, even though the exercise of them sometimes required the cooperation of an external authority. No change in government or in economic or social status ever detracted or added to the rights that a person originally possessed as a result of his being simply "man." This was "his high and only title, a higher cannot be given him" (*RM* 65). To Paine natural rights were absolute because they "appertain to man in right of his existence," no more and no less (*RM* 68). He hardly could have said this more forcefully.

These ideas directly spilled over into Paine's view of toleration, which he hated. Toleration seems a liberal notion, but it was not for Paine. He argued that toleration was always the decision of a superior to grant or recognize the beliefs of someone inferior. With toleration, there was a sense of the master ruling the servant, where the master granted permission to his servant to act or to believe something. It was as if the master said, "I deign to allow you this right. I will tolerate it." A king might tolerate his subjects' beliefs. He might even allow them free expression or freedom of religion. By the same token, he might choose to withdraw that toleration at any time, should he change his mind.

For Paine, this was simply intolerable in a free, democratic society. God alone had given men their right to a free conscience and free intellect. No ruler could interfere with the free exercise of them. Toleration as a political practice had no place in a free society. Paine despised toleration as much as he was repelled by intolerance.

> Toleration is not the *opposite* of Intolerance, but is the *counterfeit* of it. Both are despotisms. The one assumes to itself the right of withholding Liberty of Conscience, and the other of granting it. The one is the pope armed with fire and faggot, and the other is the pope selling or granting indulgences. The former is church and state, and the latter is church and traffic.
>
> But toleration may be viewed in a much stronger light. . . . Toleration, therefore, places itself, not between man and man, nor between church and church, nor between one denomination of religion and another, but between God and Man; between the being who worships, and the Being who is worshipped; and by the same act of assumed authority by which it tolerates man to pay his worship, it presumptuously and blasphemously sets itself up to tolerate the Almighty to receive it. (*RM* 85–86)

Religious freedom, the right to worship as one pleased, was a natural right, the right of conscience. Toleration had no place, only the free enjoyment of one's right to believe as one's conscience dictated.

> There is no such thing as a religion that is wrong; but if they [men] are to judge of each other's religion, there is no such thing as a religion that is right; and therefore, all the world is right, or all the world is wrong. But with respect to religion itself, without regard to names, and as directing itself from the universal family or mankind to the Divine object of all adoration, it is man bringing to his Maker the fruits of his heart; and though those fruits may differ from each other like the fruits of the earth, the grateful tribute of everyone is accepted. [*RM* 86]

A state-established church opposed this right. It channeled the people's beliefs in a single direction under a single dogma according to the authority of a single institution. State churches were products of monarchies. Hence, monarchy was "the popery of government," an idea he drew from the Protestant historical tradition that linked the person of the pope to the dreaded Antichrist (*RM* 184).[8] Only now the church in collaboration with monarchy made both monarchy and popery evil, the devil incarnate. This argument concerning religious liberty potentially augmented his contention that British revolutionary political transformation was desirable and necessary. Certainly it appealed directly to the Dissenters and Nonconformists who were outside the church.

In opposition to Burke, Paine held that all religions were worthy, especially in their most primitive, unadorned form. At first, they were "kind and benign," a peculiar comment he made without further elaboration. Later, they became corrupt, they lost their "native mildness," and they turned "morose and intolerant," as they mixed with politics and became state churches. The resultant mixture of church and state was "a sort of mule-animal, capable only of destroying, and not of breeding up. . . . It is a stranger, even from its birth, to any parent mother on which it is begotten, and whom in time it kicks out and destroys" (*RM* 87). The Spanish Inquisition and British persecution of Quakers and Dissenters had destroyed all morality in modern religion.

The right of conscience was not the only natural right that man always retained in his person. Nor was it the only right that confronted the awful face of toleration. Speech was another. "Speech is . . . one of the natural rights of man always retained" (*RM* 90). French proponents of free expression, Voltaire and Montesquieu, Rousseau, Quesnay, and Turgot, all shared the belief that people always had the right to speak their minds, although the ancien régime all too often tried to forestall that right. Still, their "writings and many others had their weight; and by the different manner in which they treated the subject of government, Montesquieu by his judgement and knowledge of laws, Voltaire by his wit, Rousseau and Raynal by their animation, and Quesnay and Turgot by their moral maxims and systems of economy, readers of every class met with something to their taste, and a spirit of political inquiry began to diffuse itself through the nation at the time the dispute between England and the then colonies of America broke out" (*RM* 94). Their example, along with the success of the American Revolution, reinforced the cause of man's restoration of his natural right to speak freely throughout the world. Free expression was a powerful right that the middle and lower classes in Britain could associate with if they wished to read works like Paine's *Rights of Man* and not face the prospect of jail for doing so.

These were, then, among the first class of natural rights that man possessed. The question now is what happened to the rights of the second class, those not of personal competency. Locke had argued that in the state of nature, the individual possessed the same intellectual rights that Paine posited, along with the right to preserve life, liberty, and property. If a person's life or liberty were threatened, that person possessed the right to defend himself.

By extension, if someone threatened a neighbor's life, liberty, or property, the person had the right to protect his neighbor's goods as if they were his own. Said Locke, "the *execution of the law of nature,* is, in that state, put into every man's hands. . . . Every man upon this score, by the right he hath to preserve humankind in general, may restrain, or where it is necessary, destroy things noxious to them, and so may bring such evil on any one, who hath transgressed that law, as may make him repent the doing of it, and thereby deter him, and by his example others, from doing the like mischief. And in the case, and upon this ground, *every man hath a right to punish the offender, and be executioner of the law of nature.*"[9]

For Locke, man "gave up" this fundamental right to protect himself and his neighbor when he entered civil society. Such protection became the exclusive right of government. The individual agreed to obey the laws in exchange for that protection.

> Every one of the members hath quitted this natural power, resigned it up into the hands of the community in all cases that exclude him not from appealing for protection to the law established by it. . . . Those who are united into one body, and have a common established law and judicature to appeal to, and with authority to decide controversies between them, and punish offenders, are in *civil society,* one with another: but those who have no such common appeal, I mean on earth, are still in the state of nature.[10]

Rousseau set forth a more complex idea, that of the general will—a collective will that came into being when society acted as an organic whole. In such a situation, citizens "have but a single will, which is concerned with their common preservation and the general well-being. Then all the energies of the state are vigorous and simple; its maxims are clear and luminous; there are no entangled, contradictory interests; the common good is clearly apparent everywhere, demanding only good sense in order to be perceived."[11] Organic wholeness meant that an individual's natural rights, or as Rousseau preferred, his natural liberty, were subsumed in the state: "What man loses through the social contract is his natural liberty and an unlimited right to everything that tempts him and that he can acquire. What he gains is civil liberty and the proprietary ownership of all he possesses. . . . [I]t is necessary to draw a careful distinction between natural liberty (which is limited solely by the force of the individual involved) and civil liberty (which is limited by the general will)."[12]

For both Locke and Rousseau, a surrender of natural to civil liberty, natural rights to civil rights, took place as the people entered political society.

Paine's Coda: The Transposition of Natural Rights

Paine's position was different from Locke' and Rousseau's. The people did not give up or surrender any rights. They retained all of them, but many of them were in a different form in civil society than in the prepolitical condition of life. In this respect, Paine's view was at once more radical and more complex than those of either Locke or Rousseau. According to Rousseau, when the individual passed from natural to civil society, he unfortunately lost his natural rights. What happened was "the total alienation of each associate, together with all of his rights, to the entire community." If this "alienation" did not take place, "the state of nature would subsist and the association would necessarily become tyrannical or hollow."[13] The result was the erection of an imperfect or defective general will and the eventual deterioration of society.

Although Paine used several images and analogies throughout his work, he never used one from music. But music, to a degree, offers us a way to understand what Paine thought of how the people retained rights in civil society. For if the citizen did not give them up (or if they were not alienated, in Rousseau's sense), something did happen to them, something similar to what happens to a musical composition played in a key different from the one in which the composer originally wrote it.[14] Paine saw civil rights in just this way. People enjoyed their natural rights, but in a new key. Civil rights are a different order of rights than natural ones, but like the transposed (not transformed) composition, they represent a new expression of what existed before.

The second order of rights (civil rights, or those the individual possessed with defective power) did not exist in the natural world at all. They were brought into being only when people found them necessary. When music is transposed from one key to another, it is similar in form and substance to the original composition, but at the same time it is not the work of the original composer. It ranks as a different order of musical work.

Thus, some governments protected civil rights, and others did not. When a monarch made the laws, he did not create civil rights. He did not have to, although he might choose to protect his people. In a democratic republic, on the other hand, civil rights must be ubiquitous because that government, by definition, is one of law as well as rights. Moreover, it is a government which allows people to live as freely as possible in political society.[15] As natural man passed from individual solitude with all of his natural rights to political society, he took with him his natural rights but found that he needed to transpose those that he possessed with defective power into civil rights and thus to create a new order of rights. This second order of rights was never part of the individual but was instead placed in the community at large for safekeeping. Now the authority of the community resolved the defect of power each person experienced when he attempted to exercise these rights individually. Enforcement was no longer a problem. The rights were, in short, rights played in a new key.

The power of the entire community guaranteed the protection of everyone's rights. An actual net gain in rights occurred with the transposition because people gained political rights that they had not needed in a state of nature: the right to vote, the right to hold elective office, and the right of trial by jury. The people did not merely transpose the "musical composition" of rights. They also extended it by adding a coda. This coda was not a cumbersome addition but was well within the context of the original piece. The citizen now possessed not only his natural rights but a set of newly created ones as well. These rights remained both with the citizen as an individual and with the citizenry as a whole. They could never be given up or surrendered. They were rights that the citizens exchanged, as Paine had once said to Jefferson.

The musical analogy ought not be taken too far because there is a significant difference, namely that music is stagnant on the page and only brought to life through the agency of musicians. Rights, however, are always dynamic, at least for Thomas Paine. They have always existed and even when they lie dormant, they have a vibrancy that even Edmund Burke could not dispel. It also should be remembered that, in using the term *exchange,* Paine probably had the marketplace in mind. Even so, the image of musical transposition also displays an exchange. An individual exercised his natural rights through his own person as he had always done: the right to speak, to think, to have an opinion. On the other hand, he also exercised his civil or political rights through the medium of society as a collective entity.

> *Civil* rights are derived from the assistance or agency of other persons; they form a sort of common stock, which, by the consent of all, may be occasionally used for the benefit of any. They are substituted in the room of some natural rights, either defective in power or dangerous in practice, and are contrived to fit the members of the community with greater ease to themselves and safety to others, than what the natural ones could the individual in a state of nature.[16]

Paine's use of the word *substituted* lends credence to the musical analogue, the substitution of one key for another.

If a person's personal safety was central, then certainly he possessed the natural right to protect himself. In a community, an individual might not have the requisite strength to ensure his own safety against those stronger than he or against great numbers. Therefore, the right to protection became transposed into the new civil right of community.

> For instance, a man has a *natural* right to redress himself whenever he is injured, but the full exercise of this, as a *natural* right, would be dangerous to society, because it admits him a judge in his own cause; on the other hand, he may not be able, and must either submit to the injury or expose himself to greater: Therefore, the *civil* right of redressing himself by an appeal to public justice, which is the substitute [key], makes him stronger than the natural one, and less dangerous. ("Critical Remarks," *CW* 2:274–75)

The result was that a person under attack or in danger of injury now redressed himself through social institutions. He was an integral part of political society and therefore acted through society.

The same held true when a person made a plea in his own cause. Although he possessed a natural right to make his case, he was more effective if he engaged the services of a professional counselor, properly trained and experienced in these matters, to act on his behalf. He did not surrender or give up the right to plead his own cause. He merely transposed one right that he naturally possessed to society as a whole. Again, he acted through society by virtue of the new civil right of legal representation. "Therefore the civil right of pleading by proxy, that is, by a council, is an appendage to the natural right" (ibid.). Paine was quite explicit about this. He said that political society gave a person the opportunity to strengthen his individual rights as well as the rights of all the citizenry. "My idea of supporting liberty of Conscience and the rights of Citizens, is that of supporting those rights in *other people*, for if a man supports only his *own* rights for his *own sake*, he does no moral duty."[17] Moreover, the strength the citizen gained by uniting with the rest of the populace was incalculable. Because rights "always imply *inherent liberty*," the individual was never fully or even partially alienated from them, as Rousseau had suggested ("Critical Remarks," *CW* 2:275). Only the individual in collective society gave this "inherent liberty" greater viability and strength than it would have had had he remained alone.

Civil rights were, then, human inventions. They were rights the people created by convention, and, in this sense, they were similar to laws. Without civil society, an individual, as a solitary creature, made his own laws by making the day-to-day decisions he needed to survive. By the same token, without civil society, he possessed total freedom (and whatever strength he could muster) to exercise his natural rights. This image of natural man was not realistic to Paine, just as it had not been to Rousseau. Because people were naturally sociable creatures, the idea of them living alone, making their own laws, and exercising their rights in solitude was absurd. When a person lived in society, he quickly found that he had to erect government. A properly structured government provided the means of protecting his life, liberty, and material goods. In short, it protected his rights. And if it did not, he had a right to change it to ensure that it did offer that protection.

Rousseau had said that through the general will, a person "is forced to be free."[18] So it was for Paine. In the democratic republic, when a citizen's representative made laws, it was as if the citizen himself had participated in the making of those laws. The citizen did not act directly, but only indirectly through his representative. For Rousseau, "since sovereignty is merely the exercise of the general will, it can never be alienated, and . . . the sovereign, which is only a collective being, cannot be represented by anything but itself. Power can perfectly be transmitted, but not the will."[19]

Paine envisioned the same thing with a person's rights. But where Rousseau saw that people gave up their natural liberty when they entered political society, Paine said that man never totally surrendered that liberty. All people possessed it, equally, for all time, but in a new way to conform to the people's new life in a community. In this way, Paine proclaimed that everyone possessed powerful tools to reorder the political world, especially if they listened to his homiletic message of hope and encouragement. One mechanism he saw as a means to implement this power was the right to vote.

The Equal Rights of Man: The Vote

Throughout his writings, Paine often argued on behalf of the inherent equality of men. His advocacy of the principle that no man ought to be politically superior to another was a subversive doctrine which, he hoped, would inspire those who read his works, especially *Rights of Man*, to join the revolutionary tide of the times. Nowhere was this more evident than when he talked about universal manhood suffrage. In 1792, he wrote that "equality consists in the enjoyment of the same rights by each" person, a thought he consistently articulated during the early years of the French Revolution.[20] To protect natural equality, the people gave it a political expression, namely the franchise. Just as the nation possessed the right to form its own kind of government, so the people possessed the right to protect their equality through the franchise. The vote was the key component of people's ability to secure their natural equality.[21]

In civil society, voting was a political right of all citizens. It was a new right that people in association created to allow them to make collective decisions for the general community, for the common good. As a political convention, it had its roots in the people's original natural liberty, but they had transposed that liberty into a new form, the vote. Indeed, voting was the guardian of the people's natural and civil rights and liberties. If this were the case, as he believed it to be, then logically all the people must have the right to vote. Using the Old Whig language that advocated a broad franchise, frequent parliamentary elections, and equal electoral districts, Paine argued the absolute (and immediate) desirability of implementing voting for every man past the age of twenty-one. Indeed, he admired the French National Assembly because of its very broad franchise. Its members "were elected by the greatest body of men exercising the right of election the European world ever saw." As a result, France was the opposite of the corrupt electoral districts that pervaded England, where the franchise was at best haphazard, at worst evil. "They [the French delegates] sprung not from the filth of rotten boroughs, nor are they the vassal representatives of aristocratical ones" (*RM* 90). But even the electoral procedures of the French National Assembly were not founded on the widest possible franchise: on universal manhood suffrage, which was something Paine consistently advocated in the French revolutionary years.

In the French "Declaration of Rights of Man and Citizen," which Paine quoted in full in *Rights of Man*, the sixth principle stated that

> the law is an expression of the will of the community. All citizens have a right to concur, either personally, or by their representatives, in its formation. It should be the same to all, whether it protects or punishes; and all being equal in its sight, are equally eligible to all honours, places, and employments, according to their different abilities, without any other distinctions than that created by their virtues and talents. (*RM* III)[22]

There are at least four possible reasons for quoting this passage. First and simplest, since this principle was part of the "Declaration," he included it because it was there, and he really did not think very much about its meaning. Second, although the principle did not actually say anything specifically about voting, it offered a generalized, somewhat vague, statement relating to the functioning of the general will. The argument in this context was circular and would run as follows. Once the people, through their constitutional procedures, elected their executive, that executive thereafter had the authority to make and enact laws; meantime, the citizens had the right to concur with those laws, that is, to obey them, because this law was binding on them since its enactment was based on constitutional forms. After all, the election of the sovereign (assuming, in this case, the sovereign were an assembly) was constitutional. Had the people, on the other hand, not elected their sovereign in accordance with the constitution's provisions, then they would not be obliged to obey the laws.

A third possible reason for this statement's inclusion is that Paine wanted to emphasize his ideas of representation. It suggested that obligation to obey the law was contingent on participation in the actual formation—that is, the drafting—of the laws: that people had a right, prior to the passage of legislation, to say what should be in the draft itself. This meant that all citizens, no matter who or where they were, possessed the right to participate in decision making either by serving directly in government or indirectly by electing the government's officials. Service either in government or as an elector depended on one's abilities.

This consideration leads to a fourth possible perspective, namely that Paine's ideas were nothing more than an expression of a bourgeois ideology spreading throughout France. Those who merited the suffrage were the people who earned a sufficient amount of income to qualify for the right to vote or serve in government. Financial success, as the basis of social status, was the only proper index of the worth of one's citizenship.[23]

Paine's view was none of these. After studying who should vote, he concluded that all males without regard to their socioeconomic status or personal ability should, so long as they had reached their majority. Paine's universalism may well have been his desire to find an alternative to revolutionary action after the Terror, that is, the bloodshed and incarcerations (including his own) which he considered to have been the root causes of the Revolution's failure. Give the people a political outlet through the franchise and we might avoid revolution and its excesses. There is a shift in his writings after his release from the Luxembourg Prison, though his style continued to be homiletic and his advocacy of radical change was no less salient.

The French Constitution of 1795 defined the citizen as one who first paid a tax, real or personal, to the French republic as an indication of status. On reading this, Paine responded negatively in strong terms. "If those only who come under the above description are to be considered citizens, what designation do you mean to give the rest of the people? I allude to that portion of the people on whom the principal part of the labor falls, and on whom the weight of indirect taxation will in the event chiefly press. In the structure of the social fabric this class of people are infinitely superior to that privileged order whose only qualification is their wealth or territorial possessions."[24] If the government expected a citizen to concur with a law at its formation, he must automatically have the suffrage, which Paine conceived of as universal manhood suffrage. (Paine, it appears, had no concept of women voting).

Once again, Paine mythicized history by imagining a contract between God and the people. If we were to return to the people's natural origins, we would find that this contract was binding for eternity on both God and the people. "And that as the relation and condition which man in his *individual person* stands in towards his Maker, cannot be changed, or anyways altered by any human laws or human authority . . . all laws must conform themselves to this prior existing compact" (*RM* 113n.). At that time, God alone established human dignity without prejudice. A sovereign who tried to distort this dignity violated that original contract. Of course, Paine offered no proof that such a contract actually existed, nor could he. The contract, however, offered Paine additional ammunition to assert the right of all men to vote (and now, hopefully, avoid revolution). Because all laws have to "conform themselves to this prior existing compact," then Paine thought that he had proof that "every citizen is a member of the sovereignty" (*RM* 143). A properly constituted republic, with a natural constitution, "operates to embrace the whole of the Nation" (*RM* 144).

Sovereignty must never rest only on the shoulders of a single person, a monarch, or a group of men who were unaccountable to society. Sovereignty, because of that original compact between God and the people, always remained with the people themselves. Usurpers might violate that sovereignty, but the people always retained the natural right to govern themselves as they pleased. The right to restore sovereignty to its original and rightful place, to restore it to the people themselves, was inviolable. Abolish monarchical sovereignty "and sovereignty itself is restored to its natural and original place, the Nation" (*RM* 144). Only in the democratic republic would we find that "every man is a proprietor of government" (*RM* 184).

Now, in 1795, he argued that the right to vote was different from other rights. The common stock of society contained these other rights but not the right to vote. That right the individual always retained, for only he alone could directly exercise it. This right was personal, inviolate, and immediate. All citizens possessed it as individuals. In this sense, it was a right more like the natural right to think for oneself, to have an opinion. Such "personal rights, of which the right of voting for representatives is one, are a species of property of the most sacred kind" (*Dissertation, CW* 2:578). Clearly, by 1795, Paine had modified his view toward a more conservative position in his attempt to avoid future revolutions like the one in France.

In *Agrarian Justice* (1796), long regarded as Paine's most radical economic work, he reiterated his position on voting, but now it was a clear substitute for revolution. He explained that "the right of voting for persons charged with the execution of the laws that govern society is *inherent* in the word liberty, and constitutes the equality of personal rights" (*CW* 1:607). Every citizen had responsibility for the enactment of the laws through the franchise. This right was so precious and so important that if anyone tried to take it from a citizen, that man should face punishment by losing his own voting rights. That would be the worst penalty such a person would face. "He that would employ his pecuniary property, or presume upon the influence it gives him, to dispossess or rob another of his property or rights, uses that pecuniary property as he would use fire-arms and merits to have it taken from him" (*Dissertation, CW* 2:578).

Paine thus stated unequivocally that "every man has a right to one vote" (ibid., *CW* 2:577). This was true of both rich and poor, and neither class could with justice exclude the other from voting. As far as he was concerned, any attempt at exclusion never amounted to the poor moving against the rich. The issue was always the attempt by the rich to deny the poor their human nature. "It is investing themselves with powers as a self-created part of society, to the exclusion of the rest" (ibid., *CW* 2:578). Most eighteenth-century writers, the most radical among them, advocated some property qualifications for voters. Thomas Spence and Thomas Paine did not.

Paine's ideas paralleled those of writers like Spence, who opposed property qualifications and based the right to vote on humanity. "It is dangerous and impolitic, sometimes ridiculous, and always unjust to make property the criterion of the right of voting. If the sum or value of the property upon which the right is to take place be considerable it will exclude a majority of the people and unite them in a common interest against the government and against those who support it; and as the power is always with the majority, they can overturn such a government and its supporters whenever they please." Avoid this danger by dropping all property qualifications. Even if the smallest quantity of land or wealth were required,

> it exhibits liberty in disgrace, by putting it in competition with accident and insignificance. When a broodmare shall fortunately produce a foal or a mule that, by being worth the sum in question, shall convey to its owner the right of voting, or by its death take it from him, in whom does the origin of such a right exist? Is it in the man, or in the mule? When we consider how many ways property may be acquired without merit, and lost without crime, we ought to spurn the idea of making it a criterion of rights. (Ibid., *CW* 2:579)

By the same token, not only must voting be open to all men, so should political positions in government; that is, all men must have the opportunity to serve as public officials. This was the last of Paine's rejections of the Burkean demand for rule by an aristocracy or the Calvinist ideal of the rule of the Elect. For "wealth is often the presumptive evidence of dishonesty. . . . If therefore property, whether little or much, be made a criterion, the means by which that property has been acquired ought to be made a criterion also." Remove either the right to vote or the right to serve in government, and you "reduce a man to slavery, for slavery consists in being subject to the will of another, and he that has not a vote in the election of representatives is in this case. The proposal therefore to disfranchise any class of men is as criminal as the proposal to take away property." As for the latter, the poor, like the rich, had the same right as everyone "of electing and being elected" (ibid.).[25] Remove those rights, and nations would face revolution and possibly disaster, as the French found between 1793 and 1794.

Still, Paine's idea of political participation, founded on his concept of equality of rights, was well in advance of the great Reform Bills of the nineteenth century. As it was, his was a forceful statement for equality. The protection of these rights was the main function of a democratic republic, and the vote and governmental participation (or at least opportunities for participation) were the foundation of this protection. Using the Old Whig theories of political equality and a homiletic demonstrating what was desirable about this equality, Paine presented to his audience, especially his British audience, one of the most radical late-eighteenth century proposals for voting reform.

Of course, for Burke, an inherent danger resulted in extending the right to vote and political participation to the masses of society, to the rabble, who would destroy the entire political structure and in turn destroy centuries of history and experience. But for Paine, the consequences of denying that protection could be even more disastrous. They could lead to far-reaching destruction and hopelessness, as he witnessed in France. The universal vote was part of the answer to avoiding future revolutions. His radical views on man's equal right to property round out this picture.

The Right to Property

Paine's strong adherence to the principle of private property has led some modern commentators to associate him with bourgeois radicalism.[26] It is true that he argued in several places that private property was a civil right and that he opposed its abolition. He never called for a general leveling of society, though his enemies often accused him of just that. They associated him with the seventeenth-century Levellers, whose leader John Lilburne, they thought, was the model of an absolute, empty-headed egalitarian.[27]

In reality, Paine placed the right to own private property in the same category as all other civil rights. Like the right to vote, the right to own property belonged to the individual. But unlike the right to vote and more like the right to security and protection, the distribution and control of property was beyond the individual. They were within the realm of the community as a whole because money was required for one person to convey property to another. Money, Paine said, was part of the common stock of society. Property thus occupied a halfway point between individual and collective rights. But this made no difference to Paine. People had the right to own property if they could afford it.

Private property was a man-made invention. When God created the earth, he gave it to all men for their use and enjoyment, an observation Locke had made more than one hundred years earlier. Only later did the institution of private property evolve, an institution in which individual men could purchase domains for their own selfish use at the expense of their fellows. Just as God had created all men equally, so no initial distinctions existed between natural and artificial or private property.

Paine knew, however, that people in fact differed, that mental capabilities distinguished one person from the next. "It is impossible to control Nature in her distribution of mental powers. She gives them as she pleases. Whatever is the rule by which she, apparently to us, scatters them among humankind, that rule remains a secret to people. It would be as ridiculous to attempt to fix the hereditaryship of human beauty, as of wisdom. Whatever wisdom constituently is, it is like a seedless plant; it may be reared when it appears, but it cannot be voluntarily produced" (*RM* 175).

So it was with property. Natural and artificial property were different. As Paine said, "firstly, natural property, or that which comes to us from the Creator of the universe—such as the earth, air, water. Secondly, artificial or acquired property—the invention of man" (*Agrarian Justice, CW* 1:606). Curiously, falling into the first of these categories was the individual's ability to labor, which was to Paine a personal form of property. Work was part of a person's nature and indeed part of nature itself. It was sacred. "The faculty of performing any kind of work or services by which he acquires a livelihood, or maintaining his family, is of the nature of property. It is property to him; he has acquired it; and it is as much the object of his protection as exterior property, possessed without that faculty, can be the object of protection to another person" (*Dissertation, CW* 2:581).

Paine's major concern in addressing the issue of property was not to concentrate on a person's ability to work. He was, rather, interested in private property as something that developed largely by accident. In other words, he was not really interested in seeing how people obtained property—that is, how they acquired the wealth to purchase it—but rather what they did with it after they possessed it. He once wrote that "oppression is often the *consequence,* but seldom or never the *means* of riches; and though avarice will preserve a man from being necessitously poor, it generally makes him too timorous to be wealthy" (*CS* 72).[28]

Unfortunately, the social consequences of artificial or acquired property could be devastating. Poverty, for example, was repugnant to him. It was an unfortunate consequence of civilization itself. It had never existed when man resided in a natural condition. His famous passage with the line that "the life of an Indian is a continual holiday, compared with the poor of Europe" demonstrated his awareness of the depth of European poverty (*Agrarian Justice, CW* 1:610). If poverty were a consequence of civilized life, Paine might have advocated a return to uncivilized or prepolitical life, to a state of nature or natural equality. This was not the case. Instead, he preached the necessity of society as a whole intervening to ameliorate the problems of the poor. His was a deeply moral position, couched in a style of overstatement he had hardly used since *Common Sense:* "An army of principles will penetrate where an army of soliders cannot; it will succeed where diplomatic management would fail: it is neither the Rhine, the Channel, nor the ocean that can arrest its progress: it will march on the horizon of the world, and it will conquer" (ibid., *CW* 1:622).

But his position was also pragmatic because the equal access to property was yet another means to avoid revolution. Since all members of society were responsible for poverty, society must respond to it. The people must attack the problem at its source to "remedy the evils and preserve the benefits that have arisen to society by passing from the natural to that which is called the civilized state" (ibid.). A general leveling of society was impossible because the limits of human equality had extended only to the point of human rights. This limitation was not due to a moral imperfection in nature or in God's creation. It was a consequence of the nature of things. The people had progressed too far to return to their origins to eliminate the inequities of civilization.

One such inequity was private property, and here Paine undoubtedly displayed his least radical moment. Property could not be distributed on an equal basis because all people had not "contributed in the same proportion" to the development of private property (ibid., *CW* 1:606). Individuals invested a certain amount of money and labor in an enterprise. As a result, they expected a return, a legitimate return, assuming that the enterprise was successful. Men therefore acquired private property through their industriousness and capital, and society had no right to divest them of what they had worked hard to obtain. "Every man is a proprietor in society, and draws on the *capital* as a matter of right" (*RM* 69).[29] All citizens had a right to expect some compensation from society in the form of a subvention since

God had once long ago given them a share of the earth. They now no longer had that share because of the vast changes that had taken place.

This subvention was the foundation of Paine's famous land rent proposal in *Agrarian Justice*. It had the dual effect of ameliorating poverty and skirting revolution. As Locke and Jefferson had both argued, God had given man the earth to hold in common.[30] Jefferson's famous dictum that "the earth belongs in usufruct to the living"[31] was repeated in Paine's later formulation that God had given men and women "the earth for their inheritance" (*Agrarian Reform, CW* 1:620). No matter who occupied a given piece of the earth, it always belonged to everyone on an equal basis.

A twofold problem arose. First, too many people lived in the world at present for the earth to support a population of hunters and foragers. People now needed to cultivate the earth and had already begun to do so. "As it is impossible to separate the improvement made by cultivation from the earth itself, upon which that improvement is made, the idea of landed property arose from that inseparable connection" (ibid., *CW* 1:611). Second, although no one person had the right of individual proprietorship, the cultivator did own the improvements he had made to the land he worked. He had occupied the land only fortuitously and certainly without the consent of society. His occupation obliged him to pay the community what he now owed to it in exchange for that occupation.

Paine's ground rent proposal was an inheritance tax whose revenues went to the common treasury for those who were landless. This proposal, most likely designed to appeal mostly to his British lower-class readers, no doubt alienated those in the middle class who felt that yet another burden was being placed on their labor. Even so, it was a point he wished not to give up in light of what he perceived to be the inequality that had been brought about through inequitable land distribution. Because the landless were also human beings, they too never gave up ownership of the land that was now under fortuitous occupation. "It is nevertheless true, that it is the value of the improvement, only, and not the earth itself, that is individual property" (ibid.).

This was a fiction, of course, but a convenient fiction. Paine used it to assert what he thought was the best, perhaps only, alternative to revolution, on the one hand, and a full-scale agrarian law, on the other. A law of this kind, like that which Thomas Spence proposed, would turn the economic and financial stability of society upside down. Paine called his proposal "agrarian justice," an idea destined to go nowhere in the waning years of the eighteenth century. For Paine, however, contemporary society was obliged to support not only democratic-republican government but also an economic and social system that promoted distributive justice. "I care not how affluent some may be," he said, "provided that none be miserable in consequence of it" (ibid., *CW* 1:617).

This was not charity but justice. For in the end justice was related to a person's "ultimate need," his security and safety in the community. "It is only in a system of justice that the possessor can contemplate security" (ibid., *CW* 1:621). Men must therefore learn to live in a state of economic inequality until all were financially independent. Paine here may have been attempting to assuage middle-class readers who were unsettled by his inheritance tax proposal. Until economic equality existed, social diversity was acceptable as long as people retained their rights, including the right to be equal (even if the practice of equality did not yet exist).[32]

> That property will ever be unequal is certain. Industry, superiority of talents, dexterity of management, extreme frugality, fortunate opportunities, or the opposite, or the means of those things, will ever produce that effect, without having recourse to the harsh, ill-sounding names of avarice and oppression; and besides this there are some men who, though they do not despise wealth, will not stoop to the drudgery or the means of acquiring it, nor will be troubled with it beyond their wants or their independence; while in others there is an avidity to obtain it by every means not punishable; it makes the sole business of their lives, and they follow it as a religion. All that is required with respect to property is to obtain it honestly, and not employ it criminally. (*Dissertation, CW* 2:580).

For Paine, the right to own property was a civic right brought into being with civil society. But the ownership of property could never stand as the basis for the people's other civil or political rights, such as the right to vote or hold office. Once property is mixed in politics this way, then "it is a total departure from every moral principle of liberty, because it is attaching rights to mere matter, and making man the agent of that matter" (ibid., *CW* 2:583).

Paine's recommendation in the late nineties was clear. Using an imperative tone, he seemed to say, go forth and acquire property, as much as you can, but be prepared to compensate the propertyless if you want to fulfill your civic duty and avoid revolution. His inheritance tax, heavy though it might be, was a tax full of moral implications as he attempted to address head-on the problem of the poor. This idea was not really attempted in America until the Progressive Era at the end of the nineteenth century, and it was not fully successful until the Depression stimulated the onslaught of the New Deal.

If his idea of agrarian justice were to become the law of the land, nations might avoid insurrection. Had France established a good constitution (no doubt one with his subvention idea as one of its provisions), "the violences" would "have been prevented. . . . But, instead of this, a revolutionary government, a thing without either principle or authority, was substituted in its place; virtue and crime depended upon accident; and that which was patriotism one day became treason the next" (ibid., *CW* 2:583). The right to own property was a function of civilization, a function which meant the property owner now owed a large financial debt to society.

In the meantime, man's concrete rights were, as from the beginning, universal and inviolable. To deprive the people of their ability to exercise these rights was a shocking denial of God's will. Human rights—all of them, from free speech to the vote to service in public office—extended beyond the freedom of the individual in the community. That individual also possessed some serious responsibilities. Man was, after all, a social creature who was obliged to work to improve the lot of his fellows. How he chose to do this did not really matter. A life lived without creating improvements was a life hardly fulfilled, and rarely satisfying. For this reason, Paine proclaimed that "when we speak of right[s] we ought to unite it with the idea of duties: Rights become duties by reciprocity" (ibid., *CW* 2:579–80). The duty to invent, to create things for the improvement of the human condition, was a duty of all people, without exception. This duty was the main consequence of the rights of man, and in a political context it meant that man must create an equitable economic order and a good constitutional arrangement.

❧ 6 ❧

National Unity, Revolution,
and the Debt

Thomas Paine did not expend all his energy and enterprise on delineating the political rights of man. His concerns also fell into the financial and economic arena as well. Here, his tone was always sober but still there are elements of the homiletic: his message was gently explanatory, his intention to convince his readers, especially in America, of the impending crash of the British economic system, based as it was solely on a war economy. Later, writing in the second part of the *Rights of Man*, his tone became more imperative and compelling. Although he never favored leveling society, he advocated several social welfare programs designed to ameliorate the condition of the poor and ultimately lower the level of class conflict.

Part of the issue for Paine was the natural sociability of human beings. Although it was natural for them to live among their fellows, they did not always display their social affections. In England, those who deprived others of their rights might live in society, but they in no way demonstrated their love of humanity. America, however, was different. America offered the opportunity of political life in a new key; men could change the political and constitutional composition to reflect their natural characteristics and qualities. There they could achieve the public good through their natural sense of unity in a common struggle against oppression. It was also a place where new economic relations could potentially assure the financial security of all the people.

If anything bothered Paine as much as political oppression, it was economic and financial tyranny. After all, natural rights included the right to live in a world where natural plenty was accessible to all. Men had the ability to overcome poverty through the emerging science of political economy and thus to live well sheltered, clothed, and fed. In political society, economic rights, like others in nature, were transformed into civil rights. Paine's attention to economic and financial issues was neither particularly unusual nor distinctive in the late eighteenth century. Certainly Adam Smith, David Hume, and Edmund Burke were the best-known analysts of political economy, which focused on the relationship between economics, politics, and culture.[1] In a world undergoing rapid political and economic change, this new science helped men develop the instruments to determine the best financial direction society could take.

Specifically, political economy was the vehicle for writers such as Burke, Hume, and Smith to study the origins and development of a nation's wealth and financial administration. The appeal of this new science was largely partisan. It was the discipline of those who more often than not supported, or were at the very least only mildly critical of, the established Whig government in Great Britain, whose policy based the economy on the issuance of paper money, the expansion of public credit, and a large national debt. These three elements supported a large navy and a professional standing army, prerequisites for Britain's growing international power. Adam Smith in 1776, in *The Wealth of Nations,* showed how a monied economy operated in actual practice.[2] Hume also favored such an economy, though in 1776 (the year of his death), he feared that a large debt could potentially bankrupt England. Burke, in 1790, defended a monied economy in his *Reflections on the Revolution in France.*[3]

In a broader context, political economy in the eighteenth century provided these analysts with the tools to examine the moral and ideological foundations of society. According to J.G.A. Pocock,

> It is and was also possible to use the term to denote a more complex, and more ideological, enterprise aimed at establishing the moral, political, cultural, and economic conditions of life in advancing commercial societies: a commercial humanism, it might not unjustly be called, which met the challenge posed by civic humanism or classical republicanism to the quality of life in such societies.

As a political economist, Burke attacked the critics of British finance and commerce in just this way. He was after all "a defender of Whig aristocratic government. . . . Whig government was identified with the growth of commercial society . . . [and] Burke saw the Revolution as a challenge to the Whig order, arising within the conditions that order made possible; and . . . he employed the language and categories of political economy in order to analyse the revolutionary threat and respond to it."[4]

Paine, of course, opposed Burke's political and economic ideas, especially after 1790. Even so, political economy was not a science reserved only for the Whig supporters. Paine used the language of political economy, or a radical version of it, to preach how people could naturally live in a highly developed economy to secure the rights of man. They could construct a better economy if they overcame society's financial problems. In this way, they could achieve an economic "public good," a term he used but defined only late in life (see below). In general, an economic public good paralleled the people's political accomplishments when they erected a democratic republic. It encompassed what they achieved in the economic sphere largely through commercial enterprise. Men therefore had to create economic democracy, which would be attained when the financial good of all exceeded, on an economic scale, what they might gain under other forms of government.

Paine focused on a series of issues to prove his point: American national unity, the rise of the national debt, and the growth of a system of public credit. He also investigated the nature and causes of class divisions. His position was that if men were free and equal creatures, they must reduce the conflict that these divisions produced. In arguing his points, Paine often spoke the language of political economy, even if he did not specifically use the term. In this way, he sharply criticized the British financial system and its imminent bankruptcy. In the end, he tried to preach a convincing argument about how men could develop a virtuous economic and commercial environment markedly different from the deplorable conditions experienced in monarchical states. As the state modernized politically, so too must it economically and financially, creating an equitable foundation in society for all citizens.

As an admirer of Adam Smith, whose work he often cited but with which he did not always agree, Paine followed Smith in asserting that a nation prospered through the economic self-interests of its citizens. Human beings, said Smith, had a dual propensity, a self-regarding nature and a communal one. "It is not from the benevolence of the butcher, the brewer, or the baker that we expect our dinner," he said in a famous passage in *The Wealth of Nations*, "but from their regard to their own interest." We thus "obtain from one another the greater part of those mutual good offices which we stand in need of, so it is this same trucking disposition which originally gives occasion to the division of labour."[5] Talent, divided throughout society, worked ingeniously in a free market, to benefit not only one person but all citizens. This is the self-interested public good.

On the other hand, in the American revolutionary years, unlike Smith, Paine spoke of a more generalized good that went beyond the particular interests of the individual. What he was talking about was the "collective" public good; although he didn't use the term. The self-interested and collective public good were opposite sides of the same economic coin. First, individual citizens could do certain things to increase their own wealth. Such citizens were the producers or productive elements of society. Farmers, merchants and manufacturers, mechanics and craftsmen were all involved in modern exchange relations to ensure their own private economic welfare. As they prospered, their increased wealth accrued to the nation as a whole. This amounted to a Smithian free market, an eighteenth-century version of "supply-side economics" with its own "trickle-down effect." Farmers, artisans, and manufacturers circulated their crops and goods in a free-flowing economic system that brought them the wherewithal to purchase additional materials to increase their production. Merchants made their profits by conveying the goods throughout the nation. The nation as a whole grew in the same proportion as these individuals prospered. The market could be, in short, the means toward achieving the wealth of the nation.

In the meantime, certain activities transcended economic self-interest. Some automatically accrued from the very start to the good of the nation as a whole, and not initially to individual wealth. The disposition of the western lands was an example. In a 1780 work with the title "Public Good," Paine referred specifically to the collective or community good that would benefit the entire United States, rather than the individual states or their citizens, when Congress gained access to all western lands. "Mutual happiness and united interests" were the goals that would be accomplished when such a transfer took place (*CW* 2:304–5). In this context, the public good was national unity. Indeed, first on Paine's economic agenda was the future of America as a united national entity, and the disposition of the western lands made unity a difficult political and economic matter.

The National Union

To Paine, American national unity was the logical extension of the collective public good.[6] During the war against Britain, Congress wanted the states to overcome their distinctiveness and to become a nation in reality, not thirteen individual, at times competing, states united only momentarily to pursue the common goal of independence.

Paine did not satisfactorily define what he meant by the public good until 1795, when he gave it a highly Rousseauistic definition. At that time, he wrote that it was "not a term opposed to the good of individuals; on the contrary, it is the good of every individual collected. It is the good of all, because it is the good of everyone: For as the public body is every individual collected, so the public good is the collected good of those individuals"

(*Dissertation, CW* 2:372). This definition was written after the Revolution, but even during it Paine attempted to supersede Smith's individualism and to argue the need for the collective good of national unity. The collective good could be achieved if all the states were united in the common cause of growth and prosperity. Economic justice worked only if its principles were applied equally to all citizens. If one person failed to benefit from these principles, all citizens suffered.

During the American Revolution, national self-interest was a major concern. The danger was loss of the public good should the United States became financially bankrupt. After all, the states failed to provide sufficient capital for the war effort. With their myopic vision, the states could not see the collective economic good that underlay the imposition of the 5 percent import tax, for example, which Congress proposed in 1782 to raise revenues. This impost was to enable the United States to pay the interest on a loan contracted from Holland. Under the Articles of Confederation, a tax of this sort required the unanimous consent of all states. Georgia and Rhode Island dissented, though Georgia eventually agreed. Paine, under the pay of Congress, wrote six letters to convince the citizens of Rhode Island, and indeed of the United States collectively, of the necessity and morality of the tax. In his argument, he went beyond the problem of war financing and instead demonstrated the long-term positive economic outcome that the states would experience when they worked together in unity.

Paine's language was the same he used to describe the collective, as opposed to the self-interested, good. Rhode Island (and all other states, too) must understand that if the United States was to survive beyond the temporary crisis that the war presented, it must agree on "a law as shall operate with equal justice over all, inferring at the same time the necessity of her cordially going hand and hand with the States as far as they have already gone, and refer herself in common with the rest to a legislative decision of the whole. In this regard, Paine told his political ally, the wealthy merchant Robert Morris, that his goal was "to enjoin the necessity of a stronger union, for at present we hang so loosely together that we are in danger of hanging one another."[7] National economic unity for the collective good was a necessity that must become a reality, and soon. Renegade states, though accustomed to their own decision making, must become conscious of the collective nature of the emerging American economy. This unity was a vision writ large for Paine. To him, it was self-evident. He could not understand why Rhode Island failed to perceive it as clearly as he did.

He urged the citizens of Rhode Island to consider the connection between American independence and the national union. "We have only to deserve prosperity," he told them. "I am no enemy to genteel or fashionable dress, or to the moderate enjoyment of those articles of indulgence we are furnished with from abroad; but they ought to bear their proportion of the public expence as well as the soil we live on, and not be solely consigned as a revenue to the persons who import them, or the foreigners who bring them."[8] America would be economically independent only when all Americans fully realized that union was the sole means to achieving economic justice.

The prosperity that Americans could reach would arise through an intricately united commercial network of states and their trading partners.

> Commerce is not the local property of any State, any more than it is the local property of any person, unless it can be proved, that such a State neither buys nor sells out of its own dominions. But as the commerce of every State is made up out of the produce and consumption of other States, as well as its own, therefore its regulation and protection can only be under the confederated patronage of all the States.
>
> Besides, the European world, or any place we may trade to, knows us only through our national sovereignty, as *United States*. Any infringement on our rights of commerce must be lodged before the United States, and every redress for any such injury must come to us through that line of sovereignty; consequently the regulation of it must reside in the same power.
>
> The United States are likewise accountable to foreign powers for all misconduct committed under their flag; and as it is their flag which privileges our conduct abroad, and on the seas, it cannot therefore be expected, that the United States should be thus accountable on the one hand, and afford protection on the other, to all the rights of commerce, without receiving an[y] aid and assistance from it.

From this network, America would see itself as "one extended family, one imperial Commonwealth" ("Six Letters," *CW* 2:350–52).

America's newness embodied her potential greatness. She could start the world over again, economically. The "one imperial Commonwealth," he preached, would bring this greatness to the rest of the world. Economic democracy in the United States, like the country's political structure, would prevail on an international plane. "The States, either unitedly or severally, have a moral as well as a sovereign character to support. Their reputation for punctuality and integrity ought to stand as high as their reputation for liberty. To be free is a happiness—but to be Just is an honor, if that can be called an honor which is only a duty" (ibid., *CW* 2:357).[9] The moral implications of this advice were clear to his American readers: anything that worked against this unity was dysfunctional. Unity was a moral imperative, it was the Americans' duty to be united. Lack of unity inevitably destroyed economic justice and with it any hope of reaching the collective good. More particularly, a huge national debt (as in Britain) was counterproductive to the achievement of unity and prosperity.

A good deal of confusion has arisen over Paine's position on the national debt. As with the collective versus the self-interested public good, he was often ambiguous about the debt. The problem is resolved, however, when the debt is discussed in the context of national unity. The manner in which the British incurred their debt had negative implications for the British people; especially when we inquire into why they developed a debt in the first place. Now, the Americans too had a debt, but theirs was not destructive. The American debt actually helped effect national unity. For the British, debt led only to war and ultimately bankruptcy.

The Debt and War Finance

Paine's view of a national debt seemed decidedly to shift depending on the historical context in which he was writing or the audience he was addressing. In 1776, speaking to Americans only, he argued in *Common Sense* that "no nation ought to be without a national debt. A national debt is a national bond" (*CS* 102). He thus directly linked unity with indebtedness. Exactly twenty years later when he was addressing a British audience of middle- and lower-class readers in *The Decline and Fall of the English System of Finance*, he lashed out at the British national debt because it had created a financial system that "will expire in a bankruptcy of the government" (*CW* 2:654). His goal was again unity but this time the unity of these two classes to oppose the British monarchy and system of government. In both instances, he saw the morality of unity and vehemently asserted, sometimes in imperative terms, that it was necessary to overcome financial and economic deprivation. Everybody had an obligation to work for universal prosperity.

Are the two positions (the one in 1776, the other in 1796) reconcilable? Did Paine simply grow more sophisticated economically over the course of twenty years? The problem may be resolved when his 1776 prodebt position is aligned with his ideas about American national unity. Here he himself made an important distinction between a good American debt, which would lead to the development of the American economy, as opposed to a bad British debt, which had already demonstrated its destructiveness as Britain plunged into war after war which depleted its national resources.

Some commentators have argued that Paine's position was not contradictory because he was willing to accept a national debt as long as it was moderate. Such a debt enhanced the United States' ability to fight the British because it gave the Americans needed finances to prosecute the war. Others have suggested that Paine actually believed, in the words of J.G.A. Pocock, "that a national debt was benign and helped hold the nation together, and that only aristocratic mismanagement ensured disaster."[10]

These assessments, although true as far as they go, are incomplete. Paine's views of the debt were more exacting than either conclusion. Analysis shows that he held specific ideas about the proper use of the debt and the limits to which it should go. First, in 1776, Paine distinguished (spuriously, perhaps) between debts with and debts without interest. He never identified those debts that bore no interest, but he gave the impression that interest rates were more important than the debt itself. The full statement from *Common Sense* runs as follows:

> No nation ought to be without a debt. A national debt is a national bond; and when it bears no interest, is in no case a grievance. Britain is oppressed with a debt of upwards of one hundred and forty millions sterling, for which she pays upwards of four millions interest. And as a compensation for her debt, she has a large navy. America is without a debt, and without a navy; yet for the twentieth part of the English national debt, could have a navy as large again. The navy of England is not worth at this time more than three millions and a half sterling. (*CS* 102)

The key idea here was how a debt could arouse national unity. He was aware of the ideological opposition to the English debt in America and England. Indeed, in the same breath in which he touted an American debt, he also attacked English indebtedness with the exclamation that "Britain is *oppressed* with a debt." Thus, the English debt was bad, the American potentially good.

Just before his announcement that nations should not be without a debt, he revealed his underlying motive, using a typical eighteenth-century motif pitting virtue against corruption, the new against the old. America, as a new nation, was different from old, corrupt ones, like England. "Debts we have none," he said, "and whatever we may contract on this account will serve as a glorious memento of our virtue" (*CS* 101). America was "young and capable of infinite improvement," he argued in *The American Crisis* (1778), whereas "England has got to her extent of age and growth." America possessed vast, unoccupied lands, but England had none. "The one is like a young heir coming to a large improvable estate; the other like an old man whose chances are over, and his estate mortgaged for half its worth" (*CW* 1:149–50).

The youth and vigor of America meant that even with a tax revenue eleven times less than England's, America could easily pay her costs of the war (even if the states were reticent about paying their share). Paine relied on his own calculations to figure out war expenses, which he determined were annually two million pounds sterling. He estimated that this came to thirteen shillings per person for every man, woman, and child. America could afford this. England could not. He charged in a 1780 *American Crisis* piece that

> the condition of that country, in point of taxation, is so oppressive, the number of her poor so great, and the extravagance and rapaciousness of the court so enormous, that, were they to effect a conquest of America, it is then only that the distresses of America would begin. . . . Their manner of reasoning would be short, because they would naturally infer, that if we were able to carry on a war of five or six years against them, we were able to pay the same taxes which they do. (*CW* 1:175)

America's struggle against England, then, went farther than resolving the political and economic problems that centered around some oppressive legislative enactments. America was also engaged in a struggle that concerned her very survival as a nation "with a settled form of government, an independant constitution of its own" (*CS* 101). If a national debt guaranteed these things, then the expenditure of any amount of money was justifiable, legitimate, necessary, and moral. Even at the risk of incurring a debt of great significance, America must act, and act soon.

A national debt was, therefore, the counterpart of a national bond in the sense that a nation needed to prove that its population was collectively willing to do anything to fight tyranny. By this reckoning, England's indebtedness was both illegitimate and immoral. England possessed no high ethical values like national unity, which the Americans desperately needed. The English debt had grown from the selfish desires of the few (kings and lords) to extend English imperial power beyond its island nation to the Continent, and then to America. This was not virtue. The British debt was wholly due to its war economy, a state of affairs that Paine found especially repugnant.[11]

The English economy originated in the seventeenth century. From it came England's main industry, war, a self-perpetuating state of affairs. A wartime economy required a continual source of revenue to cover the debts that accrued with each successive war. No amount of internal taxation adequately funded these wars. "If taxation, or any thing else, be taken in its room, there is no proportion between the object and the charge. Nothing but the whole soil and property of the country can be placed as a possible equivalent against the millions which the ministry expended" (*American Crisis, CW* 1:144). Indeed, insofar as America was concerned, the extraction of revenue from the colonies (legal or illegal, wholesale or in part) would never sufficiently cover the outflow of money necessary to support a nation continually at war. "No taxes raised in America could possibly repay it. A revenue of two millions sterling a year would not discharge the sum and interest accumulated thereon, in twenty years" (ibid.).

The British had to look beyond colonial control to the actual plundering of their colonies. They had already bled dry the East Indies, "and the profligacy of government required that a new mine should be opened, and that mine could be no other than America, conquered and forfeited. They had no where else to go. Every channel was drained; and extravagance, with the thirst of a drunkard, was gaping for supplies" (ibid.). Total conquest, total subjection of America was necessary, though Paine was at a loss to explain why England needed total conquest. The British might have been able to achieve their goal short of war. He surmised only that this was the true nature of the British beast. Once the warmongering began, no one could stop it. "You enjoyed the whole commerce before. It could receive no possible addition by a conquest, but on the contrary, must diminish as the inhabitants were reduced in numbers and wealth" (ibid., *CW* 1:145).[12]

America, on the other hand, had never developed, nor would she ever develop, a war economy. America was not aggressive. Moreover, her war against Britain was defensive. Acting together on a united front, the states worked for a common purpose, for America's resources were plentiful. Her resources must now be made ready: men as well as "tar, timber, iron and cordage" (*CS* 103). A nation's economic resources were natural gifts from God to man, but they were only worth anything when they were put to good use. At the moment, their best use was to combat British tyranny.

This was why America had to raise a navy. A navy was a military expedient, but it also solidified both commerce and security. If America were to satisfy her future commercial goals after the war, she would need a navy to protect the sealanes and coastline. "To unite the sinews of commerce and defence is sound policy; for when our strength and our riches play into each other's hand, we need fear no external enemy" (*CS* 106). A time might come when America would neither want nor need a navy. "If we want them not, we can sell; and by that means replace our paper currency with ready gold and silver" (*CS* 103). Until then, the need for a navy was obvious.

After the war, America could easily liquidate the debt because of her vast natural resources. In focusing on these resources, Paine articulated the Lockean labor theory of the value of mixing labor with land to increase its worth. By being used, these resources became more valuable. Thus, Paine built a powerful argument to convince Americans of the positive consequences of separation. For now, he hoped America was engaged in what would be a successful war against England.

His consciousness of America's vastness and natural richness was un-doubtedly a consequence of his fascination with the natural world. Without a king lavishing borrowed money "on his worthless dependants," Americans could quickly discharge the present debt (*CS* 107). They could therefore use their resources for the dual purpose of individual wealth and national pros-perity, for the collective and the self-interested public good. Paine preached this theme consistently throughout his argument for American independ-ence. So far as he was concerned, the American debt was only temporary. Once the war ended, the United States could shift to individual and general economic growth. Commerce, "well attended to, will secure us the peace and friendship of all Europe" (*CS* 86). In this context, the meaning of the state-ment that "commerce diminishes the spirit of both patriotism and military defence" becomes clear. It was impossible to focus attention at the same time on matters patriotic and commercial.

The British had tried and failed to create a permanent war economy and then to erect commercial prosperity on that economy. Paine observed that the war economy was the major fault in England's economic and financial system. In *The American Crisis,* he pointed out that "war and desolation have become the trade of the old world," and he warned that an America not free from British control became "a sharer of [Britain's] guilt, and a partner in all the dismal commerce of death" (*American Crisis, CW* 1:81).

War and commerce were, then, incompatible. "To make war with those who trade with us, is like setting a bull-dog upon a customer at the shop-door." This was the behavior of "piratical nations" like Britain. In the war against the United States, England had suffered great economic losses when she broke her commercial ties with America. "Besides the stoppage of trade in time of war, she exposes more of her own property to be lost, than she has the chance of taking from others" (ibid., *CW* 1:145–46).

The result was that now the English national debt would have to in-crease at an appalling pace. Unwittingly, some Englishmen viewed this in-creased indebtedness as a means to enhance "their riches; that is, they reckon their national debt as a part of their national wealth." Paine found this paradox mystifying. It would be tantamount to a person mortgaging his property, then adding back the amount borrowed to the full value of the property. In fact, England's annual revenues could barely pay even the yearly interest charged to the debt. "This is nearly the case with England, the interest of her present debt being at least equal to one half of her yearly revenue, so that out of ten millions annually collected by taxes, she has but five to call her own" (ibid., *CW* 1:149).

If during the Revolution Paine used the theme of the national debt to enhance his argument for American national unity, twenty years later he was still using the argument, but for different purposes. No longer was his interest focused on America's public good, but rather the good of Europe, especially Britain. With the French Revolution, he was convinced that a general renovation not only in politics but in finance was about to take place. His main hope was that England would be the next country to fall, a country to which he devoted his most sophisticated, impassioned work on the national debt, *The Decline and Fall of the English System of Finance*, published in 1796.

To legitimize the figures he cited in that work, he turned often to the authority of Adam Smith. When he argued that the national debt had risen from 2.5 million to 400 million pounds sterling from 1697 to 1793, he turned to "Smith in his chapter on Public Debts" (*CW* 2:654). Paine's central point was to project what would happen if England continued to maintain its economy on a war footing. He concluded that the costs of war had increased by one-half for each new war. This ratio worked out in practice because he was "led to the idea merely by observing that the funding system was a thing in continual progression, and that whatever was in a state of progression might be supposed to admit of, at least, some general ratio of measure, that would apply without any great variation." This was based on concrete scientific evidence, the kind Newton himself undertook in his exploration of the physical world. "I have not *made* the ratio any more than Newton made the ratio of gravitation. I have only discovered it, and explained the mode of applying it" (ibid., *CW* 2:657).

Within four wars, British costs would have risen to 3,200 million pounds. "Is there a man so mad, so stupid, as to suppose this system can continue?" he rhetorically asked (ibid., *CW* 2:656). He was positive it could not, and he used the rest of his discourse to prove this point.

Paine was, of course, dead wrong about the strength and resiliency of the imperial system, which proved it could do quite well on the sea and in foreign possessions during the ensuing one hundred years. Still, from his perspective, the problem was that the Bank of England could never service its accumulated debt. It could not even pay the interest, let alone any principal. At 4 percent per year, the interest alone amounted to 128 million pounds per year. He estimated that the bank had only two million on hand, "most probably not more than one million; and in this slender twig, always liable to be broken, hangs the whole funding system of four hundred millions, besides many millions in bank notes" (ibid., *CW* 2:663). The bank simply would have to authorize more paper money, another consequence that Paine feared, a consequence which he attributed to the permanent system of war finance.

Inflation, now rapidly increasing, would become most burdensome for the poor and middle classes. As the government produced more paper money, the cost of goods and the interest rates on loans increased. Paine drew two conclusions from these observations. First, the system could not last more than twenty years. Second, the bank would stop paying on the debt. As for the latter, he noted that Smith had shown that this had occurred in 1696. "That which happened in 1696 may happen again in 1796." This "confession of insolvency" actually took place, though, in 1797, not 1796, when the bank halted all payments on the debt by ceasing to convert bank notes into specie (ibid., *CW* 2:664). David Freeman Hawke, Paine's biographer, notes that Paine may have been successful in forging a convincing argument concerning the impending doom of the English system. "For the moment," says Hawke, "Paine appeared to the world as an acute economic prophet."[13]

The consequences of British indebtedness were inevitable: social revolution. All past cases of high national debt alienated the lower and middle classes when they found that they had to pay more money for fewer goods. It also alienated those financiers holding bank notes who saw nothing in return when the entire system failed. They were the ones who had provided the financial wherewithal for the government to prosper through "the fair way of trade" (*Decline & Fall, CW* 2:663). It was to these groups of people that Paine addressed *The Decline and Fall* tract.

The projected social revolution involved more than merely a political transformation. Projecting what would almost certainly be an economic apocalypse for Britain, Paine argued that this transformation would almost certainly lead to the total reordering of English society. With "the decline and fall of the English system of finance," royal and aristocratic control of the economy would end. The French monarchy and first revolutionary government had already fallen because of "a failure in the finances of France" (ibid., *CW* 2:664). In America, the same thing had happened during the period of the Articles of Confederation. The French and Americans both had become impatient with the financial instability and irresponsibility of their government. And now it was England's turn.

In America, it was not a question of reordering society to end royalty and aristocracy since they were not present there anyway. The Americans did want, however, a government responsive to their social needs and financial investments, a government which could oversee national unity and the public good. For Paine, British financial exigencies set forth the beginning of political and economic renewal. Until then, the ministry, whose finances were based on war, was voracious. The issue simmered down to two broad considerations. First, such an economy was wasteful, immoral, and divisive. It required an ever-increasing amount of money, the consequence of which was leading to a proportionally increasing indebtedness. Second, because it could not pay this debt (it simply did not possess enough hard specie), it had to have complete control over the bank. Adam Smith, said Paine, had found the connection between the government and the bank a positive one. He quoted Smith on this account. "'The stability of the bank is equal to that of the British Government'" (ibid., *CW* 2:672–73).

Paine responded that Smith was wrong. Not only would the government fail, but the bank and everyone else would as well. When Paine asserted that "the English system of finance is on the verge, nay even the gulf of bankruptcy," he was referring not only to the English government but to the entire population. This financial and moral failure was due, in the final analysis, surely to the debt, but also to the proliferation of public credit through the issuance of paper money and bank notes. The problem of paper currency was so great that the debt, by comparison, appeared to be only "a trifle" (ibid., *CW* 2:673–74).

These economic problems arose because the relationship between government and the bank, between a private and a public institution, was too intimate. In America in the 1780s, Paine advocated the establishment of the Bank of North America. It too was an element in the American national unity, a force in nation building (see chapter 7). The issue for England was, however, different. There the bank was not an independent agency, as it was in America, but an agent of British imperial power and economic corruption. In England, the government controlled the bank. With that control, the government destroyed the bank's financial stability and that of the nation as a whole. It turned the bank into its own private producer of cash by issuing paper money. "This is the connection that threatens to ruin every public bank. It is through this connection that the credit of a bank is forced far beyond what it ought to be, and still further beyond its ability to pay" (ibid., *CW* 2:669).

This unholy alliance between the government and the bank reflected the linkage between bankruptcy and war. There was a "mysterious, suspicious connection between the minister [Pitt] and the directors of the bank" (ibid., *CW* 2:670). Like court politics, it brought out the worst self-interest in men. In effect, it was very un-Smithian, because this self-interest did not beget national prosperity at all. The collective public good received nothing. Now the bank's investors have "to get their money and take care of themselves" (ibid.). Selfishness was rampant, and it was all due to the purveyance of paper credit. Paine's critique of this form of credit ranks among the most devastating of the eighteenth century. It strengthened his argument that while America had the opportunity to create a nation based on the public good, the financial system of England was inevitably doomed and a new age would soon dawn for the British people.

Public Credit and the Decline of Morals

Throughout the century, indeed since the establishment of the Bank of England at the end of the seventeenth century, as Pocock has described, several writers had addressed the problem of paper money as a cause of the nation's economic woes.[14] The Whig opposition called the major supporters of paper money the "monied interest" because of their corruption as a result of involvement in court politics. They did not acquire wealth and position as did the autonomous and independent men from their freehold. They relied instead on places and pensions from the court or from their investments in the bank and other institutions. They were the rentiers, stockjobbers, and landlords whose interest was to assure the movement of credit, especially in the urban areas, to insure their prosperity.

Paine's animus against paper money was quite different from that of the Whig opposition. He was not interested in autonomy through the acquisition of a freehold or in support of a landed gentry. Paper currency was simply worthless because gold and silver (natural species) did not support it. In this respect, Paine might have been thinking philosophically. Men should be close to nature. His desire for natural species as a means of exchange fits this analysis quite well. On the other hand, he was also, and more importantly, pragmatic. Paper money was an unproductive resource. It was not a stable means of exchange because nothing of real (or natural) value supported it. The free market that Smith had envisioned would not work with false currency. With paper, people always faced high inflation rates and a depressed economy. "Paper is too plentiful, and too easily come at. It can be had anywhere, and for a trifle" (*Dissertation, CW* 2:405).

Here he again followed Adam Smith, who had defined the natural limits of an artificial means of exchange. If paper were separated from that natural limit, it declined in value and prices would climb. "The increase of paper money, it has been said," wrote Smith, "by augmenting the quantity, and consequently diminishing the value of the whole currency, necessarily augments the money price of commodities." When the value of paper money fell below the nation's worth in gold and silver, Smith advised that the holders of this currency immediately return it to the bank for conversion to specie. Otherwise a person would hold "superfluous paper."[15] A decline in the value of paper may cause some serious problems that even Smith was unaware of, namely a run on the bank "to the whole extent of this superfluous paper," thus setting off an "alarm . . . necessarily increasing the run."

Paine favored a natural economy in which the means of exchange were gold and silver.

Gold and silver are the emissions of *nature:* paper is the emission of art. The value of gold and silver is ascertained by the quantity which nature has made in the earth. We cannot make that quantity more or less than it is, and therefore the value being dependent upon the quantity depends not on man. . . . It has a capacity to resist the accidents that destroy other things. It has, therefore, all the requisite qualities that money can have, and is a fit material to make money of; and nothing which has not all these properties, can be fit for the purpose of money. (*Dissertation, CW* 2:404–5)

These observations extended beyond the economic and into the moral sphere. Man's desire to acquire great wealth through the accumulation of stacks and stacks of paper blinded him from seeing the value of the collective public good. "One of the evils of paper money is that it turns the whole country into stock jobbers," he said.

The precariousness of its value and the uncertainty of its fate continually operate, night and day, to produce this destructive effect. Having no real value in itself it depends for support upon accident, caprice and party, and as it is the interest of some to depreciate and of others to raise its value, there is a continual invention going on that destroys the morals of the country. (Ibid., *CW* 2:406)[16]

By the time Paine wrote *The Decline and Fall* in 1796, he was aware of the fluctuations in the economy when it was under the dual pressure of war finance and economic growth. Men contributed to their nation's financial stability and growth only when their nation possessed enough cash to support its debts as well as the arms to protect it.

Twenty years earlier in *Common Sense,* he had linked the potentially positive American national debt to the creation of a navy. "We ought to view the building a fleet," he said, "as an article of commerce, it being the natural manufactory of this country. It is the best money we can lay out. A navy when finished is worth more than it cost. And is that nice point in national policy, in which commerce and protection are united. Let us build; if we want them not, we can sell; and by that means replace our paper currency with ready gold and silver" (*CS* 103). By British standards, an American navy was inexpensive, but even a cheap navy with a growing economy that needed protection required the stability in currency that only gold and silver could provide.

When a nation based its economy on a means of natural exchange, prices would remain stable and the economy would grow. The organic economy that Smith had envisioned could exist quite well, and the nation as a whole prosper. Otherwise, a nation faced an economic crisis like the one that occurred in Philadelphia in 1779. At that time, Paine witnessed the decline in morals (which he spoke about in 1796) during riots, some of which led to the deaths of several people. This was especially true of the so-called Fort Wilson riot that took place in front of James Wilson's house in October of that year.[17]

He also witnessed it in the financial crisis that followed the rise of inflation rates. The more radical elements of Philadelphia tried to halt inflation by creating committees (Paine was a member of one) to oversee the regulation of prices.[18] The point is not that Paine converted from an advocate of the "just price" to one of laissez-faire. Rather, in the twenty year period (1776–96), he grappled with ideological solutions to very serious financial problems. Inflation caused violence, but violence did not solve the problem of inflation.

The end of paper currency, however, would. In 1780, the Philadelphia assembly rescinded the legal tender acts and placed the economy on the more stable species footing.[19] Along with other wealthy financiers, Robert Morris, with Paine as his pamphleteer, established the Bank of North America. They designed this institution to create economic and financial stability and growth and at the same time to overcome the paper money crisis.[20]

In arguing on behalf of the bank, Paine claimed that the bank's notes were different from paper money because hard species backed them, and the bank held this species in its reserves. Paper money, on the other hand, was like "dram drinking. . . . It relieves for a moment by deceitful sensation, but gradually diminishes the natural bent, and leaves the body worse than it found it" (*Dissertation, CW* 2:411).[21] If natural species supported the notes on an even, one-to-one basis, then paper money overcame artificiality and worthlessness. "Instead of banishing [species, paper money would] work itself into gold and silver; because it will then be both the advantage and duty of the bank and of all the mercantile interests connected with it to procure and import gold and silver from any part of the world, to give in exchange for the notes" (ibid., *CW* 2:411–12). The bank would produce a stable, natural financial system to strengthen the nation's ever-improving economy.

In the meantime, any legislator who introduced legal tender bills should face punishment. At first Paine suggested lenient punishments, saying that such a person only "merits impeachment, and sooner or later may expect it." In thinking more about this subject, he concluded that the issue was basically one of distributive justice. Impeachment was insufficient. Paper currency destroyed the moral fiber of a community, and it led to violence, death, and the destruction of property. "Tender laws, of any kind, operate to dissolve, by the pretense of law, what ought to be the principle of law and support, reciprocal justice between man and man." On second thought, "the punishment of a member [of a legislature] who should move for such a law ought to be *death*" (ibid., *CW* 2:407–8).[22] For Paine, public fraud of this kind, which led to economic divisiveness, was so wicked that the penalty must be the ultimate one.

Commerce and the Collective Good

Paine's political purposes in discussing questions of political economy were quite different from those of Burke, Smith, or Hume. He vigorously preached that economic growth was the social counterpart to political democracy. The relationship between his economic ideology and the language of political economy centered on his ideas about commercial development. He rejected the Old Whig or classical republican ideal of the autonomous citizen beholden to no man but independent because he possessed a freehold. Commercial growth secured the future of American (and later French) democracy.

With the linkage of liberty to commerce, American independence (and survival) was secure. America's natural resources were unlimited. Hence, Paine's famous dictum in *Common Sense* naturally followed. "Our plan is commerce, and that, well attended to, will secure us the peace and friendship of all Europe" (*CS* 86). Where Burke might not worry over an English national debt (though he worried about one for France), Paine's version of political economy pointed to the establishment of commercial enterprises free from public credit and national indebtedness, those immoral attributes that supported a war economy.

In his attack on the debt and paper money, Paine never once advocated a return to a debt-free world, a vision which figured in the classical-republican tradition. On the contrary, he envisioned a growing, prosperous, and stable commercial and financial economic system. He parted company, therefore, with Burke and Smith. He never once used "political economy" as a science to foster politeness and the "refinement of the passions." The very crudeness of his personal style, which he so often displayed to friend and enemy alike, argued against this interpretation.

Commerce possessed a healthy economic benefit for Americans, and it also had moral consequences. These benefits redounded not to the few (as had economic privilege) but to the many. Aimed toward achieving the collective public good, commerce was virtuous because it led to the good of the entire community. In contrast, the evil war economy of England, the hallmark of growing British imperial power, was avoidable when men turned their attention to the economic good rather than to warmongering. By the

1790s, he was already looking toward an economic rehabilitation of not only America but the world itself. "If commerce were permitted to act to the *universal* extent it is capable, it would extirpate the system of war, and produce a revolution in the uncivilized state of governments," he wrote in *Rights of Man* (*RM* 212, emphasis added). This was the meaning of his appeal to universalism.

Paine was not simply addressing issues that Bernard Mandeville earlier in the century had raised regarding man's natural selfishness, which might by chance produce public economic benefits. Indeed Paine's vision was more radical and more capitalist. Commercial relations between people had a civilizing effect. They encouraged intercourse as they diminished the desire for war. Commerce "is the greatest approach towards *universal* civilization, that has yet been made by any means not immediately flowing from moral principles" (*RM* 211–13, emphasis added). It was a mechanism men could use to achieve unity and universal civilization; it was not divisive, as was war.

Nor was commerce foreign to man. Commercial relations between people coincided perfectly with their sociable nature. God wanted people to coexist in society for mutual and communal benefit. War was an unnatural consequence of unregenerative governments ("the uncivilized state of governments"). These governments and their leaders made men behave in ways contrary to their nature such as waging war on their fellows.

On the other hand, a government that was regenerative, like a democratic republic, would allow commerce to flourish, and men could achieve the collective, the public good. Commerce "is a pacific system, operating to unite mankind," all of mankind (*RM* 212). Man's nature motivated him to join with his fellows, and commercial enterprise worked to complement that human characteristic.[23]

PART THREE

Progress

~ 7 ~

Economic Democracy

A new era of political and economic stability brought the possibility that people could erect a democratic republic and create economic democracy. These two developments would elude the dangers and pitfalls that confronted societies with undemocratic, corrupt regimes. Like his eighteenth-century contemporaries, Paine spoke of these ideas in the language of virtue, although he never precisely defined that much-used term of his time. He did suggest, however, that virtue was not natural birthright.

Paine sounded at times like a typical eighteenth-century classical republican. And yet, he was not, especially when we compare his statements to the Old Whig, Commonwealthman, or classical republican theorists. The classical republicans understood virtue as a static quality which, to endure, must be set in unchanging social and political conditions. Truly virtuous men were public spirited. Neither selfish nor inner directed, their goal was to seek the public good and the honor and fame that attended such a search. Since some men were not virtuous, government had to force them to be so. Once government was established, it could not, indeed should not, change, lest men (most men, that is) revert to their natural desire to seek their own particular good.

An alternative version of this static lifestyle was the dynamic society of fast-paced commercial relationships and economic growth. Change occurred as people mobilized their goods and services and spread them for their own profit throughout society. The classical republican theorists believed such relations in society promoted social discontinuity. They threatened to upset the delicate balance of the political order. J.G.A. Pocock has described the tension between the status quo and dynamism as a struggle pitting virtue against commerce. The classical republicans' attitude "toward change was therefore negative." They looked "to a past and [sought] to defend virtue against innovative forces symbolized as trading empire, standing armies, and credit."[1]

For Thomas Paine, virtue was not a static quality but a dynamic one. It was a quality that helped people achieve material progress. Nor was virtue, as Burke would have it, the monopoly of one class, the aristocracy. Nor was it a quality achieved only when republican institutions of the one, the few, and the many coalesced into a state of equilibrium, as classical republicans believed. Virtue resided in a society with economic and democratic equality, where people could speak a language "free, bold, and manly," a language reflecting their democratic existence (*RM* 90).

In opposing the classical republican tradition, Paine argued that the American and French revolutionary experiences proved that political progress and economic growth worked hand in hand. Just as people could create a virtuous, democratic political order with all citizens participating, they could also design a virtuous economic and financial order. Indeed, they must.

Capitalist enterprise and the alleviation of the plight of the poor through economic development were the people's responsibility. To accomplish this, they needed the freedom that existed in democratic politics. Political and economic progress were inextricably linked insofar as political revolution stimulated an economic and commercial transformation that benefited all people.

> Already the conviction that government by representation is the true system of government is spreading itself fast in the world. The reasonableness of it can be seen by all. The justness of it makes itself felt even by its opposers. But when a system of civilization, growing out of that system of government, shall be so organized that not a man or woman born in the Republic but shall inherit some means of beginning the world, and see before them the certainty of escaping the miseries that under other governments accompany old age, the Revolution of France will have an advocate and an ally in the heart of all nations. (*Agrarian Justice, CW* 1:621–22)[2]

In the meantime, Paine knew that economic differences separated the social classes. He not only observed poverty. He personally experienced it when he found himself in a precarious financial condition.

Several questions must be addressed to understand Paine's economic ideas. First is whether he possessed a class consciousness. I have argued here, for example, that he intended his writings to be read and absorbed by the lower and middle classes, and clearly he never cared a whit if his works were read by the king of England or the duke of Norfolk. But the question is whether he explicitly conceived of society as a hierarchy of differentiated classes. Did he think that society consisted of different economic orders, some of which parasitically fed on the production of others? Was such a differentiation to him natural or unnatural, and how could this condition be remedied by a true, economic democracy? Did he articulate the needs of one particular class over others?

Although Paine often referred to *class* (or, better, *classes*) to distinguish people along economic lines, his use of these terms does not necessarily mean that he possessed a class consciousness. Sometimes, for example, he used the word *class* in a way that suggested medieval estates or guilds, even professions. He might speak therefore of the various classes or estates of tradesmen or shopkeepers. Moreover, the idea of class, especially in Marxist vocabulary, which pitted owners of the means of production against an underclass of exploited workers, did not figure in Paine's writings. He was not protosocialist, nor did he in any way "anticipate" Marxist ideology.

Paine had little sympathy for Gracchus Noël Babeuf and the 1796 Babouvist revolution. He thought that Babeuf's assault on government and society was clearly counterproductive. "The defect in principle of the Constitution was the origin of Babeuf's conspiracy," he wrote in *Agrarian Justice.*

> He availed himself of the resentment caused by this flaw, and instead of seeking a remedy by legitimate and constitutional means, or proposing some measure useful to society, the conspirators did their best to renew disorder and confusion, and constituted themselves personally into a Directory, which is formally destructive of election and representation. They were, in fine, extravagant enough to suppose that society, occupied with its domestic affairs, would blindly yield to them a directorship usurped by violence. (*CW* 1:607–8)

And yet, Paine believed that exploitation existed, that one class was subject to the economic commands of another, and that an underclass was present in society. Suffering of any kind was unnatural and unjust. The people relieved this situation only when they made the political order democratic.

The French, now that they had established political democracy after the revolution must move toward economic democracy, a term he never used but one which encapsulates his ideas of financial progress. Economic exploitation was not necessarily due to the extravagance or appetites of individuals, or even to particular classes, but to the political system. As long as government remained based on the old system of monarchy and aristocracy, some men exploited their fellows. Government on the old system was an "aggrandisement of itself" and was not designed to promote economic justice (*RM*

171). Economic democracy, the financial and social counterpart to political democracy, enabled people to live in accordance with their nature. As the democratic republic was just (because it allowed full participation in decision making), economic democracy was also just (because it allowed full rewards for all members of society).

Economic Progress and Class

Paine identified at least two very broad social classes: a leading class of exploiters and an underclass of dispossessed. Given his distaste for monarchy and aristocracy, it is not surprising to find that among the exploiting class were the king and the nobility. Naturally enough, after 1802, he included the Federalists. Following his return to the United States, he used the same language to describe the Federalists that he had used twenty-five years earlier to describe the English aristocracy.

Whether king and lords or Federalists, Paine argued that these leading classes were unnatural when they set themselves up over other people. They had obviously forgotten that all people were "originally equals in the creation" (*CS* 71). The aristocracy had emerged because of the sudden appearance of private property, which was "an invention of men" (presumably not a divine creation) (*Agrarian Justice, CW* 1:606). It developed as the land became cultivated, as people mixed their labor with the land. Private property led to economic inequalities between aristocrats, who were the owners of the land, and the common man, who owned nothing. In other words, the land had been expropriated as an entailment for the few. The aristocracy's denial of natural equality through land seizure demonstrated its abject lack of virtue, its total selfishness, and its ability to exploit others.

Paine's second broad class, though a conglomerate, was conventionally termed the "middling" or middle classes in the eighteenth century. When he described this social category, Paine usually thought in terms of those employed in the laboring, professional, and entrepreneurial occupations, which covered the economic spectrum from the wealthiest financiers and lawyers, such as Robert Morris and James Wilson, to the shopkeepers, tradesmen, and artisans, such as Timothy Matlock and Charles Willson Peale.

There were also the poor. Unlike his contemporaries who decried the status and condition of the "lower sort," Paine had great sympathy for the poor, especially the laboring poor. He was certain that someday government could assist these people move upward along the economic scale to where they could achieve economic dignity. "Bred up without morals, and cast upon the world without a prospect, they are the exposed sacrifice of vice and legal barbarity. The millions that are superfluously wasted upon governments, are more than sufficient to reform those evils, and to benefit the condition of every man in a nation, not included within the purlieus of a court" (*RM* 218). These people might be poor, but not from their own doing. Historical circumstances had left them in terrible financial distress. If government were natural, that is, based on public-spiritedness (if it were the democratic republic), it could help them overcome poverty.

Does all this evince a class consciousness insofar as Paine identified with any one class, for example, the artisans, the merchants, the poor? Paine's background sheds little light on this question. His staymaker father taught his son the trade, and Paine on several occasions tried and failed to make a living as a journeyman staymaker. This occupation was clearly of the lesser sort. "Staymaking ranked low on the social scale of crafts, and in later years detractors relished the chance to ridicule 'Tom Paine the Staymaker.'"[3] He was also a shopkeeper, the owner of a small grocery and tobacco store, which eventually fell into bankruptcy. On two occasions, he worked as an excise tax collector, a profession which placed men in "peculiarly pitiable" economic straits. "A single man may barely live; but as it is not the design of the Legislature or the honorable Board of Excise, to impose a state of celibacy on them, the condition of much the greater part is truly wretched and pitiable."[4]

Some commentators have concluded that his radical political ideology and especially his economic ideas concerning social welfare originated in his lower-class, artisan background. This conclusion is not necessarily warranted, despite the simplicity and straightforwardness of Paine's style which indicate that he included the common man in his appeal. He deliberately avoided the imaginative flourishes and ringing rhetoric of an Edmund Burke.[5]

At the same time, the evidence does not conclusively prove that Paine supported any particular class.[6] It is certain, however, that he believed that economic and material progress would enhance the condition of all people, no matter what their station or class. He was quite clear about this. The issue is what exactly he meant by this progress. During America's war of separation from Britain and thereafter, he argued that America must become a strong, united commercial nation, not only to survive in a hostile world, but also to demonstrate the remarkable virtue inherent in a democratic republic.

Unlike England, the youthful America had the potential to build an economy on natural principles. If the Americans could unite the country so that no one element in society and no one state set itself against another, their future would be secure. "We are young," he exhorted, "and we have been distressed; but our concord hath withstood our troubles, and fixes a memorable aera [*sic*] for posterity to glory in" (*CS* 108). America's potential growth was limitless. "Riches in a new country, if I may so express it, differ exceedingly from riches in an old one. In the latter it only shifts hands, without either increasing or diminishing; but in the former there is a real addition of riches by population and cultivation."[7] The former was a natural form of economic growth, though it lasted only temporarily; a new country should soon develop industry and manufacturing through its inhabitants' inventiveness.

Paine wanted all Americans to be economically secure. If they were to avoid the problems of the English, they must create a nation which, as Richard Price once wrote, would be "a confederation of states prosperous and happy, without Lords—without Bishops—and without Kings."[8] America was to have no formal class distinctions, though how Paine arrived at this conclusion is complex. Early on, he was quite conscious of how class differentiated people. In 1778, he told Henry Laurens that he could identify "various classes and merits of men in society", and he set out to do just that.[9] Economic growth and stability were virtues of only one class, and that class was not one of privilege. It could not be a composite aristocracy, whether called the British nobility or the American Federalists. But why could it not include a class of privilege, especially when he himself claimed to "defend the cause of *humanity*" or said that "I speak an open and disinterested language, dictated by no passion but that of *humanity*. . . . My country is the world, and my religion is to do good."[10]

The answer is that the composite aristocracy was a class not of human beings but of parasites. The class, the single class, that Paine acknowledged consisted of those groups or guilds of producers and manufacturers who added to everyone's financial prosperity. Unlike the composite aristocracy, the class he admired contributed to society's economic stability. This class included the three useful or productive classes of society. The first useful class of citizens were the farmers and cultivators. These were the producers, the creators of basic items, such as foodstuffs, that people needed just to live. As a result, they made up what he called a class of "citizens of first necessity" because people could not survive without their services. A second class followed: "the various orders of manufacturers and mechanics of every kind," a class of people who were not citizens of first necessity because they did not produce products absolutely necessary for man's sustenance. They were those who "contribute to the accommodation rather than to the first necessities of life." They provided conveniences and luxuries which were not only worth having but also needed, although he did not specify why they were needed. This class also consisted of craftsmen and artisans, those whose lives were spent in production, but their products were not derived from the earth. The last class consisted of the merchants and the shopkeepers, who did not produce anything of first or second necessity. They were, however, an important factor in the economic structure because they conveyed and sold the goods of the first two classes to the rest of society, "living by the profits" (letter to Laurens). Although they did not live on revenues which they received from the production of crops or manufactured goods, they could do quite well financially in the towns and villages as the purveyors of merchandise.

Paine's ideas about class distinctions were fairly well developed as early as 1778. His letter to Laurens that year throws into question the conclusion that his pro-artisan activities began a year later, in 1779, during the debates over price controls. In fact, he understood the nature of the place of the artisan in society quite well. Indeed, as the son of a staymaker and a staymaker himself, he had particular insights into their contributions. This understanding in no way conflicted with his appreciation of the role of manufacturing and trade. The work of the manufacturers, merchants, and tradesmen was also important to the needs of the people. This consciousness explains why Paine was willing to ally himself so easily with the wealthy Philadelphia merchants, especially Robert Morris, and to advocate a laissez-faire economy rather than one based on strong price regulations.[11]

Merchants and manufacturers, artisans and shopkeepers, farmers and cultivators were all, then, the virtuous guilds, or more particularly members of the virtuous class. The rest of society parasitically fed on the goods and services that the virtuous and natural class produced and circulated. When Paine returned to America in 1802, he applied his vision of the producers and conveyors of goods to what he found had developed there since his departure some fifteen years earlier. In America, the Federalists occupied the same position as the nobility in Britain. They were a class of people who aggrandized their power at the expense of society. They were a *faction,* a term with the most negative features available to an eighteenth-century writer. It echoed the Madisonian warning of potential divisiveness and political disintegration.[12]

Paine's vision of the Federalists was distorted on at least two counts.[13] First, he viewed them through the French revolutionary lens he had acquired during his years in France. There, he had witnessed at first hand the parasitic character of the French aristocracy, though Lafayette was an obvious exception. Second, he attacked the Federalists so vociferously because they had vilified him.[14] He also felt that Washington had abandoned him while he was imprisoned in France during the Terror. He was certain at that time that he would be executed at any moment.[15] Still, he understood the true nature of the Adams presidency with its persecutions and Alien and Sedition Acts. As Paine put it, "It is a much greater crime for a President to plot against a constitution and the liberties of the people, than for an individual to plot against a President; and consequently, John Adams is accountable to the public for his conduct, as the individuals under his Administration were to the Sedition Law."[16]

Outraged, he often used outrageous language. He charged that the Devil himself had created the Federalists. Greed and self-interest corrupted them so that they were "beginning to contemplate government as a profitable monopoly, and the people as hereditary property." The Federalists used other Americans for their own narrow and unnatural purposes, forcing people out of their senses. People were made unaware that they had become subjected to Satan's commands. Paine reverted to the strong, religiously toned language he had made famous in *Common Sense* more than twenty-five years earlier by finding a new source of wickedness in America.

Paine used here the powerful image of "the cloven foot of faction" for its shock value in describing the Federalist evil made incarnate, which the Americans thought they had defeated with their victory over George III and his ministry. Now, true Americans had to repeat the exercise. This time, however, they would not have to use guns and artillery, only the ballot box. In America, natural virtue was stronger than in Britain and the classes of men more naturally virtuous.

> There is in America, more than in any other country, a large body of people who attend quietly to their farms, or follow their several occupations; who pay no regard to the clamors of anonymous scribblers, who think for themselves, and judge of government, not by the fury of newspaper writers, but by the prudent frugality of its measures, and the encouragement it gives to the improvement and prosperity of the country; and who, acting on their own judgment, never come forward in an election, but on some important occasion.

These independent men of independent means in 1800 had overcome Satan (the Federalist faction) with the election of Thomas Jefferson. Satan was therefore in "the agonies of death, and in proportion as its fate approaches, gnashes its teeth and struggles." Like the preacher from the pulpit who issued forth words of fire and damnation, Paine condemned the Federalists for their selfish double-dealing with the American cause.

Even now, he said, the Federalists feared Thomas Paine. On hearing of his return, they reacted like "the sight of water to canine madness."[17] Perhaps this was the real reason for his hatred of the Federalists: he resented them for daring to attack him. Or better, perhaps, he saw the origins of the Federalists in the British nobility whom William the Conqueror had created from his band of plunderers. In designating the Lords, William had foisted "a badge of disgrace upon the country." The Lords were "the defenders of his measures, and the guardians of his assumed prerogative against the people."[18]

The Federalists followed their predecessors. Their goal was to re-establish monarchy and aristocracy and thus seize financial control of America for their own aggrandizement. Commercial and economic growth blinded them to the common good. All of them, especially John Adams, had fought for independence for reasons quite different from those for which other Americans had fought. Adams, along with Hamilton, wanted independence so that their faction could lead a new hereditary executive, control a Senate with lifetime terms, and thus destroy the democratic republic. Adams was clearly the main culprit. "John was for independence because he expected to be made great by it." He thought that he eventually could be crowned king. "His head was full of kings, queens and knaves, as a pack of cards."[19]

Such sentiments, overstated as they are, underscored Paine's strong class bias. The Federalists wanted to impoverish the people "by loading them with taxes in order to load them with chains."[20] During the Adams administration, "the clamor for war" deliberately ensured the passage of increasingly higher taxes that would support a strong standing army, which these new American aristocrats would use to crush any attempt to save the democratic republic.[21] Paine thundered with all the bluster he could find that Adams and the others wanted a House of Lords in America, which like William's of old, would "place government on the corrupt system of the Old" world.[22] The Federalists were "counter-revolutionary," a term laden with both political and economic overtones since Paine was convinced that their goal was to seize political control for their later economic gain.[23] Seeking to place themselves in the same position as the British prior to 1776, they fitted perfectly into Paine's portrait of those who hindered America's economic and political progress.

Pitted against the "rattlesnake of federalism" were the natural and virtuous souls who sought to stem the tide of kingship and aristocracy. Paine's contemporary Everyman, Thomas Jefferson, won the presidency because a responsible, virtuous electorate at last understood its true interests. Americans had finally become aware of the dangers they had faced since 1796. The single term of Adams's administration had taught them their lesson easily and well. Revolution was unnecessary now because the people had voted the Federalists out of office (though barely). "Make it the interest of the people to live in a state of government, and they will protect that which protects them. But when they are harassed with alarms which time discovers to be false, and burdened with taxes for which they can see no cause, their confidence in such government withers away, and they laugh at the energy that attempts to restore it. Their cry then is, as in the time of the terror ('not to your tents, O! Israel), but to the Next Election O! Citizens.'"[24]

Economic growth was America's hope for a sound financial future. Prosperity was for the many, not only the few. In America in the new century, as everywhere in the world, the danger was that a narrow clique might subvert the new political order. Wealth was an avenue to be left open, as Adam Smith had taught, to all people. "The more riches a man acquires," said Paine, "the better it shall be for the general mass" (*Agrarian Justice, CW* 1:621). He thus preached against Federalist selfishness and for the democratic ideal of universal economic growth. "We every day see the rich becoming poor, and those who were poor before, becoming rich. Riches, therefore, having no stability, cannot and ought not to be made a criterion of right. Man is man in every condition of life, and the varieties of fortune and misfortune are open to all" (*Constitutional Reform, CW* 2:1001). Only one great class, consisting of men working together, would orchestrate the economic future of the world. The sole interest of that class was to expand financial and political power for everyone.[25]

Class Consequences: The Bank

The dangers inherent in a society with class conflict did not end with the demise of aristocrats and Federalists. Another hindrance to economic progress was social inequality. The poor were unable to participate in the schemes of the rich to control British politics and finance. Yet they directly felt the impact of these schemes because bank notes, circulating as legal tender, became the means of exchange for the unsuspecting underclass. This underclass had no choice but to use the notes, which were subject to high inflation rates. This was particularly apparent to Paine in the 1790s when he was convinced of the coming collapse of the English system of finance as the war economy boiled over. In his discussion of the bank and the eventual economic demise of Britain, Paine explained in financial terms how the collapse was to come, but he clearly allowed both his English and American lower- and middle-class audiences to understand how desirable this collapse was insofar as it contributed to revolutionary progress.

At first, he said, bank notes were printed only in twenty-pound denominations. As the government needed additional revenues to cover its voracious debt service, smaller denominations were printed until finally five-pound notes appeared. These circulated among the "little shopkeepers, butchers, bakers, market-people, renters of small houses, lodgers, etc." Such naturally virtuous people had nowhere to turn if they wanted a means of exchange. Government had played them a dirty trick. "All the high departments of commerce and the affluent stations of life were already *overstocked*" with the higher denominations. "No place remained open wherein to crowd an additional quantity of bank notes but among the class of people I have just mentioned, and the means of doing this could be best effected by coining five pound notes. This conduct has the appearance of that of an unprincipled insolvent, who, when on the verge of bankruptcy to the amount of many thousands, will borrow as low as five pounds of the servants in his house, and break the next day" (*Decline & Fall, CW* 2:673). Paine might have overstated his case, but as usual he felt certain that class inequality was destroying the British economy.

Two situations developed as a consequence of this banking policy. The British government was now controlled by an undemocratic minority of very wealthy creditors, and the economic downfall of a government unable to repay those creditors meant that the bankruptcy of the lower and middle classes inevitably followed. Not only were these orders forced to use worthless cash, they also had to shoulder the burden of increasing taxes to pay for British warmongering, while the creditors and war profiteers became wealthier. "A few men have enriched themselves by jobs and contracts, and the groaning multitude bore the burden," he wrote in 1787 of Britain's "amazing accumulation of debt, and an unparalleled burden of taxes." The lower classes' lot was to become the foundation of "the exhausted nation" and their outlook was to be "huzza'd into new taxes," as the cycle of war and taxes, debt and bankruptcy continued unabated until the nation collapsed from the sheer weight of its financial burdens (*Rubicon, CW* 2:623–25).

In America, the men of first necessity, the farmers and cultivators, were little affected by the debt, but Paine's support of one class of producers (the shopkeepers, butchers, and so forth) did not mean he had forgotten farmers and cultivators. After all, in saying that he defended "the cause of humanity," he focused on both these classes: city artisans, tradesmen, and merchants, on the one hand, and rural farmers and cultivators, on the other. Their economic and financial conditions were actually quite different. Paine's strong advocacy of the Bank of North America in the 1780s brought these differences out when he found himself, at least momentarily, pitted against the farmers and backcounty settlers, those men of first necessity whom he admired and wanted to help.

Unlike the English system, a national bank in America could do two things, Paine argued: overcome class differentiation and at the same time aid in the national unity he was seeking. America as a new nation did not face the corruptions of older nations. Support of the bank, of course, meant opposition to the western Pennsylvania farmers who wanted to repeal the bank's charter. Support of the bank also threw him in opposition to some, though not all, Philadelphia artisans who spoke against the bank as well. Indeed, support of the bank meant that he sided with wealthy Philadelphia merchants, like Robert Morris, Robert Livingstone, and others, who financed the bank in part for their own profit.

According to Eric Foner, "Paine's alliance with Morris did not represent a full break with his artisan constituency."[26] This statement is true, but it should be more broadly stated. First, Paine sought no breaks with the artisans or with the tradesmen, the merchants, or the farmers, or even the poor. Second, Paine's vision of economic growth went far beyond those of the artisans and the farmers. Paine was a longtime supporter of the bank, advocating its creation when the United States was literally running out of money and facing the prospect of being unable to support the war effort against the British. He believed that while the bank would initially profit only those who invested in it, in the long run it would have positive benefits for American society as a whole. An example of his faith was his decision to keep his own money on deposit there.[27] When Morris hired Paine to write in favor of the bank, Paine gladly accepted, but he did so from the belief that the bank was good for everyone.[28]

Paine argued that those who wanted to revoke its charter were wrongheaded and misguided. They did not understand the bank's potential for all Americans, and not just the wealthy like Morris and Livingstone. When four backcounty politicians (John Smilie, George Emlen, William Findley, and Robert Whitehill) led the fight in the Pennsylvania legislature to terminate the bank, Paine was not surprised. In his attack on their position, he twisted reality, as he was wont to do on occasion. He accused them, paradoxically, of being the "monied men," who viewed

> a public bank as standing in the way of their private interest. Their wealth is not of so much value to them as he and therefore they say down with the bank. To accomplish this point, so agreeable to their wishes, and advantageous to their wealth, they have been working through the ignorance of the late house in matters of commerce, and the nature of banks, and on the prejudices of others as leaders of that party, to demolish the bank. It might be error in the former, but it is wilful mischief in the latter; and as mischief is not lessened by the apology of error, nor encreased by the criminality of design, therefore those who sacrificed to prejudice, are, as to matters of public trust, alike the objects of public reprobation. ("Bank," *CW* 2:424)

Paine in effect accused those who opposed the bank of wanting only their own private gain at the expense of public prosperity. Had he taken the side of Smilie, Emlen, and company, he might have said the same of Robert Morris.

It might be speculated that Morris, who was interested in accumulating great personal wealth (and in fact did), knew that an economically stable America was the foundation of his wealth. He once wrote in a manner that suggested he understood the relationship between the two. "I shall continue to discharge my duty faithfully to the public, and pursue my private fortune by all such honorable and fair means as the times will admit of."[29]

How much of this was self-flattery and how much bluster is not clear. But if Paine ever heard Morris speak this way, he probably believed him. Paine's views of Morris were decidedly different from those he held of war profiteer Silas Deane, whose life, he once said, "has been fraud, and his character is that of plodding, plotting, cringing, mercenary, capable of any disguise, that suited his purpose."[30] If Morris was selfish, it was in a Mandevillian way. Smilie and Emlen were simply shortsighted. They failed to perceive how the bank was "one of the best institutions that could be devised to promote the commerce and agriculture of the country, and recover it from the ruined condition in which the war had left both the farmer and the merchant, as well as the most effectual means to banish usury and establish credit among the citizens" ("Bank," *CW* 2:415). This failure in perception was inexcusable because they were educated men, entrusted with the welfare of the people.

The farmers, however, were different. Their antagonism toward the bank did not mean that they lacked natural virtue. They were simply unaware of the bank's benefits because of their backcounty origins: the Pennsylvania frontier areas of America, in short, the wilderness. They could not help the way they thought about such matters. They were not capable of seeing the common good, of being public-spirited. Here, the natural environment actually worked against them. It was to blame for their antibank prejudices. It blinded them to the vision of modernity that the bank offered America. The wilderness was where Paine's fascination with nature encountered the wall of economic progress. He loved nature, and things natural, but when the wilderness areas, the backcounty, seemed to prohibit economic progress, he decried the myopia of those who lived there.

It may be remarked that Paine's animus toward the wilderness directly contradicted his adulation of things natural. But Paine often used arguments to suit his position, and here was no exception. Just as we find him employing scripture to emphasize a point while denying the truth of the Bible, so we may find him condemning those living in the wilderness in order to bolster his position, and that is precisely what he did at this point in his argument.

Those who opposed the bank were those "who from their remote situation feel themselves very little, if at all, interested in the prosperity of the more *settled and improved* parts of the state. Their ideas of government, agriculture and commerce, are drawn from their own frontier habitations; and their politics seem calculated to suit their particular situations, at the expense and detriment of the rest." Such people failed to understand the advantages of civil society in all its positive attributes "either because they have yet no produce to sell or export, or because they have no commercial intercourse with the market where the Bank is established at."

In this regard, Paine distinguished between the frontier and the farm, the frontiersman and the farmer, the backwoodsman and the producer, a distinction which was not immediately evident to the reader and which Paine was hard pressed to make. And yet, if he were to fulfill his goal of condemning those who opposed the bank, he had to find a means to distinguish the opponents from the bank's supporters. The frontiersman (or "settler," as he preferred to call him) "is not yet a farmer." He was uninvolved in commercial relations with his fellows. He was therefore not fully productive. He sold nothing because he produced nothing to sell. Someday he may become a full-fledged farmer-producer. Until then, he would raise only enough crops for his own family. "In the stage of the settler, his thoughts are engrossed and taken up in making a settlement. If he can raise produce enough for the support of his family, it is the utmost of his present hopes. He has none to bring to market, or to sell, and therefore commerce appears nothing to him; and he cries out, that a Bank is of no use. But the case is, he is not yet in a condition to participate in its usefulness. When he is, he will think otherwise."

When settlements became farms, a new consciousness would develop. This consciousness allowed the farmer (the former settler) to see the commercial and public value of the bank. The settler's range of vision was, until then, limited, a factor for which Paine had little patience. The settler was cut off from the commercial hub of modern civilization. "Therefore, when a back county member says that the Bank is of no use to the farmer, he means the settler, who has yet no produce to sell, and knows nothing about the matter."

The farmers' commercial consciousness developed only as a result of economic progress, which made their places of residence more like "the improved parts of the state, from whence the staple commodities of the country are brought." Until then, they would still be guided by the "monied men" in the Pennsylvania legislature who claimed to represent their interests, but who in fact were interested only in their own profit ("Bank," *CW* 2:426–27). Paine had to know that his argument was a sham. He probably realized that Smilie and Emlen and the others had no monetary interest to reap should the bank fail. He also probably knew that the accusations he hurled at them would finally be persuasive to those in the assembly who had not yet made up their mind.

In his discussion, Paine clarified what he meant when he claimed he defended the cause of humanity. *Humanity* had a narrow meaning in the context of the bank. The bank worked in the interest of all Americans who contributed to the new nation's economic strength, viability, and, perhaps most important, its modernization. These contributors, the wealthy merchants and manufacturers, the artisans and farmers, did not include backwoods frontiersmen and settlers. The latter could not at the outset use the bank, although they could potentially become full participating members who would someday share in the benefits of America's economic growth.

In this sense, the bank was not undemocratic, as Emlen and Smilie had charged, but was very democratic. The sole prerequisite for enjoying its advantages was a certain level of economic consciousness and commercial sophistication. Only those who reached this level and participated in market activities (merchants *and* artisans) were virtuous. The rest were yet in a stage of economic simplicity and were not fully aware of the common purposes that drew Americans together as a united people.

The bank's greatest asset was its ability to lend money. The settler and the frontiersman never had a need for loans. Borrowing, especially for a short term, was a great boon only to those classes which needed ready cash. These people had reached the requisite level of commercial participation and economic consciousness, a level which excluded the settler and the frontiersman. "Loans for short periods serve to pay the farmer, the miller, the tradesman, the workman, etc. and hundreds are served in the course of a year."

The same was true in farming because farmers needed cash to continue to develop their acreage and to increase their crop production. "Now that the farms are made, the best encouragement to the farmer is to provide means to buy and pay, in real money, for the produce he has to sell" ("Bank," *CW* 2:431). This the bank could do, but the backwoods people could not understand how the bank could help them; at least not until they themselves became farmers. And only then would they become conscious of the bank's purpose for America's future.

The Poor

If frontiersmen were unaware of the bank's advantages, the poor were even more so. In the 1790s, Paine seriously addressed the difficulties associated with poverty, especially the urban squalor he witnessed in Paris. He wrote on this subject at his most passionate level. He personally appreciated the effects of poverty and he often went directly to the point, which was that government's obligation was to end poverty. Much has been made of Paine's outspoken concern for the poor, especially his social welfare programs outlined in the second part of *Rights of Man* and *Agrarian Justice*. His concern for the poor corresponded to his overall understanding of a virtuous citizenry.

The poor were impoverished not because of some weakness in their character, but because those who were more powerful than they had stolen the land that God had given to all to hold in common. The thieves were able to set themselves up over the rest to rule (and oppress) them. The condition of the poor was the result of historical circumstances, especially the development of private property, rather than of anything they themselves had or had not specifically done. Paine never advocated the redistribution of property. He never favored leveling society to absolute equality by eliminating the private ownership of land.

People, he said in *Agrarian Justice,* were originally "born to property." When they moved from hunting and then to pasturage and farming, they became cultivators and thus improved the land. Over time, the land was divided among men and large parts of it gradually became privately owned. Paine refined Locke's labor theory of value by arguing that in a conventional sense the land itself never became privately owned. Only the improvements of it did. The earth itself remained the property of all men, at least in theory. Whereas Locke had argued that the land became the property of those who improved it, Paine held that the land did not change at all through cultivation, even if the few who owned property believed that it did. Since "man did not make the earth, and, though he had a natural right to *occupy* it, he had no right to *locate as his property* in perpetuity any part of it; neither did the Creator of the earth open a land-office, from whence the first title-deeds should issue" (*CW* 1:611). A person could only acquire or possess the value that he invested in the earth, not the earth itself.

This distinction is important. Undeveloped land should not at any time have become private property. Those who created a monopoly over the land had stolen it. Poverty, which he considered among the greatest of evils, inevitably followed. To rectify the theft of the land, Paine proposed the social programs in *Rights of Man* and the ground rent plan of *Agrarian Justice*. But first, everyone had to agree on the principle that "no person ought to be in a worse condition when born under what is called a state of civilization, than he would have been had he been born in a state of nature, and that civilization ought to have made, and ought still to make, provision for that purpose" (*CW* 2:613).

Paine's point was that society as a whole must overcome the impoverishment, which was the fault of the few. The theft of the land denied a fundamental right originally granted to man by God. "In advocating the case of the persons thus dispossessed," he said, "it is a *right*, and not a charity, that I am pleading for" (*CW* 2:612).[31] The end of the poor rates and of high taxation on the poor (which were not applied at all to the aristocracy) and the beginning of governmental payments to the poor and to young married couples for public education and social security, along with his celebrated ground rent, were designed with the same end in view. The essential point he preached here was that society owed the people what was by right theirs.

The poor had as much right to benefit from the land as anyone else. Perhaps their claim was even greater since they were the dispossessed. Historical circumstances prevented impoverished people from owning land. Current owners must compensate their less fortunate compatriots because their acquisition of the land was a result of historical circumstances. The poor ought to be objects of sympathy and compassion. "It is the nature of compassion to associate with misfortune," and so society's supreme duty was to help the poor in the only way it could, namely by meting out welfare on the basis of a natural (or even divine) right (*RM* 218).[32]

If poverty could be ended and economic prosperity secured for all, as Paine desired, then economic equality would be at hand. People's moral responsibility was, then, to remove the blight of poverty from the earth. To do so would accomplish the dual ends he preached in the aftermath of the French Revolution: the improvement of the poor's condition and the avoidance of revolution as a result of economic injustice.

A Single Class, A New Society

Paine's class consciousness and his ideas of economic democracy were distinctive. He possessed an acute sensibility about the causes of social differentiation, in particular how corrupt men expropriated the land that God had originally given to benefit everyone. Some people, setting themselves above the interests of the whole, were not virtuous. They were naturally self-aggrandizing. They thought only about their own wealth and status and hence delayed economic progress. Their consciousness was narrow. They could not see beyond their own profit or their own standing.

On the other hand, the virtuous "producers and conveyors" of society's goods provided benefits for all the people and saw to it that those goods were transported to all regions of the country. They demonstrated that human beings were not by nature exploitative of their fellows. These were the farmers and cultivators, the merchants and manufacturers, the artisans and craftsmen. Although they may differ in wealth and social standing, Paine considered them all of the same class. They acquired their position and riches because their work benefited all of society. They were forward looking even when they accumulated great fortunes. They represented a goal achievable by all people who would use their natural abilities. In between these two classes stood those to whom society must offer its assistance or patience. The poor and less fortunate (which included the young and the elderly) needed the community's help until they were financially able to enter into the ranks of the producers or conveyors of goods or until they died. Moreover, the settlers needed society's patience. As the frontier developed, they too would begin to see how, as full citizens, they fitted into the growth of America.

As Paine grew older, his views on the alleviation of the poor's problems grew more radical. He no longer only spoke of the middle class and how it might aid in the creation of a good American society. Now he demanded that government live up to its responsibility to care for its economic victims, to ensure peaceful progress, and, if at all possible, to sidestep revolution. To ensure these goals, he explained how the people were to erect the democratic republic.

❧ 8 ❧

Constitutional Invention

God in his perfection created nature as he wanted it. He gave man broad physical and intellectual powers for good. Human invention, a reflection of God's own creativity, opened to man the possibilities of art, politics, literature, commerce, finance, and construction. It was just as important to invent good constitutional forms as it was to write good poetry and design good bridges or make better candles. The eighteenth century was open to invention. It was, as Paine named it, the Age of Reason, an age of innovation and experimentation. In politics, each state in the new United States experimented with constitutional formation: with and without bills of rights; with one or with two legislatures, with and without judicial review. The Americans as a whole experimented with the Articles of Confederation and later with their Constitution.

Many of the people involved with these experiments were also engaged in scientific and technological developments. And some were Paine's friends. Benjamin Franklin is an obvious case in point. Scientist, inventor, diplomat, writer, and politician, Franklin once referred to Paine as his "adopted political son."[1] In England in 1774, he suggested that Paine sail to America, and he sent with him a letter recommending Paine for jobs as a schoolteacher, clerk, or surveyor. Franklin again sent letters of introduction when Paine traveled to France in 1787. The two corresponded until Franklin's death in 1790. Another close associate was Benjamin Rush, physician and politician, who like Franklin was constantly engaged in medical and scientific experimentation. And yet another was John Fitch, who "put the first successful self-propelled steamboat on a trial run up and down the Delaware River."[2] After his arrival in America in 1774, Paine found himself "on exceedingly good

139

terms" with Thomas Jefferson.[3] As the architect and builder of Monticello, the founder of the University of Virginia, and an amateur scientist and inventor, Jefferson sought the most propitious improvements through concentrated human invention.

All of these people influenced Paine and contributed especially to his vision of how men could create a better life, a vision reflected in his fascination with scientific and technological innovation, including, of course, the design and construction of bridges as well as of constitutions. Bridge building and constitution making were positive paradigms in Paine's overall outlook. Both served as natural extensions of his vision of man, the inventor of things, *homo faber*. And yet, man's creative powers also had a negative side: he was a maker of war on his fellows. Paine therefore often used the paradigm of war to understand man's complex character as maker.

The Paradigm of the Bridge

In speculating about Paine's motivations in constructing a bridge, historians have suggested possibilities ranging from a desire to continue to work as a skilled craftsman to a desire to accumulate riches and fame in construction that would match his fame as a political commentator. Simply put, Paine wanted to accomplish in the practical sciences the counterpart of his contribution in political science. "He would be as useful to America in the practical sphere as he had been in the political."[4] That Paine himself was aware of the connection between bridges and constitutions is evident in a 1775 essay which said that he could "reflect with inexpressible pleasure, on the numberless benefits arising to a community, by the institution of societies for promoting useful knowledge." Indeed, the people's duties spanned the distance between the political and the practical, for "while we glory in what we are, we may not neglect what we *are to be*."[5]

Paine claimed that his bridge was an improvement because it overcame the main problem of bridges built over water in the American climate. In the extremely frigid winters, frozen rivers and streams often destroyed piers and arches. Paine's design solved this problem "by leaving the whole passage of the river clear of the incumbrance of piers."[6] He acknowledged that his design came from nature, specifically the spider web. "I naturally supposed that when nature enabled that insect to make a web she taught it the best method of putting it together."

The bridge's portability displays a feature of Paine's approach to scientific investigation. With nature as his model, he believed that he could design "bridges capable of becoming a portable manufacture, as they may, on this construction, be made and sent to any part of the world ready to be erected; and at the same time it greatly increases the magnificence, elegance and beauty of bridges, it considerably lessens their expense, and their appearance by repainting will be ever new; and as they may be erected in all situations where stone bridges can be erected they may, moreover, be erected in certain situations where, on account of ice, in firm foundations in the beds of rivers, low shores and various other causes, stone bridges cannot be erected."[7] Paine's bridge design was to be a contribution to all people. It would "exceedingly benefit the city and county, and besides its usefulness would, I believe, be the most extensive arch in the world, and the longest bridge without piers."[8] He claimed that he was not interested in profiting from the construction and sale of his bridge, although profit may well have been an early motivation. On his return to America in 1802, after having little success in securing financial support in France or England, he wrote to Congress that he did not seek personal monetary gain from his bridge. Accordingly, he was not applying for a patent. His bridge was for the Congress, for the American people, to make "use of the construction freely" as a benefit to mankind.[9] Human invention thus brought improvements that benefited all people, and the paradigm of the bridge was an index of man as *homo faber*.

The Paradigm of War

But man was also an inventor of war. Although Paine never systematically investigated the perennial question of the just war, he did argue that each person must consider the reasons why his country chose war before deciding to join or not to join the armed forces. Paine's acceptance of some wars as just (the American war against the British, the French revolutionary wars against the European anciens régimes) is problematic given his partial Quaker background. On occasion, he acknowledged that he was a Quaker, and in 1793 Marat directly called him one after Paine's heated defense of Louis XVI.[10] If he were a Quaker with strong roots in a pacifist tradition, how was it possible for him to support American independence and French democracy when the achievement of both goals entailed violence and combat?

Paine's reply to the Quakers concerning American separation from Britain was not only a counterpoint to their pacifism, in general, and their loyalty to Britain, in particular, but also an expression of his own pragmatic spirit. In this instance, war was a necessity, a human invention, designed to achieve positive ends, although war itself was repugnant. If war was a necessity, it was an unfortunate one.

Paine addressed this question head-on when he said, "Were the Quakers really impressed and influenced by the quiet principles they profess to hold, they would, however they might disapprove the means, be the first of all men to approve of *independence,* because, by separating ourselves from the cities of Sodom and Gemorrah, it affords an opportunity never given to man before of carrying their favourite principle of peace into general practice, by establishing governments that shall hereafter exist without wars" (*American Crisis, CW* 1:83). Events had outpaced their thinking. The Quakers failed to understand the necessity of this war and to appreciate their proper role in it. "Like antiquated virgins, they see not the havoc deformity has made upon them, but pleasantly mistaking wrinkles for dimples, conceive themselves yet lovely and wonder at the stupid world for not admiring them" (ibid., *CW* 1:94). He claimed that his views a year before the American Revolution were similar to the Quakers', but only to this point: "I would gladly agree with all the world to lay aside the use of arms, and settle matters by negotiation," quickly adding that two sides in a dispute must ultimately agree if they were to settle an argument.

Because that was impossible in America's relationship with Britain, "I take up my musket and thank heaven he has put it in my power." This is necessary because "we live not in a world of angels."[11] The king and his ministry, that "set of savages and brutes" (*American Crisis, CW* 1:89), the "vile and the abandoned," proved that "the reign of Satan is not ended" (*Defensive War, CW* 2:52–53). This war was necessary, then, because above all it was not an aggressive war, but a defensive one, for the people to regain their lost rights.

Paine's interest in war as a human invention resulted from his inquiry into how Americans could best protect their natural and civil rights. All articles of war were evil. If people, however, used them for good purposes, such as the defense of rights, then a particular war was just and virtuous. The opposite was true if they were used for wrong—offensive or aggressive— reasons. Gunboats were therefore important and indeed necessary to protect American ports, especially the New York harbor. Such instruments of war were for defensive purposes only. "There is no mode or system of defense the United States can go into for coasts and harbors or ports, that will be effectual as by gun-boats."[12]

Monarchical governments always misused human inventiveness because such "governments have trained the human race, and inured it to the sanguinary arts and refinements of punishment." People must copy good examples of invention, "but it becomes us to be strictly on our guard against the abomination and perversity of monarchical examples."[13] All citizens could advance civilization by creating things for positive ends. Constitution making fell in this category.

Innovation and Historical Consciousness

In Thomas Paine's political universe, the highest form of invention was a democratic republican constitution. Paine's conception of what a constitution ought to be was a direct outgrowth of his conception of natural and civil rights. Because constitutions preexisted governments, their primary purpose was to ensure the protection of rights. When carefully drafted, they provided a physical framework for that protection. If they accomplished that purpose, they succeeded in their fundamental task.

For this reason, a constitution must be written down. Without a written constitution, a government was left dangerously unfettered. Those who ruled might try to seize unlimited power. They might choose to rule without regard to freedom and justice, without virtue, without humanity. The decisions of such rulers would be for their own narrow self-interests, and the common good would be in danger. Paine consistently charged that the English monarchy was guilty of such abuses of power. His famous challenge to Burke to produce, if he could, the British constitution was in the end answered by Paine himself when he said that "no such thing as a constitution exists, or ever did exist, and consequently . . . the people have yet a constitution to form" (*RM* 71–72).[14]

Paine defined a constitution as "a thing *antecedent* to a government," so that the government that followed from this constitution was its "creature."

> The constitution of a country is not the act of its government, but of the people constituting a government. It is a body of elements, to which you can refer, and quote article by article; and which contains the principles on which the government shall be established, the manner in which it shall be organized, the powers it shall have, the mode of elections, the duration of parliaments, or by what other name such bodies may be called; the powers which the executive part of the government shall have; and, in fine, everything that relates to the complete organization of a civil government, and the principles on which it shall act, and by which it shall be bound. A constitution, therefore, is to a government, what the laws made afterwards by that government are to a court of judicature. The court of judicature does not make the laws, neither can it alter them; it only acts in conformity to the laws made: and the government is in like manner governed by the constitution. (*RM* 71).

This passage underscored Paine's emphasis on the components of a good constitution: form, structure, and composition, all designed to provide a protective shield around the people's equal, inherent rights. But how was this to be done? What models should the people, indeed could they, use to devise a constitutional structure that would infallibly protect their rights?

No models existed. If people searched for the best forms of government, they were not to be found. Nature did not provide a model, such as Paine found in a spider's web for his bridge. People must develop a constitution through trial and error, through experimentation, because all constitutions were innovations. Because "we are a people upon experiments," he told the Americans in 1778, we "have the happy opportunity of trying variety in order to discover the best." This opportunity meant that "novelty" was the key factor in the design of a good constitution. Novelty was an idea he preached in two ways. The new constitution was a novelty, a phenomenon unlike any other that had been successful (after all, the Greeks and Romans had failed). Since all previous constitutions "have been defective, that which shall not be so, *must be a novelty*, and that which is *not a novelty*, must be defective." Innovation was the hallmark of good constitution making. The people could (and did) experiment with new forms of government on different occasions: in Pennsylvania in 1776, in the United States as a whole in 1787, in France in 1793 and again in 1795. Paine was typically unconcerned with historical precedent when it came to the design of a constitution. Perhaps men have nothing to learn from the past. "It does not appear that any form of government yet known in the world has answered the pretences of its institution. The Greeks and Romans became slaves. All forms have failed in producing freedom and security."[15]

To argue that Paine lacked a historical consciousness is to provide an incomplete picture of his sensitivity to history. The truth is not that Paine was uninterested in history, but rather that he thought that history failed to provide what people needed. From his understanding of history, Paine preached that history presented no models of a good constitution because "the science of government is so far only in its childhood." Political science had not yet advanced enough that modern constitutional innovators could cull from the annals of the past a perfect or even reasonably acceptable model. Only time and experience allowed citizens to master the frailties and inequities of government.

On the one hand, Paine preached that people had little to learn from the past, that former political models were useless, and that political novelty and experimentation were their best hope. On the other hand, he showed appreciation of the past by citing various historical personalities whose wisdom confirmed his ideas. Was this selective verification? Or was there more here than he appeared to suggest? After all, he suggested that Burke look to human origins to find the source of rights, and he searched the past for historical examples and models, though he found none to fit his vision of a good constitution.

Paine's stratagem was to assert in 1792 that whatever else he did, he made full use of the past: "I can but hope that, whatever system [of government] may be adopted, it will permit us to take advantage of the lessons of *experience*."[16] In other words, the past had several lessons to teach those who would learn them.

Americans had to be aware of the "seedtime" of the republic, for it is at that moment, at the creation of the republic, that the seeds of the political culture are sown (*CS* 82). The French must act to ensure "a bond of union" so that "every individual would [then know] the line of conduct he was to follow" (*Dissertation, CW* 2:587). Good habits must be cultivated from the beginning. Bad habits and weak institutions were difficult, if not impossible, to change later on.

The only positive lesson of history for Paine was drawn from mythicized history: his idea that men were given natural rights at their creation. That was a mythical, not a historical, moment—a creation of Paine's fantasy, designed specifically to answer Burke's prescriptive argument. All other historical events provided moral and political lessons of what men should avoid. Classical antiquity, for example, taught Paine the following:

> I cannot but help being sometimes surprised at the complimentary references which I have seen and heard made to ancient histories and transactions. The wisdom, civil governments, and sense of honor of the states of Greece and Rome, are frequently held up as objects of excellence and imitation. Mankind have lived to very little purpose, if, at this period of the world, they must go two and three thousand years back for lessons and examples. We do great injustice to ourselves by placing them in such a superior line. We have no just authority for it, neither can we tell why it is that we should suppose ourselves inferior.
>
> Could the mist of antiquity be cleared away, and men and things be viewed as they really were, it is more than probable that they would admire us, rather than we them. America has surmounted a greater variety and combination of difficulties, than, I believe, ever fell to the share of any one people, in the same space of time, and has replenished the world with more useful knowledge and sounder maxims of civil government than were ever produced in any age before.[17]

Human invention meant not that people should emulate what had gone before out of some misguided admiration of the past, but that they should try something new, that they should experiment by creating a novelty. If one novelty did not work, they should try another. Paine demonstrated this by first accepting in 1778 the idea of a unicameral legislature and then in 1786 his rejecting of it. This shift reflected his readiness to change once the experiment failed. Pennsylvania needed a second legislative house to act as a check on the first.[18]

Experiment, he admonished, to determine what would best secure rights and freedom, protect men's property, and ensure their happiness. But do not slavishly emulate the past just because it was antique. "We live to improve, or we live in vain; and therefore we admit of no maxims of government or policy on the mere score of antiquity, or other men's authority, the *old* Whigs or the *new*."[19] Once people knew what to avoid, they could learn what to do in a positive way to create a good constitution. They would inevitably make mistakes, but through trial and error, they would eventually find the best constitutional forms. This meant that the most important aspect of a constitution was not necessarily whether it called for a legislature with one or two houses or for a single or multiple executive. More important than these was a built-in mechanism for revision in response to changing times or abuses of power.

A constitution worth having, therefore, must have an amending provision that would permit the people to capitalize on and utilize the past. A historical consciousness was consequently critical. It gave the citizenry, as it gave Paine himself, not only a vision of future constitutional forms but a perspective on what failed to work in the past.

Paine based the amending provision firmly on a principle that he advocated most of his life, namely that one generation did not possess the right to legislate for succeeding ones. "When we are planning for posterity," he said, "we ought to remember that virtue is not hereditary" (*CS* 110). And yet, the independence that the Americans won and the freedom the French achieved were legacies that they must pass on to future generations. The difference was that no one legislated these revolutions. The people undertook them in order to regain the rights and freedoms they had once possessed. With rights and liberty properly back in the hands of the people, the principle that every age and generation should legislate only for itself became the obligation of all free peoples. Otherwise, they were not truly liberated from the tyranny that they had overthrown or separated from. That tyranny still existed. The people must perforce be repelled by the "idea of consigning their children, and their children's children" to a system of government that was still rooted in a tyranny that seemed unchanging and unchangeable.[20]

The Enlightenment faith in inevitable progress, the faith of the philosophes and of English writers, mainly the Dissenters, was obviously infectious to Paine. The inevitability of progress lay firmly in his belief that human beings were designers in control of their own destinies, that people must seek and work for progress, if they were ever to achieve it in the long run. "We must do nothing to impede progress," he once said. The test of a generation striving for progress was whether it legislated in its own behalf, that is, whether it made its own laws and changed its constitution as it saw fit. A future generation might well accept what was worth keeping from a past generation, or it might not. The decision was its to make. "Perhaps, their wisdom will be more profound than ours. It would be folly in us to assert a privilege to which we have not the slightest claim."

If, therefore, all constitutions included "a method of correcting [defects] as they arise," they would "be permanent."[21] This was a lesson he had learned first from the Pennsylvania Constitution of 1776 and then from the American example in 1787. His argument was based on his own experiences, and he was intent on teaching this knowledge to his American and French readers. The science of government was only in its infancy, but it was always improving. With the passage of time, citizens would gradually learn how to make constitutions more perfect and thus longer lasting. Experiment and novelty, through constitutional provisions themselves, were leading the people to a new era of government. Protected by its own constitutional framework, the democratic republic that Paine envisioned prefigured the historical development of the American Constitution over the past two hundred years. This framework, if it contained the right intentions (to protect rights and freedom), would be as crucial to the life of man as were his everyday, practical inventions.

The Democratic-Republican Constitution

Until the end of the eighteenth century and the appearance of the works of Jean-Jacques Rousseau and Thomas Paine, many writers believed that democracy was a highly unstable form of government. Aristotle had taught that it possessed a negative form into which it could always potentially degenerate—namely mob rule or anarchy. Both Paine and Rousseau thought of *democracy* in a positive sense; it described the constitutional form that best protected the equal rights of man. They both made, however, a number of qualifications about the nature of democracy. For Rousseau, democracy "is the form of government most appropriate to men not far removed from their natural freedom."[22] Paine agreed insofar as in democracy "the whole of [man's] faculties," his mind and his conscience, "could be employed . . . to bring forward, by a quiet and regular operation, all that extent of capacity which never fails to appear in revolutions" (*RM* 176). In a democratic polity, a person could achieve his fullest potential, and he exercised his rights in an environment that no external authority encumbered. He was at once governed and free.

But now the qualifications. Democracy had two meanings. First, democracy was a form of government essentially suited only for small, self-contained states. Rousseau believed this as well. Indeed, Paine may have adopted the idea of democracy for small states from Rousseau. His most highly developed views of democracy were formed during and after the French Revolution, at a time when he was particularly susceptible to the Genevan's ideas of democracy.

Rousseau had written that "there has always been a great deal of argument over the best form of government, without considering that each one of them is best in certain cases and the worst in others. If the number of supreme magistrates in the different states ought to be in inverse ratio to that of the citizens, it follows that in general democratic government is suited to small states."[23] In such a state, everyone knew everyone else on sight, they possessed few if any sophisticated customs and traditions, they were practically equal in wealth and rank, and they were unencumbered by luxuries.

Paine agreed with this assessment. As the Greeks had discovered, no matter how theoretically desirable it might be, democracy would not work as a practical matter in an extended or large, complex state. As "democracies increased in population, and the territory extended, the simple democratical form became unwieldy and impracticable; and . . . the consequence was, they either degenerated convulsively into monarchies, or became absorbed into such as then existed" (RM 177). These governments failed because they were unable to adapt to changing or new conditions. Their failure did not condemn democracy per se, but only democracy in its simplest form.

The second meaning Paine gave to democracy was more important than the first. This was "the public principle" of democratic government. If the citizens could not implement this principle in its simplest form in a large state, then some fine tuning, some political innovation, was necessary. Their constitution must have a system of representation erected on the foundation of democracy.

Representation created the democratic republic (or representative democracy—the name itself did not particularly interest him). Representation overcame the problems of a simple democracy in a large territory. "Simple democracy was society governing itself without the aid of secondary means. By ingrafting representation upon democracy, we arrive at a system of government capable of embracing and confederating all the various interests and every extent of territory and population; and that also with advantages as much superior to hereditary government, as the republic of letters is to hereditary literature" (*RM* 180).

Here Paine departed from Rousseau, who objected to representation under any circumstance. Rousseau thought that representation was a modern innovation, a product of human contrivance. "In the ancient republics and even in monarchies, the people never had representatives. The word itself was unknown." He vociferously argued that the general will was neither alienable nor divisible; in other words, it was the reverse of what a system of representation provided for. When men made laws, all the people needed to be present to give their direct consent to them. "The moment a people gives itself representatives, it is no longer free; it no longer exists." After all, "the law is merely the declaration of the general will;" thus, "it is clear that the people cannot be represented in the legislative power."[24]

For Paine, representation, when connected to democracy, worked and worked well. America had already demonstrated this. "It has fixed the form by a scale parallel in all cases to the extent of the principle. What Athens was in miniature, America will be in magnitude. The one was the wonder of the ancient world; the other is becoming the admiration and model of the present. It is the easiest of all forms of government to be understood, and the most eligible in practice; and excludes at once the ignorance and insecurity of the hereditary mode, and the inconvenience of the simple democracy." Representative democracy would work in France or wherever the people established it. "It adapts itself to all possible cases." The representative system was so superior to any other that it was unfortunate that the Athenians never discovered it. It was good even for small states, he said, and "Athens, by representation, would have outrivalled her own democracy" (*RM* 180–81).

The best form of representative democracy was the mixed regime, the triadic model provided by the Americans and rooted in the Old Whig delineation of the one, the few, and the many. This government was an organic whole in which each part survived only as long as the other parts remained vital and functioning. The precise form that this government would take depended on those charged with its framing in the constitutional convention, itself an entity that worked well through representation. In the meantime, form was only a matter of opinion. All that was necessary was "that all parts be conformable with the *principle of equal rights;* and so long as this principle be religiously adhered to, no very material error can take place, neither can any error continue long in that part which falls within the province of opinion" (*Dissertation, CW* 2:584).[25]

Paine gave primary importance not to the form of government but to its procedures, especially in matters of law making and the dangers of a runaway or potentially tyrannical majority. In addressing this question, he returned to the central role of human rights. If a person were conscious of his rights, he could avoid despotism. Certainly a powerful majority might deem the rights of a minority null and void, given the institution of slavery in Paine's time.[26]

Perhaps Paine's faith in human generosity was somewhat overbearing here. His position was that the "minority has been composed of men possessing property, as well as of men without property; property, therefore, even upon the experience already had, is no more a criterion of character than it is of rights." If people overcame the class basis of governmental decision making, they could get on with the business of government. When a majority was wrong and the minority right, experience dictated the direction that change ought to take. "The error will reform itself by the tranquil operation of freedom of opinion and equality of rights" (*Dissertation, CW* 2:585).[27]

Without a constitution to define the role of the representative bodies in a government and to limit the powers of these bodies, laws would inevitably be "irrational and tyrannical, and the administration of them vague and problematical" (*RM* 195). This was the main difficulty with the English Parliament, which included not only the Lords, but the Commons and the king as well. The "so-called" English constitution, he exhorted in 1776, consisted of two ancient tyrannies, king and Lords, "compounded with some new republican materials," the Commons (*CS* 68). As far as Paine was concerned, the people should forget about having a king. As for aristocrats, they were, he warned the French almost twenty years later, "an excrescence growing out of corruption" (*Dissertation, CW* 2:586).

The third element, the Commons (the only true representative of the people), could take any form: a uni-, a bi-, or a multi-cameral house. The important factor was that the legislature enact "laws that are consistent with the foundation and principles of the constitution. Otherwise, the legislative power would be pure despotism, call it by what name you will." If this body were to be truly representative (that is, if all the eligible people were empowered to vote), it would constitute a check on the executive, that branch of the government "associated, some way or other, in our minds with the idea of arbitrary power." The nation, in other words, would be better off and indeed safer and more secure when the "*elected* legislature controls the executive." This is not to say that the legislature itself elected the executive but only that it should have a negative power, a veto, over the actions of the executive, just as the Americans provided for in their Constitution, allowing the Congress to override a presidential veto.

As for the executive, its responsibility lay in its "power of enforcing the laws."[28] Paine was especially adamant about law enforcement. As God had made natural laws that people had to respect and obey, so legislatures, as legally constituted representatives of the people, made civil law. Citizens must also obey these laws because they had elected those charged with enacting the law. The law was made, so to speak, as if the people themselves had actually made it. This was the republic in its highest manifestation: a representative democracy.[29]

In terms reminiscent of Whiggish vocabulary, Paine noted that the word *republic* was "no other than government established and conducted for the interest of the public, as well individually as collectively. It is not necessarily connected with any particular form, but it most naturally associates with the representative form, as being best calculated to secure the end for which a nation is at the expense of supporting it" (*RM* 178). In referring to the government as "republican," Paine in no way sought to dilute its democratic elements. The democratic republic, after all, achieved the good of all by working through a procedure akin to a modified general will, an idea that Paine adopted during his long years in France. "Now, however, the law is all powerful, and as it is the expression of the general will, it is the interest of everyone to see that it is executed."[30] People must respect the law, and if they did not, the defect lay most likely in the constitutional structure. In this case, the invention must be changed, again and again, if necessary, until it was right.

Above all, the citizenry must never allow the two principal elements of government, the executive and the legislative, to come into conflict with each other. They must work together for common cause. Together, they would constitute "a single edifice," he said, "in which all is united and harmonious." In this way, a people avoided the constitutional crises that the British always faced because most decisions were made by a prime minister who "waves over [the people] his sleep-compelling wand, and they are at once plunged in the slumber of servitude."[31] The British prime minister could impose this despotic servitude because Britain had no constitution, and if it had no constitution, it was a despotism. For Paine, no middle ground existed. A nation either had a formal constitutional structure organizing the government as well as "regulating and restraining the powers . . . given" to it, or it did not (*RM* 192). A government unrestrained in its political action was by definition despotic.

The evolution of the English government from William the Conqueror might prove to some that the common law, parliamentary statutes, and other legal and judicial developments had all produced the unwritten constitution. But not to Paine. As long as Britain was unable to produce a written constitution, it could not prove it possessed one. Such instruments as the Magna Carta or the Bill of Rights as well as the historic relationship of the crown to the parliament, when all taken together, did not comprise a constitution. The people believed, without warrant, that they resided under a constitution which provided them with protection and security. In reality, only the appearance of constitutional form existed; this was a shadowy reflection of a constitution because in Britain, election and representation, the two key elements of a constitutional structure, were separate and distinct. Such a structure makes "the candidates [for election] . . . candidates for despotism" (*RM* 193).

Of course, Paine either refused to or simply could not see the historic restraints that Parliament had placed on the crown and court of Britain. Nor did (perhaps could) he envision British parliamentary developments after his own time. Even so, his condemnation was always intemperate, always couched in negative terms. For him, British politics had no redeeming virtues.

The American experience proved to the world how human ingenuity crafted a good constitution and how constitutions could be one of the most beneficial of all human inventions. "The first thing" men must understand then "is, that a nation has a right to establish a constitution" (*RM* 198). People gathered together as a nation possessed the right to form a government of their own choosing. This act amounted to one of the newly created rights that they acquired when they exchanged their natural right of self-determination for the civil right to produce and constitute a government. The right to develop this constitution was akin to the new civil rights all people acquired when they obtained the right to vote, the right to serve as an elected public official, or the right to a trial by jury. They were the rights that they themselves had guaranteed in the democratic republic.

But what if a constitution failed to restrain government so that it forced its subjects to do its (as opposed to their) will? What if this government denied to its people their right to change the polity? In answer, Paine addressed one of the most extreme, but at times necessary, rights that the citizenry always possessed: the right to revolution. On this subject, his tone was exhortatory at least until the mid-1790s, when he found that revolutions are dangerous matters not only for kings and lords but for Thomas Paine as well.

Revolution as Invention

As the people had the intellect and skill to design and erect bridges and constitutions, so they possessed the wherewithal to know when and how to make revolutions. The right to resist reflected another example of man's ability to create a positive entity. Only now, rather than building a constitution, he was a maker of revolution. Revolutionary action was legitimate for a people under a corrupt and despotic regime. Moreover, revolution was both a right and an obligation, and Paine at times used an imperative voice to emphasize this position. His own time gave people the opportunity to rise and realize that they could recast government in the interests of all people everywhere. Revolution as a worldwide phenomenon opened "a new era to the human race" (*RM* 178, 162).

Although he held this view of revolution for a long time, his last writings clearly modified it. In the years before the Terror, Paine wrote in his most radical political style, arguing an age or a new day of revolutions, a new era, and a need for people to act now to save themselves and the world. Following the downfall of Robespierre and St. Just, he became much more cautious and certainly more conservative. Revolutions should be undertaken warily, lest those who led them fall themselves into tyranny and despotism. He saw how even a well-intentioned revolution could fail with the worse possible consequences, some of which he himself had experienced. He began to see in the power of the vote and in the amendment provision of constitutions alternatives to revolutionary action, alternatives which he hoped would make revolutions unnecessary.

But even before his view changed, he never thought that revolutions broke new ground. In *Rights of Man,* he wrote that they were vehicles that enabled people to restore their rights when usurpers denied them. When "government has arrived at its dotage, and requires to be renovated," he wrote, it was the people's duty to begin revolutions (*RM* 197). They in effect restored something that had been stolen from the people. They awakened them from their "dormant state" because they could "create genius and talents" (*RM* 176). Revolution unlocked the people's creative ability to make good inventions. "It excites it to action" (*RM* 176). As the examples of America and France demonstrated, revolutions stimulated "a renovation of the natural order of things" (*RM* 144). Thus, revolution helped people to seek something they had lost. Only after the revolution could they make progress by creating new political forms. Revolutions were restorative only, not progressive for human improvement.

At what point do people decide when revolution is necessary? Logically, one might think that Paine at his most radical would hold that revolution was necessary whenever people found themselves without constitutional government. At one point in *Rights of Man,* he remarked that "a Nation has *at all times* an inherent indefeasible right to abolish any form of Government it finds inconvenient, and establish such as accords with its interest, disposition, and happiness" (*RM* 143, emphasis added). This sentiment, on the surface, appears to be a blanket statement concerning the right to revolution.

But Paine was much more circumspect than to accept revolution on demand. Paine here was addressing only the *right* of revolution, not the issue of when revolution ought to take place. For Paine, again using Rousseauistic terms, sovereignty resided in the people, or what Paine preferred to call the Nation. Government "is not and from its nature cannot be, the property of any particular man or family, but of the whole community, at whose expense it is supported; and though by force or contrivance it has been usurped into an heritance, the usurpation cannot alter the right of things. Sovereignty, as a matter of right, appertains to the Nation only, and not any individual" (*RM* 143). Therefore, when the will of the nation, the general will, called for revolution, then the people should rise up against their oppressors. Revolution became an imperative choice at the moment when a universal will regarded it as the correct choice.

While these may have been the ideas of the Thomas Paine of *Rights of Man,* they were not those of the Thomas Paine of 1795, who two years earlier witnessed the excesses of revolution and suffered his own harrowing experience incarcerated in the Luxembourg Prison. After Thermidor, he reverted instead to the Lockean notion that revolution should be only a last resort. Locke had written that

> revolutions happen not upon every little mismanagement in public affairs. Great mistakes in the ruling part, many wrong and inconvenient laws, and all the slips of human frailty, will be born by the people without mutiny or murmur. But if a long train of abuses, prevarications, and artifices, all tending the same way, make the design visible to the people, and they cannot but feel what they lie under, and see whither they are going; it is not to be wondered, that they should then rouze themselves, and endeavour to put the rule into such hands which may secure to them the ends for which government was at first erected.[32]

After 1795, Paine argued that the grounds the people should use to undertake revolutionary action were the same for all radical transformations. Oppression alone was not sufficient for revolution. Under a constitution, "nothing, therefore, can justify an insurrection, neither can it ever be necessary where rights are equal and opinions free" (*Dissertation, CW* 2:587).

Good constitutions obviated the need for revolution. Without a constitution, however, revolution could well be necessary, but it should be undertaken with a great deal of caution. Insurrection was the alternative only when people faced despotism because despotism did not change by itself. Once the revolution rid the country of its despots and their cohorts, the new rulers, to preserve liberty, must "permit to themselves a *discretionary exercise of power* regulated more by circumstances than by principle, which, were the practise to continue, liberty would never be established." The revolution must cease as soon as possible.

The people, then, must not take revolutions lightly. Once begun, they must end, and end quickly, so the business of governing can begin. Revolutions were unnecessary in democratic republics which had sufficient channels to rectify oppression, should it occur. Even in republics, some dangers arose when revolutions lasted too long. Revolutionaries must avoid the urge to become like those whom they had overthrown.

This was the problem in France during the Terror. "The moral principle of revolution is to instruct, not to destroy." France had failed to establish a strong democratic constitution in 1793, one that could have stopped the Terror and its miserable consequences. Rather than creating a democratic republican government, the National Convention (of which Paine was a member) failed in its task. It allowed France to transform itself into

> a revolutionary government, a thing without either principle or authority. . . . Virtue and crime depended upon accident; and that which was patriotism one day became treason the next. All these things have followed from the want of a constitution; for it is the nature and intention of a constitution to *prevent governing by party,* by establishing a common principle that shall limit and control the power and impulse of party, and that says to all parties, *thus far shalt thou go and no further.* But in the absence of a constitution, men look entirely to party; and instead of principle governing party, party governs principle. (*Dissertation, CW* 2:587–88)

A few years later, on his return to America, Paine found that party and faction were potentially tearing America to pieces the way they had in France. The virtue of the American Constitution was that the electoral process had worked, that the Federalists were voted out of office (though barely), and the Jeffersonians were in ascendancy (at least for the moment).

This proved that a vigilant citizenry protected its rights by means of a good constitution, one that kept party and faction in check. Such a constitution allowed citizens to have a high awareness of the day's public issues. For only when they were fully acquainted with the issues could they confront and resolve them. In other words, the people's natural political character forced them always to employ their inventive powers. As long as the constitution protected their fundamental civil and political rights, they could use them to undertake gradual, necessary changes as the conditions of life changed. Man as *homo faber,* properly a maker of good inventions, reflected the intentions and image of God.

❧ 9 ❧

The Vision of the Future

Thomas Paine saw man as an inventive creature capable of creating the social and political environment that best suited his nature. This environment entailed those institutions in government and economics, culture and society, which allowed man to live to his full potential. Such institutions were never stagnant or enslaving. Man was after all God's greatest creation. When God created man in his image, he imparted to him the same qualities that he (God) possessed, though on a human scale: goodness and creativity, justice and wisdom. The Bible, of course, was wrong in its depiction of God as "a changeable, passionate, vindictive" being. Creation teaches us "a contrary idea—that of unchangeable and of eternal order, harmony and goodness."[1]

Man in his own person reflected these qualities. A consistent theme in Paine's work was man's ability to improve himself. From the time of his arrival in America at the end of 1774, he understood that man could achieve positive changes in the world if he took advantage of his natural capabilities. At times people turned away from their natural abilities, denied them, and consequently became denatured. And yet men always had the opportunity to build a new society, a new politics, where all would be free and equal in a just and earthly paradise. These thoughts reflected Paine's vision of the future.

Using these themes, Paine promoted one of the most advanced political and social critiques of the eighteenth century. In his appeal to reason and nature, Paine is among the most influential writers in the age of the American and French revolutions.[2] He never looked backward to a lost past which he hoped men could somehow recapture. Rather, he envisioned a future in which (inevitably he thought, though he was less optimistic later in life) men

156

would achieve universal harmony, or as he called it "universal civilization."[3] This harmony, a reflection of God's universal, eternal order and wisdom, would come when men made full use of their reason, for this faculty gave shape to both present and future change.

His emphasis on universal political and social change was phrased not only in the language of revolutionary politics. At times, he employed elements of another available language, that of the coming republican apocalypse, to describe the perfectibility that men might experience in this life. Paine's secular millennialism lay deeply embedded in his vocabulary, and at the same time it paralleled his iconoclastic, antiscriptural deism. It was a language that he used with great relish, even if he did not fully accept its ideology. For him, millennialism was yet another means of appealing to the believing lower- and middle-class readers he thought he was addressing in England and America.

The millennialist theme ran throughout his works from the 1770s until his death in the first decade of the nineteenth century. His was a millennium that depended not on God's intervention but on human action. To 1795, he believed the millennium would be brought about by revolution, certainly not by Christ's return. After that date, he believed that democratic procedure, in particular the vote, would initiate the new age. And this age would not be a divine paradise but the secular Eden of the democratic republic in which freedom and harmony would prevail.

His most clearly articulated millennialist writings came in the 1790s, when he spoke of a coming age of earthly perfection inaugurated by the French Revolution. Yet, even in the seventies, we find him preaching the millennial nature of the new nation which the Americans could achieve through their revolution. These two perspectives—his revolutionary outlook and his secular millennialism—were quite compatible. He used them both frequently, sometimes interchangeably, to inform his common-man readers in England and America that his vision of a coming time of political perfection was based on his assessment of the human events which he himself had witnessed.[4]

Paine's millennialism did not match that of mainstream eighteenth-century thinkers, and this should make us suspicious of his use of the language. In fact, there were many dissimilarities between him and more traditional millennialists. After all, he denied that God played an active role in the world. The scriptures were for him fabulous and mythological. His faith was based on what men could and ought to do, not on what God could do for them. He believed in God only insofar as he (Paine) was a witness to God's creative energy as he had expressed it when he made the universe and all that was in it. The millennium, for Paine, was not God centered and not even nature centered. Its advent was, in the final analysis, totally up to the people who would work to bring into being a highly secularized society of peace, justice, equality, and most of all, democratic institutions.

In contrast, one writer who did fit into the more conventional millennialist mainstream was Joseph Priestley, scientist, preacher, and prolific writer on the subject. Through his scientific explorations and theological inquiry, Priestley undertook a lifelong, deliberate, and exhaustive search of Biblical scripture to determine when God would fulfill the great prophecies of last days. His search ultimately led him to conclude that the end would occur, not in some distant future, but in his own time or at the very least (he sometimes hedged) shortly after his time. Priestley's ideas serve as excellent counterpoints to Paine's vision of the future.[5]

Priestley and Paine: The Coming Apocalypse

Paine's theological views lack the necessary ingredients of a genuine millennialism. He displayed, for example, neither sensitivity to nor belief in the compelling elements of biblical prophecy that moved Priestley. As a result, Paine was never as explicit as Priestley about these matters. According to the latter, the prophets of the books of Daniel and Revelation had correctly foretold the events relating to the coming perfection of the world which were being worked out in his own time. In May of 1795, Priestley wrote to his friend and associate Theophilus Lindsey that his interest in European politics was due only to "the attention I give to the fulfillment of prophecy."[6] A few months later, in a letter to Thomas Belsham, he noted that "the great events are those we are now looking for."[7]

Paine had no patience with such matters. Prophecy, as he explained in *The Age of Reason* (1794–95), was little more than what its original meaning signified: poetry or music. The prophets were musicians or poets, little else. The distinction between the greater and lesser prophets was superfluous. Some were simply better than others at music and poetry. The idea that God informed someone of a future event was itself meaningless because no one could prove that this really happened. Besides, prophecy was usually so "loose and obscure" that any convenient event could be made to fit its so-called fulfillment. Paine condemned the prophet as "a character useless and unnecessary; and the safe side of the case is to guard against being imposed upon by not giving credit to such relations" (*Age of Reason, CW* 1:511).

While Priestley also denied portions of biblical scripture, he did not question the prophecies concerning the resurrection and the future state. For Priestley (as indeed for Paine), a person must apply a test of reason to each scriptural element to determine its validity and truth. The Gospels have instructed the faithful to "search the Scriptures," he noted, "and what faculty can we employ for this purpose, but that which is commonly called *reason,* whereby we are capable of thinking, reflecting, comparing, and judging of things?"[8] On this basis, he rejected an array of orthodox doctrines: atonement, the Trinity, and the preexistence of Christ.

He refused to deny, however, those prophecies that foretold the return of Christ and the inauguration of the millennium. Priestley, like most conventional millennialists, believed that a series of events must take place before the Second Coming. These events warned of a future time of troubles when the Turkish Empire would crumble, the Jews would be restored to the Holy Land, and the Antichrist would be destroyed. In 1798, Priestley wrote that his study of the prophecies proved that "the fulfillment of the most important of them is, no doubt, at hand." Soon, we must expect "the restoration of the Jews," though "the Turkish empire must fall, before that event." Indeed, "great changes in the dispositions of men may take place in a short time, and things least expected come to pass. Of this we have lately seen many instances."[9]

Like Priestley, Paine applied tests of reason to scripture, but rather than being selective, Paine rejected almost everything. The notable exception was creation, because he could actually see the results of it. "We can only know God through His works," Paine commented in *The Age of Reason* (*CW* 1:601).[10] A few years later, he expanded on this subject.

> Contemplating the universe, the whole system of Creation, in this point of light, we shall discover, that all that which is called natural philosophy is properly a divine study. It is the study of God through His works. It is the best study, by which we can arrive at a knowledge of His existence, and the only one by which we can gain a glimpse of His perfection."[11]

At one point in *The Age of Reason,* he suggested that egoism caused man to believe that God had created only one world, as *Genesis* described. The universe really consisted of a plurality of worlds, each with a multiplicity of civilizations. He speculated that some creatures inhabited all the planets that revolved around the sun and they all "enjoy the same opportunities of knowledge as we do" (*Age of Reason, CW* 1:503). The belief that God had created only one world was illogical as was the idea that the first man's sin and the prophecies of the messiah's coming and returning affected only the inhabitants of this earth.

Paine, using the ridicule so characteristic of him when he approached a distasteful subject, offered an alternative view that would never have occurred to a pious believer like Priestley or to the prosecutors of *The Age of*

Reason. He speculated that interplanetary deicide was a distinct possibility. After all, certainly each of these other worlds "in the boundless creation had an Eve, an apple, a serpent and a redeemer. . . . In this case, the person who is irreverently called the Son of God, and sometimes God himself, would have nothing else to do than to travel from world to world, in an endless succession of deaths, with scarcely a momentary interval of life" (*CW* 1:504).

Rather than relying on fabulous stories, Paine preferred to use his own rational tests to question every event in the Bible. Whereas Priestley could believe a great many elements in scripture, Paine ridiculed the same texts, often without offering a cogent reason for rejecting them. On the virgin birth, he wrote that "were any girl that is now with child to say, even to swear it, that she was gotten with child by a ghost, and that an angel told her so, would she be believed? Certainly she would not. Why, then, are we to believe the same thing of another girl, whom we never saw, told by nobody knows who, nor when, nor where?" He concluded that common sense would demonstrate that this story contained an inherent "absolute impossibility and imposture!" (ibid., *CW* 1:574). In the same way, he spent considerable time and energy comparing the contradictory and "absurd" accounts of Christ's last days as reported in the Gospels. They were "all fabulous inventions, dishonorable to the wisdom and power of the Almighty" (ibid., *CW* 1:582–83). The Gospels had had little impact on men.

> Talk with some London merchants about Scripture, and they will understand you mean *scrip,* and tell you how much it is worth at the Stock Exchange. Ask them about theology and they will say they know of no such gentlemen upon 'Change. Tell some country squires of the sun and moon standing still, the one on the top of a hill, the other in a valley, and they will swear it is a lie of one's own making.
>
> Tell them that God Almighty ordered a man to make a cake and bake it with a turd and eat it, and they will say it is one of Dean Swift's blackguard stories. Tell them it is in the Bible and they will lay a bowl of punch it is not, and leave it to the parson of the parish to decide. Ask them also about theology and they will say they know of no such a one on the turf.[12]

Paine here was probably referring to the kinds of people who most likely would sit on a jury to judge *The Age of Reason.* In his opinion, scripture had the effect portrayed here on most people. It is no wonder that so many people, including Priestley, thought he was an atheist.[13]

Paine was no atheist, of course, but a man who believed in God as creator, whose spirit was immanent in every living, natural being. God had given people a moral and universal order. Their duty was to reflect this order in their lives and, in this manner, to be the mirror image of the divine. When religion made them aware of this, it fulfilled its only purpose. Twice at the end of *Rights of Man,* Paine commented that "every religion is good that teaches man to be good" (*RM* 260, 270). For religion to go beyond this precept was the unfortunate fate of Christianity, which had proved itself to be "too absurd for belief, too impossible to convince, and too inconsistent for practise." And finally, in ringing condemnatory tones, he proclaimed that "as an engine of power, it serves the purpose of despotism" (*Age of Reason, CW* 1:600).[14]

What, then, might suggest that Paine was a millennialist? In a conventional or traditional sense, he was not, especially if we take Priestley as a model eighteenth-century millennialist. Priestley accepted as true the prophecies pronouncing Christ's return during a time of upheaval and the subsequent establishment of an earthly paradise. To him, his own time was the best of times. The chaos that the Revolution in France unleashed and the wars that followed caused him to comment that the final storm had begun and though it might "blow over," the end of time was surely not to be "deferred long." Soon, men would surely see the "sudden, and most unexpected, coming of Christ."[15] At one point, he even wondered whether God had appointed Bonaparte to herald the return of Christ.[16] And, curiously, he once speculated to Thomas Belsham that "Jesus is no doubt living and on earth, and he cannot be unemployed. No intelligent being, who is awake, is or ought to."[17] After Priestley's death, Belsham recalled that Priestley always knew that "the second appearance of Christ was very near at hand. "'You,' says he, 'may probably live to see it; I shall not. It cannot, I think, be more than twenty years'" away.[18]

Although Paine did not think along these lines, his language articulated a vision which contained millennialist elements, only without Christ and without the scriptural foundation of the biblical prophets. Men would have to bring the millennium into reality through their ingenuity and through the use of their rational faculty. Reason was a divine gift, an instrument that helped men succeed in their struggle to overthrow tyranny and injustice. Paine was deeply aware of his own divinely appointed role and the purposes for which he used his reason. He often said that his life was part of a larger plan that God had set forth at the moment of creation. God would not fulfill this plan. Men would, he exhorted. They were to use their natural inclinations and capabilities to push forward the processes of progress, freedom, and enlightenment. This was the foundation of a Painite millennium: a secular paradise of justice, harmony, and equality. This secular paradise is Paine's counterpart to the political and economic perfection he hoped men might strive for, even if they never achieved it.

God's gift of reason and ingenuity to Paine meant that he occupied a special place to help set the world aright. He could say with absolute equanimity in *Rights of Man* that "I am fully satisfied that what I am now doing, with an endeavor to conciliate mankind, to render their condition happy, to unite nations that have hitherto been enemies, and to extirpate the horrid practise of war and break the chains of slavery and oppression, is acceptable in His sight, and being the best service I can perform, I act it cheerfully (*RM* 271). Late in life, after his persecution by Robespierre, after the reversals of the French Revolution, after his return to America, where he was constantly under personal attack in the Federalist press and by those who thought he was the Antichrist, after all of this, he could still write as late as 1806, three and a half years before his death, that he was optimistic about man's future.

He had devoted his political writings "to rescue man from tyranny and false systems and false principles of government, and enable him to be free, and establish government for himself." He told John Inskeep in 1806 that he had written his religious works for the same reasons: "to bring man to a right reason that God has given him; to impress on him the great principles of divine morality, justice, mercy, and a benevolent disposition to all men and to all creatures; and to excite in him a spirit of trust, confidence and consolation in his creator, unshackled by the fable and fiction of books, by whatever invented name they may be called."[19] Pulled from their context, these words echoed conventional Enlightenment language. Paine always set his political, social, and economic criticism in the context of God's perfection. Man's coming perfection reflected God's own perfection, and his progress was part of God's plan. Man's responsibility, individually and collectively, was to work gradually toward this goal. In arguing in absentia against the prosecution of *The Age of Reason*, he said unequivocally that he believed in "the perfection of the Deity" (*Prosecution, CW* 2:737). He was not rejecting God but rather the unnatural state in which tyrannical forces had placed men.

Thus, he decried both Judaism and Christianity as fabulous theologies. They forced men to believe in ideas which they would ordinarily reject, given their natural proclivities. The obverse of the theological realm was the political. Tyrannical forces enslaved vast numbers of human beings for the good only of those in control. Most men had to be made aware of these negative conditions of life that tyranny, whether religious or political, promoted. God's intention in making man in his image was for man to be a kind of subcontractor to make the world into what its potential called for. In that same 1806 letter in which he described the thrust of his political and theological writings, he added that he was always profoundly grateful that throughout his life he was able to perform what God had wanted him to do.

Here, he echoed a theme from *Rights of Man*. "I am happy in the continual contemplation of what I have done, and I thank God that he gave me talents for the purpose and fortitude to do it. It will make the continual consolation of my departing hours whenever they finally arrive."[20] God did not speak directly to him to tell him what to do. God did not speak directly to anybody. Paine wrote in 1797 that "for my own part, I believe that all [the prophets] are imposters who pretend to hold verbal communication with the Deity. It is the way by which the world has been imposed upon."[21] In *The Age of Reason,* he noted that the prophecies were in reality not based on conversations with God, but were simply the ancients' way of explaining the "unintelligible." Besides that, they were so vague, told "in such a loose and obscure manner," that they were open to a variety of interpretations (*CW* 2:511).

Even so, although God never once spoke directly to him, Paine was convinced of his specially appointed role to preach the coming perfection through man's agency. God's cause, the cause of liberty, legitimized the work of the political activist and theological reformer. These roles united in the person of Thomas Paine. If liberty was a natural condition for men, then someone like Paine must demonstrate that fact. He was therefore responsible for exposing the errors of men's ways and removing the veil of tyranny that the unnatural and ungodly forces of the world had perpetrated to enslave them. Free expression was the handmaiden of free government and free representation. Man lived most naturally under a constitution that allowed for these three. It had worked in America until the satanic Federalists appeared, and it worked in France until the persecutions of Robespierre and his associates. The search for freedom was not, however, over; it was an ongoing process. That search was for those like Paine, who possessed the requisite vision to continue the pursuit of freedom.

Like Jeremiah, he was "fully satisfied" with the part God had assigned to him. Though twice disillusioned (once in America, once in France), he was always prepared to continue in his appointed role. He told Jefferson in the middle of the latter's second administration that if the president needed a special envoy to go to France to help settle the war in Europe, he was available. "I think you will find it proper, perhaps necessary, to send a person to France in the event either of a treaty of peace or of a descent, and I make you an offer of my services on that occasion to join Mr. Monroe. I do this because I do not think there is a person in the United States that can render so much service on the business that will come on as myself."[22] The ramblings of a self-flatterer? Perhaps. Perhaps not. Almost three years earlier, he told the president that if Britain should ever be ready for a genuine written constitution, he was ready "to make another passage across the Atlantic to assist in forming" it.[23] The age of revolution may have been over, for the moment at least, but he still saw himself fostering whatever was needed in the service of human freedom. So if it was self-flattery, such adulation properly belonged in the larger context of the good he sincerely thought he had brought and could yet bring as God's earthly agent.

Such thinking might have been easier in the immediate aftermath of the French Revolution. In 1790, he said that progress and his role in furthering it would continue indefinitely (his role would continue, of course, only until his death). Although the revolution passed through "little ebbings and flowings," "the full current of it is, in my opinion, as fixed as the Gulf Stream."[24] The revolution was, in short, on a course as fixed as any natural phenomenon. But even natural phenomena, as he found, could undergo alteration. Man's natural tendencies could be drastically transformed when tyranny masked his natural affective and rational capabilities, when tyranny forced him into a dependent state, putting him totally at the will and whim of the tyrant.

Years later, his view of the future was still positive, though totally sobered by his experiences with the horror of imprisonment and the Reign of Terror. In 1805, three years after his return to the United States, he used the same language that he had first employed thirty years earlier when he spoke to his American compatriots in *Common Sense.* The great significance of the American Revolution, was "the opportunity of *beginning the world anew,* as it were; and of bringing forward a *new system* of government in which the rights of *all* men should be preserved that gave *value* to independence." He himself had played the proper role in this. He continued. "The pamphlet *Common Sense,* the first work I ever published, embraced both those objects."[25] He specifically fulfilled here the role that God had ordained for him. He would continue to undertake it in publicly denouncing John Adams and the Federalist faction, who, because they worked against the cause of America, worked simultaneously against God's cause.

Such were, then, his ideas about his personal role in life. It was a consistent belief. His will, drafted six months before his death in 1809, attested to this fact. Everything he had achieved, he said, was a natural outcome of his divinely ordained role. In the will, he rehearsed his major achievements, outlined his principal writings, and then distributed his worldly goods. This was all quite conventional. He then added a final statement. "I have lived an honest and useful life to mankind; my time has been spent in doing good, and I die in perfect composure and resignation to the will of my Creator, God."[26] The nonsense of an old and sickly man on his deathbed who was now prepared to reconcile himself to God? Perhaps. And yet, in the context of his expression of his role throughout life, these words go beyond nonsense. They demonstrate the sentiment of a man who, to the moment of his death, knew that he had devoted his life to the accomplishment of a higher purpose, namely to help bring into being a new world of peace, justice, and democracy.

Paine's Secular Millennial Vision

Paine's view of the future joins together the various components of his secular millennialism: his denial of the scriptures, his belief in political progress, and man's individual responsibility (especially Paine's own) in furthering God's cause. Although he did not fit into the mainstream millennialist tradition, he had a fairly clear picture of a utopian human condition that could be the likely outcome of world revolution or political progress and the continued efforts of people like himself. His idea of a future state in which there would be "happiness beyond this life" was definitely not couched in the vision of an afterlife. It was, rather, well within his positive thinking that even if the earthly paradise of peace, freedom, and justice were not achieved in his time, it would be soon (*Age of Reason, CW* 2:464). He told Gilbert Wakefield in 1795 that he used his talents to teach "men to preserve their liberties exclusively, leaving to that God who made their immortal souls the care of their eternal welfare."[27] In defending himself against the prosecutors of *The Age of Reason*, he argued that religion was a matter of conscience, "a private affair between every man and his Maker, and no tribunal or third party has a right to interfere between them. It is not properly a thing of this world; it is only practised in this world; but its object is in a *future* world" (*CW* 2:743, emphasis added).

These views are not mere rhetoric, especially when they are placed alongside ideas which paralleled Priestley's more conventional millennialism. Paine's theology did not necessarily have to be either Christ centered or prophetic. Two elements in his thinking are particularly striking: his view of revolution, and his idea of universal reformation. They both suggest that he might seriously have believed in a coming perfection at the end of time. He even used, at least on one occasion, though only in a letter, the figure of a thousand years, though not in the context of the millennium.[28]

Like Priestley, Paine saw the world as a place where a cosmic struggle between the forces of good and evil was taking place on a universal scale. The outcome of this struggle would be as profound as Priestley thought it would be: the creation on earth of a republican paradise where all men would forever live in freedom and happiness. This vision became especially evident in his assessment of the revolutions in America and France, where as far as he was concerned, events of world history rapidly revealed to mankind the prospects of a future far beyond anything ever before witnessed. America's inevitable separation from Britain was such an event.

He noted in *Common Sense* his certainty that God had made America his new chosen nation. God's grace was originally reserved for the Jews, but they had lost that grace when they relinquished their republican government and asked God for a king "to judge us like all other nations" (*CS* 74).[29] Paine recalled how the prophet Samuel vehemently tried to dissuade the Jews from having a king, but without success. He concluded from this story that the scriptural account of their request and God's reaction to it proved that God had unequivocally "entered his protest against monarchical government," a thought that conveniently fitted into Paine's absolute distaste for monarchy (*CS* 76). Hence, Paine could say, on the one hand, that scripture was nothing more than lies and myths and could accept, on the other hand, the *lesson* that it taught, when that lesson agreed naturally with his own political views.

Here, Paine made use of the image of the pope as the Antichrist, who in both English millennial thought and the Protestant historical tradition must be destroyed before the return of Christ. Monarchy, he said, was nothing more than "the popery of government" (*CS* 76).[30] It was ungodly because it had "laid (not this or that kingdom only) but the world in blood and ashes" (*CS* 80). America, as God's choice to create a virtuous republic, was now the focus of divine grace. Indeed, the hand of "the Almighty" was present when America was first discovered, "to open a sanctuary to the persecuted in future years, when home should afford neither friendship nor safety." This grace, along with the physical distance between America and England, demonstrated the separate nature of the two nations. "The authority of the one over the other, was never the design of heaven" (*CS* 87). The only outcome was that an entirely "new era for politics is struck—a new method of thinking has arisen" (*CS* 82).[31] Man now had unlimited opportunities for future perfectibility, and these opportunities were in the Americans' hands. Not since Noah had the world been prepared for such a marvelous transformation. "A situation, similar to the present, hath not happened since the days of Noah until now" (*CS* 120). Another friend and close associate of Joseph Priestley, Richard Price, echoed these sentiments when he noted in 1784 that "next to the introduction of Christianity among mankind, the American Revolution may prove the most important step in the progressive cause of human improvement."[32] Paine went even further when he exclaimed in two of his most ringing, and most often quoted, phrases. "We have it in our power to begin the world over again," because "the birthday of a new world is at hand" (*CS* 120).

If the events in America held out the promise of a new day in that land, by the time of the upheavals in France after 1789, he was certain that he could convince the world to fulfill the same promise. The political rhetoric of *Rights of Man* is well known: the frontal attack on Burke, Paine's sympathetic review of the events in Paris in 1789, and his espousal of liberty and rights in direct opposition to Burkean prescription and historical tradition.

Paine consciously used here the same millennialist language that he had earlier used in *Common Sense* to demonstrate the universal significance of the French Revolution, which brought into the open more than ever before the underlying tension between the evil forces of sin (monarchy, princely power, hereditary privilege) and the valiant thrusts of virtue (liberty, republicanism, and representation). Paine characterized the storming of the Bastille in terms that go beyond simple depiction of events. Now he used distinct Manichean terms. The tower was either to be the assailants' victory or defeat, their "prize," as he termed it, or their "prison." But it was not merely the securing of this one building that was at issue. The stakes were much higher in an ultimate sense, for the fall of the tower "included the idea of the downfall of Despotism: And this compounded image was become as figuratively united as Bunyan's Doubting Castle and Giant Despair" (*RM* 52).

In Bunyan's allegory, Christian and Hopeful lose their way and are caught one morning on the grounds of "Doubting Castle," whose owner, Giant Despair, captures them and puts "them into his castle, into a very dark dungeon, nasty and stinking to the spirits of the two men. Here then they lay from Wednesday morning till Saturday night, without one bit of bread, or drop of drink, or light, or any to ask how they did; they were therefore here in evil case, and were far from friends and acquaintance."[33]

"Despotism," with its uppercase "D" in some editions of *Rights of Man*, symbolized not only the injustices and the illiberality of the French monarchy. It was also a universalized evil pitted against a universal good. The same understanding held true in Paine's account of the earlier plot by the comte d'Artois (Louis XVI's younger brother) to disband the National Assembly. The comte represented the evil forces of darkness of all old regime governments. In contrast, the forces of good, virtue, and light would accomplish his defeat. No person better possessed these latter characteristics than Lafayette, who, like a knight of old bringing forth the Holy Grail, offered the *Declaration of Rights* to the people. As Paine put it, "every thing was now drawing to a crisis. The event was to be freedom or slavery," a choice between the artificial evils of monarchy and the natural goodness of democracy, and nothing in between (*RM* 54). The struggle had a cosmic significance; it pitted Gog and Magog against the kingdom of God, as it had appeared in Revelation. On the one side stood those who would attack the hated prison. "An enthusiasm of heroism" inspired them. Against them were their archenemies, those who stood on "the high altar and castle of despotism" (*RM* 56).

Paine's language was obvious. Despotism was an evil form of government, and virtuous men had to eliminate it. Those who supported it stood on its "altar," as if they either prayed for its everlasting success or were willing to be sacrificed for it, as in pagan times when human sacrifices were made to the gods and spirits that demanded them. On the other side were those who were spiritually "enthused" with heroic attributes and with the knowledge (which undoubtedly came with this same enthusiasm) that they were on the side of right and virtue, the natural and ultimately the godly. The virtuous could accomplish their victory in only one way: through revolution. Revolution was to have a purifying and cleansing effect on the sordid evil of despotism. The British had already experienced this in 1688, although that revolution was not fully effective. In fact, its results were "already on the wane, eclipsed by the enlarging orb of reason, and the luminous revolutions of America and France" (*RM* 91). All kings and their courtiers were satanic. They were the embodiment of the Antichrist, which must be destroyed, just as the mainstream millennialists believed. And revolution was the means to destroy them, for "that which is a blessing to nations, is bitterness to them" (*RM* 139).

This "blessing to nations" was highly reminiscent of such millennialist writers as Richard Price and the American preacher Levi Hart. Both Price and Hart argued in terms of the cosmic struggle involved in the "sacred blessing of liberty," as Price put it in 1787, or the "sacred cause of liberty," as Hart said in 1775.[34] For Paine, the struggle now taking place opened a new era in which the Americans went to war against England. The same struggle progressed even further because of the transformations in France. Men were living in an "age of revolutions" in which "*every thing* may be looked for" (*RM* 146, emphasis added). This vision echoed both Price's and Priestley's emphasis on universal reform and world peace when political distinctions between all nations would end. And yet his use of the "blessings of liberty" never once suggested that this blessing was divine, as Price and Hart believed. It was a blessing, a good thing, that men themselves had achieved in their quest for their own millennial moment.

All three writers, Paine, Price, and Priestley, envisioned a future time when war between nations would cease, an image that mirrored the prophet Isaiah's prospect of nations turning their swords into plowshares and spears into pruning hooks. In 1776 and again in 1790, Price spoke of the formation of a "general confederacy" among nations that specifically led to the fulfillment of Isaiah's prophecy.[35] Priestley, in 1793, noted that once the calamities Europe currently faced were over, events of the "greatest magnitude" would occur, events which would lead to the "final, happy state of the world" in peace and justice.[36]

Paine's style would not allow him to invoke the words of Isaiah or any other prophet for that matter. The same image was present, however, in his overall outlook for the future. War, he said, would end when virtuous men called "a confederation of nations . . . to abolish it." Following this call, a congress of European nations would convene "to patronize the progress of free government, and promote the civilization of nations." The result would inevitably be the end of war (war was for governments of "the old construction"), and "universal civilization would lead to lasting peace and security, balanced carefully, though sturdily, on a foundation of universal rights and justice." His vision was naturally never as explicit as were Price's and Priestley's views, but it contained hints of and phrases from his idea of a new world exempt from tyranny and terror. "We can foresee all Europe may form but one great republic, and man be free."

Revolution and reform, then, went hand in hand in this cosmic struggle between the forces of tyranny and justice. Like the more conventional millennialist writers, Paine speculated about when the end of corrupt government and the spread of revolution would come. He did not think that "monarchy and aristocracy will continue seven years longer in any of the enlightened countries in Europe" (*RM* 156). He had high expectations that not only would Europe benefit, but also the nations of Asia and Africa. Once revolutions began, as they already had in America and France, "it is natural to expect that other revolutions will follow" (*RM* 161).[37]

In 1791, he wrote the following to Condorcet, Bonneville, and Lanthénas. "How can a single individual [a king] become familiar with the affairs of an extensive territory embracing a multiplicity of diverse interests? His helpless ignorance of matters that affect the people must necessarily lead to the establishment of a tyrannical form of government. As evidence of the truth of this proposition, we have only to point to Spain, Russia, Germany, Turkey and the whole of Asia. That I may live to see freedom of these lands is my ardent desire" (*CW* 2:1316). Revolutions in these lands would soon lead to the establishment of the universal civilization, unity, and peace that he had foreseen. After all, the transformations and renewal of the world he predicted were already the "subjects of universal conversation, and may be considered as the *order of the day*." If men were to accomplish these goals, they would do so only because they successfully engaged in revolutionary activity, activity inspired by God himself. The world must change, for the present condition of the world was "not the condition that heaven intended for man" (*RM* 161).

Just what did "heaven intend for man?" Priestley had argued that the republic was the form of government best suited for the earthly kingdom of Christ. He admired the mixture of the monarchical, aristocratic, and democratic elements in British government and the balance that men must ideally achieve between them. As a classical republican thinker, his outlook was understandable and logical. Britain had a republic with a king because of its long historical development. America, however, was different. Because she had no previous experience with monarchy, the American republic would not need a king.

Whereas Priestley was intellectually prepared to accept a monarchical element in British government, Paine was not. A republic with king, said Paine, "is eccentric government" for either Britain or America (*RM* 181). It inevitably would lead to tyranny by the monarchical and aristocratic elements, as the British system had already proved countless times in the past. "The nearer any government approaches to a republic, the less business there is for a king," he had told the Americans in 1776. "It is somewhat difficult to find a proper name for the government of England. Sir William Meredith calls it a republic; but in its present state it is unworthy of the name, because the corrupt influence of the crown, by having all the places in its disposal, hath so effectively swallowed up the power, and eaten out the virtue of the house of commons . . . that the government of England is nearly as monarchical as that of France and Spain" (*CS* 80–81). That system denied the very meaning of *res publica*. Republican government must be democratic. Democracy allowed society to govern itself directly without intervening or "secondary means," such as the king and his court. The Americans accomplished this goal with their ratification of the United States Constitution. The French were quickly following suit, and soon afterwards so would the rest of the world, or so he thought.

As he used Manichean images to portray the cosmic struggle between good and evil at the Bastille, Paine also used them to articulate his detestation of monarchy and his admiration of democratic, representative government. He portrayed monarchy as the embodiment of the Antichrist, which a mainstream millennialist like Priestley believed had to be destroyed before the millennium. Paine alluded to the role of the Antichrist, as he had in *Common Sense*, when he again referred to monarchy as "the popery of government."

At the opposite extreme was democratic government, based on law, justice, and above all the rights of man. A new era had opened, and indeed a new Bible, with a new Book of Genesis, was being drafted following America's success in 1783. In *Rights of Man*, he repeated almost verbatim the world history language he had used in *Common Sense*. "The case and circumstances of America, present themselves as in the beginning of the world" (*RM* 185). The foundation stone of this beginning was the American Constitution, once the war with Britain was successful. The cosmic dimensions of this new era extended to all written constitutions because they composed "the political *bible* of the state" (*RM* 187).

Like Price and Priestley, Paine genuinely believed he was living at a special moment, in which God had given him a specially appointed role. He felt that he had already been indispensable in stimulating the Americans to separate from Britain, and he was certain that his *American Crisis* series had spurred them on to victory. Now, with *Rights of Man* and the aftermath of the French Revolution, the same was true, for him, in regard to the French struggle to depose their tyranny. Revolution was the means by which men achieved their ultimate victory over evil and recreated the natural forms of government. Price and Priestley understood this in the context of the prophetic texts of the Bible. Paine understood it no less. Only now the scriptural content was absent. In its place lay Paine's conviction that the entire world was to pass through a revolutionary transformation.

Paine was never as explicit about these matters as either Price or Priestley. He did not express the great political changes the world would experience in the same millennialist terms as Price and Priestley used. But for Paine, universal reformation was the order of the day. With clear political changes taking place before him, Paine could remark, using a Biblical referent, that "the present generation will appear to the future as the Adam of a new world" (*RM* 268). Change had originated with the decision by the Americans to cast off their British chains, and it was reaching fulfillment when the French and perhaps scores of others would end their thralldom, when "it winds its progress from nation to nation, and conquers by a silent operation" (*RM* 210).

Though no millennialist in the tradition of Joseph Priestley, Thomas Paine was certain of the coming of a new moral order as soon as the struggle between good and evil, freedom and tyranny, the natural and unnatural ended with the victory of the virtuous and the just. With that victory, the final spread of the great principles of 1776 and 1789 followed. Though broken, ill, and disillusioned in his last years, and largely ignored and forgotten, he remained hopeful in his will. He exhorted Marguerite de Bonneville to raise her children well: "Give them a good and useful learning, and instruct them in their duty to God and the practise of morality" (*CW* 2:1500). If she did that, they would be able to fulfill the role that God had allotted to them. Right to the end he preached in the same homiletic language, the same imperative tone, with which he had begun so many years earlier, even if now there were only one lonely, mournful person left who would listen.

❧ 10 ❦

Conclusion

Throughout his work, Thomas Paine's principal goal was to preach to men what they must do if they were to live most naturally and if progress was to continue. Their own moral progress would inevitably follow social and political reform if they created a world free from oppression and poverty, a world where institutions developed to advance the forces of progress. Paine's homiletic style of argument, his self-righteous attitudes of knowing the "Truth," and his overall vision of man and nature, all colored his manner of expression. In his own way, he developed a powerful homiletic style which was apparent from his earliest essays in Philadelphia to the last letters from New York. Year after year, he preached to his readers, first to those in America, then later to those in Britain, that they possessed the power to create good democratic and lasting governments with solid constitutional frameworks and they must always help in the formation of a just society.

Like a firebrand preacher intent on warning his flock of the possibility of burning in hellfire for eternity, Thomas Paine admonished his readers that they would suffer far worse than hell on earth unless they used their creative potential and common sense to bring changes to the world. Paine appealed to lower- and middle-class English and American audiences in the closing decades of the eighteenth century in homiletic writing, ranging in tone from didactic to imperative, from hortatory to the explanatory. He never intended for his readers (first limited principally to Americans, but then gradually shifting to include the English) to be wellborn, highbred, or wellstationed. Paine consciously wrote for the common man, the artisans, the craftsmen, the tradesmen, as well as the self-made financiers and manufacturers. He despised those whose pretensions set them above other men, namely those who claimed a royal or aristocratic status. And he despised their apologists, men like Edmund Burke, who developed seriously fallacious arguments to convince their readers that kings and lords were the sole protectors of the people so that it was their duty alone, their right, to control government and society. Paine would have none of this: his detailed and vivid arguments, always delivered in a direct, straightforward style and packed full of richly rehearsed imagery and metaphor, were designed to refute the Burkes of the world. In this way, through the power of the language of his homiletics, Thomas Paine became one of the most influential writers of his age, indeed of any age.

He thought his duty, his God-appointed duty in fact, was to rail against injustice and slavery wherever he saw it. Consequently, he saw men-devils running to and fro throughout the world in the form of kings, lords, Federalists, and others who would prevent men from being their natural selves with natural freedoms and rights. Paine taught that people must awaken from the political slumber in which tyranny placed them. The worst part of their oppression was how tyranny successfully destroyed their self-worth and self-identity by numbing their common sense. Tyranny caused them to forget their duty to renovate social and political institutions for the happiness, security, and prosperity of everyone. Their humanity alone gave them the foundation for improving the political and social conditions of life. If they lived naturally, they could actively promote social and political progress. Oppressed, they could never be fully human as God intended them, and progress would be stunted, if not impossible.

All was not lost, however, because writers like Thomas Paine were there to instruct them and awaken them from the tyrannical sleep into which they had been lulled. Paine always claimed that he never sought the role of preacher, though he willingly accepted it. From the very first appearance of *Common Sense*, he was aware of his important purpose to inform the people that they could escape their oppression: "O ye that love mankind!" he thundered, "Ye that dare oppose, not only the tyranny, but the tyrant, stand forth!" (*CS* 100). Almost fifteen years later, in a more sober mood, he alluded to "a morning of reason rising upon man on the subject of government, that has not appeared before," because someone like himself helped men become aware of the dawn that accompanied that new morning of reason (*RM* 230).[1]

He was singularly proud of his contribution toward arousing men's common sense. Through its use, men could establish a political and social order of liberty and justice. As an international writer on political and social affairs, it was "the best service I can perform," he wrote in *Rights of Man* (293). Once he and others like him helped people pass from their infantile state of dormancy, like plants in late winter, they would pass to a springtime of social and political progress. In this spring, they would secure their rights. Paine was always optimistic about this throughout his life. Only during periods of terrible fear or frustration (the Reign of Terror in France and his last years in America) did he express doubts about man's future.

And yet, even in times of depression and fear, he was certain that the future must be better than the past. On his return to America in 1802, he found factional strife everywhere. This was due, he told his fellow Americans, to the Federalists, who planned to establish monarchy in America. Within a short time, in the era of peace and stability secured in the Jefferson administration, the threat of factional politics subsided. By 1805, he wrote that "the country at this time, compared with what it was two or three years ago, is in a state of tranquility. . . . It is by keeping a country well informed upon its affairs, and discarding from its councils every thing of mystery, that harmony is preserved or restored among the people, and confidence reposed in the government."[2]

Paine's personal role was then always to preach, to use the language of the homiletic. His congregation of lower- and middle-class British and American readers, an audience of common men, not inadvertently included those, like Burke, who disagreed with him. He never wanted to alienate his primary audience, his flock, but only to preach to them. This was true even when he couched his message in the most advanced tones of the era. Had he advocated a position that was too radical or too advanced for his time, he would have lost his audience, or at least a substantial part of it. One might argue that at times he uncontrollably allowed his passion to outweigh his reason. He sometimes made outrageous accusations and assertions without real foundation. Overall, however, he chose his facts carefully and presented them in language that was immediately understood.

There are, of course, some things about Paine that we will never be certain about, but we can speculate. Without going too far, we may assume that despite his passion, which was great, he never consciously said anything unacceptable to *all* his readers. He must have figured that at least some portion of his audience of common men would accept part of his message. He was always aware that his audience was diverse, consisting not only of artisans and mechanics, but also of wealthy, middle-class merchants and manufacturers. Just as he was not solely a spokesman for the skilled workmen and mechanics, neither did he address only the emerging bourgeoisie of America, England, or France. He wrote simply, so that as many people as possible would read his work. But it was the common man that he most often addressed. If his message was clear and understandable to common people, he believed he had fulfilled his goal. And yet much of his agenda was more advanced, especially in terms of his economic views, than anything any nation in the century had implemented: his ideas of universal suffrage and universal right to hold office regardless of economic standing placed him beyond most of his contemporaries' versions of political participation; his view of man's affective and rational powers went beyond most writers of his time; he cleverly reversed Burke's aristocratic views to demonstrate the centrality of human rights; and finally, his social welfare program placed him on the radical fringe of eighteenth-century social criticism, where he was perhaps exceeded only by Thomas Spence.

He himself thought his political and social ideas were advanced, though achievable. Created in God's image, men were creators, inventors of good and useful things. They could restore to themselves everything that tyrants and "their banditti" had stolen from them, especially their rights. Accordingly, in a totally, though wildly, compelling argument, he told Burke that human rights actually preexisted creation in eternal time. Because God designated man to be the most advanced of all his creations, he gave him a secondary power of creation (secondary because God alone possessed primary power): from (great and not so great) works of literature and philosophy to (sound and not so sound) bridges and constitutions and even an (equitable and not so equitable) economic system. Barriers to man's creative powers hindered not only his natural powers but God's intentions. Interference in God's plan to allow men to use their common sense was the greatest of all blasphemies. To take back what the few had taken from the many, the many had to act, and act quickly. Although he advocated a program of radical social and political transformations, Paine's constant focus on the natural abilities of the people always tempered his radicalism. Like his Whiggish contemporaries, he too advocated a return, but not to a lost past of political perfection. Rather he wanted men to return to their own nature. Unlike Rousseau, he believed that natural man, free from all tyrannical constraints, could create a good, sound political and social order that would allow him to function as God intended.

All government was evil because it inherently restricted men's actions. But government was necessary to insure that they always acted in a morally responsible way. This was why he argued that if government is in fact necessary, it had better be a good government. If left alone, people were not virtuous all the time. They were not perfect, in or out of nature. Only good government, the democratic republic, would make people conscious of their fellows' needs. Good government supplied the defect in man's moral virtue and at the same time set the political conditions for economic democracy (*CS* 66).

Thomas Paine devoted his professional life to developing a writing style which would awaken the common man from the torpid state in which tyranny had placed him. In this sense, Paine was a dreamer like Rousseau, though he thought that dreams tended to separate a person from the harsh realities of life.[3] He once claimed he did not like dreams because they distorted reality. Dreams stimulated the imagination to flourish while judgment and memory slept. "How absurd it is to place reliance upon dreams." The major elements of his moral and political outlook (nature, reason, and affection) served as a shield to protect people from obscurantism, nightmares, and superstition.

> All the efforts that *nature, reason* and *conscience* have made to awaken man . . . have been ascribed by priestcraft and superstition to the working of the devil, and had it not been for the American Revolution which, by establishing the universal right of conscience, first opened the way to free discussion, and for the French Revolution that followed, this Religion of Dreams had continued to be preached, and that after it had ceased to be believed.[4]

Despite his admonitions, he did dream of a future world that would benefit all people, a world he designed in his reverie that permitted imagination, judgment, and memory to remain awake and alive and not numbed or somnolent. His dream consisted of his vision of the democratic republic and economic democracy. At times, he became discouraged. But although political rights and economic freedom were part of his dream, he thought they resided in man's happy future. For Thomas Paine, they were always obtainable. His was a bold dream, a dream, he thought, that fitted well with man's humanity in all its vast diversity, magnificent character, and natural creativity. Paine's writings about humanity gave his works wide popularity. Plain, ordinary people were directly touched by his open and direct homiletic style. They could also agree with him as the new world he envisioned opened before them.

NOTES

Preface

1. Letter to John Inskeep, mayor of the city of Philadelphia, *Philadelphia Aurora,* 10 Feb. 1806, in *The Complete Writings of Thomas Paine,* edited by Philip S. Foner (New York: Citadel Press, 1945), 2:1479–80.

2. Edmund S. Morgan, *Visible Saints: The History of a Puritan Idea* (New York: New York University Press, 1963). Morgan was interested, of course, in early American history. He applies the term *visible saints* to the English reformers of the period as well.

3. See the monumental work by Perry Miller, *The New England Mind: From Colony to Province* (Cambridge: Belknap Press of Harvard University Press, 1953).

4. As examples of studies in the arena of civil religion, see the seminal work of Carl Bridenbaugh, *Mitre and Sceptre: Transatlantic Faiths, Ideas, Personalities, and Politics, 1689–1775* (New York: Oxford University Press, 1962); Alan Heimert, *Religion and the American Mind* (Cambridge: Harvard University Press, 1966); Cushing Strout, *The New Heavens and the New Earth: Political Religion in America* (New York: Harper & Row, 1974); and Robert N. Bellah, *The Broken Covenant: American Civil Religion in the Time of Trial* (New York: Seabury Press, 1971). See also Catherine L. Albanese: *Sons of the Fathers: The Civil Religion of the American Revolution* (Philadelphia: Temple University Press, 1976), and Edwin S. Gaustad, *Faith of Our Fathers: Religion and the New Nation* (San Francisco: Harper & Row, 1987).

5. Winthrop S. Hudson, ed., *Nationalism and Religion in America: Concepts of American Identity and Mission* (New York: Harper & Row, 1970), 36–37.

6. John F. Berens, *Providence and Patriotism in Early America, 1640–1815* (Charlottesville: University Press of Virginia, 1978), 143.

7. *Rights of Man,* edited by Henry Collins with an introduction by Eric Foner (Harmondsworth: Penguin, 1984), 271. References to *Rights of Man* (*RM*) are to this edition.

8. He languished for ten months in the Luxembourg Prison in Paris from 1793 to 1794, and he was worried then about his fate, particularly during the Terror, when several of his prisonmates were executed. See his correspondence in *Complete Writings,* 2:1338–75, and letter to George Washington, 30 July 1796, *Complete Writings,* 2:691–723.

9. Letter to Inskeep, *Complete Writings,* 2:1480.

Chapter 1. Introduction: Language, Homiletics, and Audience

1. *The Age of Reason* (1794), in *The Complete Writings of Thomas Paine,* edited by Philip S. Foner (New York: Citadel Press, 1945), 2 vols. Unless otherwise noted, references to works by Paine are to this edition, which is abbreviated *CW.*

2. See Alfred Owen Aldridge, *Benjamin Franklin and Nature's God* (Durham, N.C.: Duke University Press, 1967).

3. For the view that Paine may have been part of a larger, growing culture of secular preaching, see Nathan O. Hatch, *The Democratization of American Christianity* (New Haven: Yale University Press, 1989).

4. Though the publisher, Robert Bell, priced the first edition at 2 shillings. Paine subsequently increased its size by a third and demanded the price be halved. See David Freeman Hawke, *Paine* (New York: Harper & Row, 1974), 44–46, for the publication history.

5. Hatch, *Democratization of American Christianity,* 213.

6. *Common Sense,* edited by Isaac Kramnick, (Harmondsworth: Penguin, 1976), 87, 96, 100. References to *Common Sense* (*CS*) are to this edition.

7. James T. Boulton, *The Language of Politics in the Age of Wilkes and Burke* (Westport, Conn.: Greenwood Press, 1975), 134–50; Olivia Smith, *The Politics of Language, 1791–1819* (Oxford: Clarendon Press, 1984), 35–67. David A. Wilson, *Paine and Cobbett: The Transatlantic Connection* (Montreal: McGill-Queen's University Press, 1988), 34–64.

8. *Rights of Man,* 66–115.

9. Paine's idiosyncrasies are well documented: the failures in love and profession in the first thirty-seven years of his life; his journalistic successes after that; his unwillingness to accept even a penny from the profits of his work; his wandering from England to America, back and forth from England to France, then finally back to America; his unkempt personal nature and his tendencies, especially late in life, to drink too much.

10. "Remarks on R. Hall's Sermon," *Prospect,* 18 Feb. 1804, *CW* 2:792–93.

11. Wilson Carey McWilliams, *The Idea of Fraternity in America* (Berkeley: University of California Press, 1973), 170 (emphasis added).

12. Myra Jehlen, *American Incarnation: The Individual, the Nation, and the Continent* (Cambridge: Harvard University Press, 1986), 5. See for similar perspectives on Hobbes, Locke, and Rousseau: Andrzej Rapaczynski, *Nature and Politics: Liberalism in the Philosophies of Hobbes, Locke, and Rousseau* (Ithaca: Cornell University Press, 1987), and on Jefferson: Charles A. Miller, *Jefferson and Nature: An Interpretation* (Baltimore: Johns Hopkins University Press, 1988).

13. David Schofield Wilson, *In the Presence of Nature* (Amherst: University of Massachusetts Press, 1978); Richard Feingold, *Nature and Society: Later Eighteenth-Century Uses of the Pastoral and Georgic* (New Brunswick, N.J.: Rutgers University Press, 1978); Raymond Phineas Stearns, *Science in the British Colonies of America* (Urbana: University of Illinois Press, 1970); Ronald L. Meek, *Social Science and the Ignoble Savage* (Cambridge: Cambridge University Press, 1976), 37–67; Robert Godwin-Jones, "The Rural Socrates Revisited: Kleinjogg, Rousseau, and the Concept of Natural Man," *Eighteenth-Century Life* 7 (Oct. 1981): 86–104. One is reminded of Locke's sentiments in the *Second Treatise* that "in the beginning all the world was America," (John Locke, *Second Treatise of Gov-*

ernment, edited by C. B. Macpherson [Indianapolis: Hackett, 1980], 29). On Paine's rejection by the American Philosophical Society, see Hawke, *Paine,* 114, and on his later acceptance, Philip S. Foner, "Editor's Introduction," *CW* 2:39.

14. *American Crisis,* no. 13 (19 Apr. 1783), *CW* 1;231. See R. R. Fennessy, *Burke, Paine and the Rights of Man: A Difference of Political Opinion* (The Hague: Martinus Nijhoff, 1963), 35–37, 69–70.

15. Eric Foner, *Tom Paine and Revolutionary America* (New York: Oxford University Press, 1976), xii–xiii. See Judith N. Shklar, *Men and Citizens: A Study of Rousseau's Social Theory* (Cambridge: Cambridge University Press, 1969), 1, which could have been speaking of Paine.

16. See, for example, the following: John J. Meng, "The Constitutional Theories of Thomas Paine," *Review of Politics* 8 (July 1946): 283–306; Joseph Dorfman, "The Economic Philosophy of Thomas Paine," *Political Science Quarterly* 53 (Sept. 1938): 372–86; Howard Penniman, "Thomas Paine—Democrat," *American Political Science Review* 37 (Apr. 1943): 244–62; Henry Hayden Clark, "Toward a Reinterpretation of Thomas Paine," *American Literature* 5 (May 1933): 133–45, and "An Historical Interpretation of Thomas Paine's Religion," *University of California Chronicle* 35 (1933): 56–87.

17. See the bibliography in A. Owen Aldridge, *Thomas Paine's American Ideology* (Newark: University of Delaware Press, 1984), 316–17.

18. Moncure D. Conway, *The Life of Thomas Paine* (New York: Putnam, 1892); Hawke, *Paine;* Alfred Owen Aldridge, *Man of Reason: The Life of Thomas Paine* (Philadelphia: Lippincott, 1959); Audrey Williamson, *Thomas Paine: His Life, Work and Times* (London: George Allen & Unwin, 1973); David Powell, *Tom Paine: The Greatest Exile* (New York: St. Martin's Press, 1985); George Spater, "The Early Years, 1737–74," "American Revolutionary, 1774–89," and "European Revolutionary, 1789–1809," in Ian Dyck, ed., *Citizen of the World: Essays on Thomas Paine* (London: Christopher Helm, 1987), 17–70.

19. Foner, *Paine and Revolutionary America,* xiii. See also Gregory Claeys, *Thomas Paine: Social and Political Thought* (Winchester, U.K.: Unwin Hyman, 1989).

20. For the theoretical approach taken here, see the following: Quentin Skinner, "Introduction: the Return of Grand Theory," in *The Return of Grand Theory in the Human Sciences* (Cambridge: Cambridge University Press, 1985), 1–20; "The Limits of Historical Explanation," *Philosophy* 41 (July 1966): 199–215; "Meaning and Understanding in the History of Ideas," *History and Theory* 8 (1969): 3–53; "Hermeneutics and the Role of History," *New Literary History* 7 (Autumn 1975): 209–32. John Dunn, "The Identity of the History of Ideas," *Philosophy* 43 (Apr. 1968): 85–104; *Rethinking Modern Political Theory* (Cambridge: Cambridge University Press, 1985). J.G.A. Pocock, "The History of Political Thought: A Methodological Enquiry," in *Philosophy, Politics, and Society,* edited by P. Laslett and W. G. Runciman (London: Basil Blackwell, 1962), 2d ser., 183–202; *Politics, Language and Time: Essays on Political Thought and History* (New York: Atheneum, 1973), esp. chaps. 1 and 8; *Virtue, Commerce, and History: Essays on Political Thought and History, Chiefly in the Eighteenth Century* (Cambridge: Cambridge University Press, 1985) esp. chap. 1 and its notes.

21. For models of the methodology in recent historical works, I have in mind particularly the following: Quentin Skinner, *The Foundations of Modern Political Thought* (Cambridge: Cambridge University Press, 1978); "The Ideological Context of Hobbes's

Political Thought," *Historical Journal* 9 (1966): 286–317; "Hobbes' *Leviathan*," *Historical Journal* 7 (1964): 321–33. John Dunn, *The Political Thought of John Locke: An Historical Account of the Argument of the "Two Treatises of Government"* (Cambridge: Cambridge University Press, 1969). Pocock, *Virtue, Commerce, and History, passim; The Machiavellian Moment: Florentine Political Thought and the Atlantic Republican Tradition* (Princeton: Princeton University Press, 1975), passim. For a study of Paine's style of argument, see Smith, *Politics of Language,* 35–67.

22. For a discussion of how this approach to historical study has come under attack, see the following exchange in *American Historical Review* 94 (June 1989): David Harlan, "Intellectual History and the Return of Literature," 581–609; David A. Hollinger, "The Return of the Prodigal: The Persistence of Historical Knowing," 610–21; Harlan, "Reply to David Hollinger," 622–26. See especially the extensive notes in Harlan's first piece.

23. Pocock, *Virtue, Commerce, and History,* 5.

24. See Isaac Kramnick, *Republicanism and Bourgeois Radicalism: Political Ideology in Late Eighteenth-Century England and America* (Ithaca: Cornell University Press, 1990).

25. The now standard works on the Old Whigs or classical republicans are Zera S. Fink, *The Classical Republicans: An Essay in the Recovery of a Pattern of Thought in Seventeenth-Century England* (Evanston, Ill.: Northwestern University Press, 1945); Caroline Robbins, *The Eighteenth-Century Commonwealthman: Studies in the Transmission, Development and Circumstances of English Liberal Thought from the Restoration of Charles II until the War with the Thirteen Colonies* (Cambridge: Harvard University Press, 1959); Bernard Bailyn, *The Ideological Origins of the American Revolution* (Cambridge: Harvard University Press, 1967); Gordon S. Wood, *The Creation of the American Republic, 1776–1787* (Chapel Hill: University of North Carolina Press, 1969); Pocock, *Machiavellian Moment.*

26. The phrase is from Christopher Hill, *The World Turned Upside Down: Radical Ideas during the English Revolution* (New York: Viking, 1972), who drew it from the New Testament book of Acts. For the suggestion that Paine may have been a Puritan or Cromwellian thinker, see Pocock, *Politics, Language and Time,* 84. For Paine's ideas as forming a "civil religion," see Wilson Carey McWilliams, "Civil Religion in the Age of Reason: Thomas Paine on Liberalism, Redemption, and Revolution," *Social Research* 54 (Autumn, 1987): 447–90.

27. See Aldridge, *Paine's American Ideology,* 95–157, for an attempt at the impossible task.

28. Caroline Robbins, "The Lifelong Education of Thomas Paine (1737–1809): Some Reflections upon His Acquaintance among Books," *Proceedings of the American Philosophical Society* 127 (June 1983): 135–42.

29. Late in life, he wrote, "I have never read Locke nor even had the work in my hand, and by what I heard of it . . . I had no inducement to read it. It is a speculative, not a practical work, and the style of it is heavy and tedious, as all Locke's writings are." Such a statement is open to question, given his wide use of Lockean themes and ideas. Letter to James Cheatham, 21 Aug. 1807, in the American Philosophical Society, Thomas Paine Collection of Colonel Richard Gimbel, Philadelphia.

30. J.G.A. Pocock has suggested that we could think of influences in the context of a climate of ideas as an "influenza," germs in the air infecting (and affecting) those who

come in contact with them. (Comment at the Folger Institute Center for the Study of British Political Thought, Feb. 1987.)

31. *To the Citizens of the United States,* "Letter IV" (3 Dec. 1802), *CW* 2:926.

32. J. L. Talmon, *Origins of Totalitarian Democracy* (New York: Norton, 1970), 69. The similarities between the two pamphlets are too irresistible to let pass, despite Talmon's singular intentions in his now-famous work. On the other hand, see R. C. De Prospo, "Paine and Sieyès," *Thought* 65 (June 1990): 190–202.

33. He told Benjamin Franklin the following: "As soon as I can get ready by the April packet I intend not omitting the opportunity. My father and mother are yet living whom I am very anxious to see, and have informed them of my coming in the ensuing summer." Letter, 31 Mar. 1787, *CW* 2:1260.

Chapter 2. Natural Man and Common Sense

1. In *CS* 65, Paine first said that government is always a necessary evil. See Mc-Williams, *Fraternity in America,* 172.

2. *Letter to the Abbé Raynal* (1782), *CW* 2:258.

3. "A Serious Address to the People of Pennsylvania on the Present Situation of Their Affairs," *Pennsylvania Packet* (1 Dec. 1778), *CW* 2:286.

4. Although these remarks are from *Rights of Man,* it will soon become apparent that the dehumanization of kings (and his cabinet) and the consequent anesthetization of the citizenry were both arguments used extensively in *Common Sense.* The writer is indebted here to J.G.A. Pocock for the observation that this work contains arguments designed to be irrefutable and indeed couched in absolutist, totalitarian (to use a modern concept) terms.

5. See, for example, Jay Fliegelman, *Prodigals and Pilgrims: The American Revolution against Patriarchal Authority, 1750–1800* (Cambridge: Cambridge University Press, 1982), 103, 289, n. 4, which says that "by arguing from the assumption of moral sense theory rather than from rationalist assumptions, Paine's *Common Sense* in one stroke radically redefined the issue, took it outside the realm of rational argumentation."

6. As is well known, Benjamin Rush took credit for suggesting the title of *Common Sense* for Paine's pamphlet. Said Rush, "When Mr. Paine had finished his pamphlet, I advised him to shew it to Dr. Franklin, Mr. Rittenhouse, and Saml. Adams, all of whom I knew were decided friends to American independence. I mention these facts to refute a report that Mr. Paine was assisted in composing his pamphlet by one or more of the above gentlemen. They never saw it till it was written, and then only by my advice. I gave it at his request the title of 'Common Sense.'" *The Autobiography of Benjamin Rush,* edited by George W. Corner (Princeton: Princeton University Press, 1948), 114.

7. Shaftesbury's elitism, which would have been wholly anathema to Paine, was outlined in Lois Whitney, *Primitivism and the Idea of Progress in English Popular Literature of the Eighteenth Century* (Baltimore: Johns Hopkins University Press, 1934), 33. For this reason, he receives only a mention here. For a revisionist view, see Michelle Buchanan, "Savages, Noble and Otherwise, and the French Enlightenment," in *Studies in Eighteenth-Century Culture,* vol. 15 (Madison: University of Wisconsin Press, 1986), 97–109. See also Robert Voitle, *The Third Earl of Shaftesbury, 1671–1713* (Baton Rouge: Louisiana State University Press, 1984), and Alfred Owen Aldridge, *Shaftesbury and the Deist Manifesto* (Philadelphia: American Philosophical Society Transactions, vol. 41, pt. 2, 1951).

8. Thomas Reid, *An Inquiry into the Human Mind,* edited by Timothy Duggan (Chicago: University of Chicago Press, 1970), 19.

9. For Rousseau's notion of common sense, which is quite close to Paine's, see the passage in *Emile* which recounts the "Profession of Faith of the Savoyard Vicar." "I am not a great philosopher," the Vicar said, "and I care little to be one. But I sometimes have good *sense,* and I always love the truth. . . . Reason is *common* to us, and we have the same interest in listening to it. If I think well, why would you not think as do I?" *Bon sens* is indeed, for Rousseau here, reason as a universal attribute of men. *Emile, or On Education,* ed. Allan Bloom (New York: Basic Books, 1979), 266 (emphasis added). See the entire "Profession of Faith," 266–313. I am indebted to Anthony La Vopa for this citation.

10. Fliegelman, *Prodigals and Pilgrims,* 103, relates Paine's idea of sensibility to nature by saying, "It is nature, not reason, that cannot forgive England." He thus makes clear the conjunction between nature and affection (in common sense), but he does not cite in full this statement, in which Paine himself conjoined nature with *both* moral affection and reason.

11. He did not say it was "the age of common sense"!

12. See McWilliams, *Fraternity in America,* 182.

13. *American Crisis,* No. 5 (21 Mar. 1778), *CW* 1:125.

14. Letter to Sir George Staunton, Esq., Spring 1789, *CW* 2:1041.

15. *American Crisis,* no. 7 (21 Nov. 1778), *CW* 1:143.

16. *Letter to Abbé Raynal, CW* 2:252.

17. Ibid., 253.

18. "Reasons for Preserving the Life of Louis Capet," (16 Jan. 1793), *CW* 2:551–55; "Should Louis XVI Be Respited?" (19 Jan. 1793), *CW* 2:556–58 (the latter includes Marat's interruptions of Paine's speech). Paine's impassioned plea for the life of Louis XVI may be attributable to a number of things: his maturity by 1793, his realization that the French under Louis were helpful during the American war against Britain, or perhaps his awareness that the revolution itself was potentially heading toward a negative end. See Note 21 below on the symbolic killing of the king.

19. *Letter to Abbé Raynal, CW* 2:253.

20. See Robbins, "Lifelong Education of Paine," 141–42.

21. Winthrop D. Jordan, "Familial Politics: Thomas Paine and the Killing of the King," *Journal of American History* 60 (Sept. 1973): 294–308.

22. For the debate over whether Paine wrote this poem, see the editor's note and Alfred Owen Aldridge, "The Poetry of Thomas Paine," *Pennsylvania Magazine of History and Biography* 79 (Jan. 1951): 89–93.

23. *American Crisis,* no. 7, *CW* 1:142.

24. "To the Abbé Sieyès," *Moniteur* (16 July 1791), *CW* 2:520. For a prayerful Paine, see his "Reasons for Preserving the Life of Louis Capet." *CW* 2: 551–55, esp. 553–54.

25. For additional later references during the French revolutionary period, see *RM* 168, 199.

26. "An Essay for the Use of New Republicans in Their Opposition to Monarchy," *Le Patriote français* (20 Oct. 1792), *CW* 2:542.

27. Ronald Paulson, *Representations of Revolution (1789–1820)* (New Haven: Yale University Press, 1983), 76–78. For the full context of the parent-child symbol of British-American relations, see Edwin G. Burrows and Michael Wallace, "The American Revo-

lution: The Ideology and Psychology of National Liberation," *Perspectives in American History* 6 (1972): 167–306.

28. "Thoughts on Defensive War," *Pennsylvania Magazine* (July 1775), *CW* 2:52–53.

29. An obvious tour de force, given the fact that he was referring to the Terror under Robespierre and St. Just, and not to kings and noblemen. Quoted by Hawke, *Paine*, 287.

30. Child sacrifice was discussed by Locke, and cannibalism by Montesquieu.

31. Kramnick's edition of *Common Sense*, which is based on the second edition of 14 Feb. 1776, has a considerable number of blank spaces, such as "the royal _____ of Britain." See, for example, 92f., 107, 112, 113. Foner, meantime, reproduces the names, as does the 10 January 1776 original in the British Museum, London.

32. While Paine had used the Bible at the beginning of *Common Sense* as a source to attack kingship, it did not necessarily follow that the adulation of live monarchs was devil worship, even if he suggested that moderns had gone further than the less advanced ancients by turning their living monarchs into gods.

33. McWilliams, *Fraternity in America*, 177, sees a trace of antisemitism in Paine's characterization of the Jews here.

34. For a different view, see Fliegelman, *Prodigals and Pilgrims*, 176–77.

35. See Aldridge, *Paine's American Ideology*, 116; *Shaftesbury and the Deist Manifesto*, 56–57; also Whitney, *Primitivism and the Idea of Progress*, 27–41; Voitle, *The Third Earl of Shaftesbury*, 125–63.

36. John Dunn, *The Political Thought of John Locke*, 87–119. Although Aldridge, *Paine's American Ideology*, has argued that Locke did not directly influence Paine, Lockean ideas permeate *Common Sense*, and *The Age of Reason* was Paine's response to Locke's *Reasonableness of Christianity*. See *Paine's American Ideology*, 119, also J.A.W. Gunn, *Beyond Liberty and Property: The Process of Self-Recognition in Eighteenth-Century Political Thought* (Kingston: McGill-Queen's University Press, 1983), 121, 173, 184–88.

37. See H. T. Dickinson, *Liberty and Property: Liberal Political Thought in Eighteenth-Century Britain* (New York: Holmes & Meier, 1977), 66–67, 199, 244; Nathan Tarcov, "Locke's 'Second Treatise' and 'The Best Fence against Rebellion,'" *Review of Politics* 43 (Apr. 1981): 198–217; and J.C.D. Clarke, *English Society, 1688–1820: Ideology, Social Structure and Political Practice during the Ancien Regime* (Cambridge: Cambridge University Press, 1985), 45–50, 64.

38. On Dissent, see Anthony Lincoln, *Some Political and Social Ideas of English Dissent* (New York: Octagon, 1971). Although published originally in 1938, this book has yet to lose its importance. For Burke, see chap. 4 below.

39. On Paine's primitivism, see Whitney, *Primitivism and the Idea of Progress*, 226–29.

40. See Pocock, *Machiavellian Moment*, 462–505.

41. "A Serious Address to the Citizens of Pennsylvania," *Pennsylvania Packet* (1 Dec. 1778), *CW* 2:279. For a full account of this affair, see Foner, *Paine and Revolutionary America*, 107–44.

42. *Letter to the Abbé Raynal, CW* 2:220.

43. See also *American Crisis*, no. 6 (20 Oct. 1778), *CW* 1:136–37.

44. *Letter to the Abbé Raynal, CW* 2:220.

45. Ibid., 220, 242.

46. See The Forester's Letter No. III (24 Apr. 1776), *CW* 2:80.

47. See Pocock, *Machiavellian Moment*, 37, and *Virtue, Commerce and History*, 37–50;

also the editor's introduction to Niccolo Machiavelli, *The Discourses*, edited by Bernard Crick (Harmondsworth: Penguin, 1970), 57–60.

48. On renovation, see Pocock, *Machiavellian Moment*, 78–79, 508–13.

49. "To the People of England on the Invasion of England," *Philadelphia Aurora* (6 Mar. 1804), *CW* 2:683.

Chapter 3. Nature and Man's Democratic Calling

1. Renato Poggioli, *The Oaten Flute: Essays on Pastoral Poetry and the Pastoral Ideal* (Cambridge: Cambridge University Press, 1975), 1.

2. See McWilliams, *Fraternity in America*, 178–80; "The environment, after all, had been the basis for the messianic hopes that European visionaries held for America. Ours was the environment of nature, where man could begin again" (178). See also chapter 9 below.

3. Richard Price, *Observations on Reversionary Payments*, second ed. (London, 1772), 276.

4. See A. Owen Aldridge, "The Apex of American Literary Nationalism," in *Early American Literature: A Comparative Approach* (Princeton: Princeton University Press, 1982), 186–208, esp. 296, and Robert Hole, *Pulpits, Politics and Public Order in England, 1760–1832*. (Cambridge: Cambridge University Press, 1989), 115–18.

5. These are discussed later in this chapter.

6. Robbins, "Lifelong Education of Paine," 138, admonishes that we ought not exaggerate Paine's debt to Rousseau. Certainly the emphasis on nature in both suggests a greater debt than Robbins concedes.

7. Poggioli, *Oaten Flute*, 216, 214. For Paine's relation to William Blake in regard to things natural, see Robert N. Essick, "William Blake, Thomas Paine, and Biblical Revelation," *Studies in Romanticism* "William Blake, Thomas Paine, and Biblical Revelation," *Studies in Romanticism* 30 (Summer 1991): 189–212.

8. While Paine's bucolic vision was rooted mostly in the French landscape, his feelings about America indicate an earlier preoccupation with the physical landscape. Thus, he offered a grand vista ranging from the far reaches of the western lands to the newly cultivated frontier to the rural countryside near and around the towns of America. See Thomas Paine, *Public Good* (1780), *CW* 2:303–33, esp. 332. For the power of the physical landscape in the late eighteenth and early nineteenth centuries, see Peter S. Onuf, *The Origins of the Federal Republic: Jurisdictional Controversies in the United States, 1775–1787* (Philadelphia: University of Pennsylvania Press, 1983); R.W.B. Lewis, *The American Adam: Innocence, Tragedy, and Tradition in the Nineteenth Century* (Chicago: University of Chicago Press, 1955); Charles L. Sanford, *The Quest for Paradise: Europe and the American Moral Imagination* (Urbana: University of Illinois Press, 1961); Leo Marx, *The Machine in the Garden: Technology and the Pastoral Ideal in America* (New York: Oxford University Press, 1964); Henry Nash Smith, *Virgin Land: The American West as Symbol and Myth* (Cambridge: Harvard University Press, 1950).

9. Paine thought the wilderness, which he once called a "savage uncivilized life," was a kind of state of nature (*RM* 211). Intriguing comparisons could be made with Rousseau, especially the "Idyll of the Cherries" in the *Confessions*. See James Miller, *Rousseau: Dreamer of Democracy* (New Haven: Yale University Press, 1984); Christopher Frayling and Robert Wokler, "From the Orang-Utan to the Vampire: Towards an Anthropology

of Rousseau," in *Rousseau after Two Hundred Years: Proceedings of the Cambridge Bicentennial Colloquium,* edited by R. A. Leigh (Cambridge: Cambridge University Press, 1982), 109–29. Parallels can also be found in Crèvecoeur, though there is no evidence Paine even heard of this rural Tory writer in New York State. See J. Hector St. John de Crèvecoeur, *Letters from an American Farmer and Sketches of Eighteenth-Century America,* edited by Albert E. Stone (Harmondsworth: Penguin, 1981), 7, 55–56, 61, 67, 69, 70–71; Myra Jehlen, "J. Hector St. John de Crèvecoeur: A Monarcho-Anarchist in America," *American Quarterly* 31 (Summer 1979): 204–22; and Marx, *Machine in the Garden,* 107–16.

10. Conway, *Life of Paine,* 1:6.

11. Audrey Williamson, *Thomas Paine,* 21, 27. See Alyce Barry, "Thomas Paine, Privateersman," *Pennsylvania Magazine of History and Biography* 101 (October 1977): 451–61.

12. Barry, "Privateersman," 460–61.

13. Williamson, *Thomas Paine,* 29, 43.

14. One of his early pieces in the *Pennsylvania Magazine* (Feb. 1775) was "Useful and Entertaining Hints," an essay which was in part an admiring ode to nature. There, he remarked that

> in such gifts as nature can annually re-create, she is noble and profuse, and entertains the whole world with the interest of her fortunes; but watches over the capital with the care of a miser. Her gold and jewels lie concealed in the earth, in caves of utter darkness; and hoards of wealth, heap upon heaps, mould in the chests, like the riches of a necromancer's cell. It must be very pleasant to an adventurous speculist to make excursions into these Gothic regions; and in his travels he may possibly come to a cabinet locked up in some rocky vault, whose treasure shall reward his toil, and enable him to shine on his return, as splendidly as nature herself. (*CW* 2:1023)

15. Even Paine's idea of his bridge came from the natural world. "I took the idea of constructing it from a spider's web, of which it resembles a section, and I naturally supposed that when nature enabled that insect to make a web she taught it the best method of putting it together." Letter to Sir George Staunton, Bart., Spring 1789, *CW* 2:1044–45. See also *RM* 181–82 and letter to Joseph Banks, 25 May 1789, cited in Aldridge, *Man of Reason* 109.

16. Paine seems to approach a rudimentary theory of utility here, but he never explicitly says that he believed that all natural phenomena, like natural disasters, were good.

17. Edmund Burke, *Reflections on the Revolution in France,* edited by Conor Cruise O'Brien (Harmondsworth: Penguin, 1969), All references are to this edition.

18. Boulton, *Language of Politics,* 137, calls this passage an "allegory . . . as simple as biblical parable[;] its message is clear and the experience it draws on is universal." See also Smith, *Politics of Language,* 35–67. For comparison with other revolutions, see Ronald Paulson, "Revolution and the Visual Arts," in Roy Porter and Mikulas Teich, eds., *Revolution in History* (Cambridge: Cambridge University Press, 1986), 240–60, esp. 254.

19. See Paulson, *Representations of Revolution,* 73–74.

20. Ibid., 41–47, 75–76.

21. This festival actually took place. See Mona Ozouf, *Festivals and the French Revolution,* translated by Alan Sheridan (Cambridge: Harvard University Press, 1988), 83–84, 172–74.

22. Ernest F. Henderson, *Symbol and Satire in the French Revolution* (New York: G. P.

Putnam's, 1912), 357–58. See also Bronislaw Backo, *Lumières de l'utopie* (Paris: Payot, 1978), 263–71.

23. Horace Walpole to Hannah More, 10 Sept. 1789, in *Horace Walpole's Correspondence*, edited by W. S. Lewis Vol. 31 (New Haven: Yale University Press, 1961), 323.

24. Henderson, *Symbol and Satire*, 361–62.

25. Jean-Jacques Rousseau, "Letter to M. d'Alembert on the Theatre," in *Politics and the Arts*, edited by Allan Bloom (Ithaca: Cornell University Press, 1968), 125–26.

26. James H. Billington, *Fire in the Minds of Men: Origins of the Revolutionary Faith* (New York: Basic Books, 1980), 48. The transformation of the Bastille into "a ballroom beneath the trees" (a public park) is from Ozouf, *Festivals*, 149.

27. J. Tiersot, *Les Fêtes et les chants de la révolution française* (Paris: Hachette, 1908), 40.

28. Quoted by Ozouf, *Festivals*, 129.

29. For a quite different set of arguments for his American audience, see Paine's view of an urban institution, the bank, in chapter 6 and chapter 8 for his cosmic use of this nature imagery.

30. Arthur Schlessinger, "Liberty Tree: A Genealogy," *New England Quarterly*, 25 (Dec. 1952): 435–48.

31. Jordan, "Familial Politics," 294–308. See also Ozouf, *Festivals*, 217–61.

32. Edmund Burke to the Duke of Richmond, 15 Nov. 1772, in *The Correspondence of Edmund Burke*, edited by Thomas W. Copeland (Cambridge: Cambridge University Press, 1960), 2:377.

33. Burke, *Reflections*, 194; 181.

34. "Address and Declaration" (London, 1791), *CW* 2:534. See also *RM* 58, where Paine makes his famous statement, "Lay then axe to the root, and teach governments humanity."

35. Jean-Jacques Rousseau, *On the Social Contract*, edited by Donald A. Cress (Indianapolis: Hackett, 1983), 79.

36. For a different view, see Aldridge, *Paine's American Ideology*, 104 and 304, n. 33.

37. "Liberty Tree," *Philadelphia Evening Post* (16 Sept. 1775), *CW* 2:1091–92. See A. Owen Aldridge, "Poetry of Thomas Paine."

38. *Prosecution of "The Age of Reason"* (1797), *CW* 2:729, 732.

39. Margaret C. Jacob, *The Radical Enlightenment: Pantheists, Freemasons and Republicans* (London: George Allen & Unwin, 1981), 110.

40. *Prosecution of "The Age of Reason"*, *CW* 2:745. See McWilliams, *Idea of Fraternity*, 182, 203–9.

41. Foner, *Paine and Revolutionary America*, 252–53; Hawke, *Paine*, 326; Jacob, *Radical Enlightenment*, 154; Williamson, *Thomas Paine*, 237. Jacob says that Paine was a Freemason. Williamson says there is no proof he was. Aldridge and Hawke say nothing. The conclusion now is that we do not have enough evidence to make a final judgment.

42. *Prosecution of "The Age of Reason,"* *CW* 2:747. See also "The Existence of God" (Paris, 1797), *CW* 2:248–56.

43. "Origins of Freemasonry" (unpublished, 1805), *CW* 2:833.

44. Aldridge, *Man of Reason*, 255–56; Hawke, *Paine*, 332; Williamson, *Thomas Paine*, 249–50, 253; Billington, *Fire in the Minds of Men*, 42 (on Paine's introduction to Bonneville in 1791).

45. Aldridge, *Man of Reason*, 271–72, 186–87; Williamson, *Thomas Paine*, 274; Hawke, *Paine*, 394. The youngest son, Benjamin, became an important military officer in the United States and the subject of a biography by Washington Irving.

46. Thanks largely to the nefarious biography by Paine's enemy, James Cheetham, a great deal has been made over whether Marguerite de Bonneville was Paine's paramour, whether Paine really fathered her two youngest sons, and ironically, whether Paine was impotent during most of his life. Paine's biographers discount all of this. On Bonneville's detention in France, see Conway, *Life of Paine*, 2:432–33.

47. Aldridge, *Man of Reason*, 146, claims he was. For the history of this extraordinary group, see Gary Kates, *The Cercle Social, the Girondins and the French Revolution* (Princeton: Princeton University Press, 1985).

48. Billington, *Fire in the Minds of Men*, 39, 66.

49. Nicholas de Bonneville, *The Jesuits Driven from Free Masonry* (Paris, 1788), 1:26, quoted in Billington, *Fire in the Minds of Men*, 97.

50. C. Delacroix, "Récherches sur le Cercle Social (1790–1791)," Doctoral thesis, University of the Sorbonne, 1975, 33–34, quoted by Billington, *Fire in the Minds of Men*, 39.

51. Nicholas de Bonneville, *On the Spirit of Religions* (Paris, 1792), quoted in Billington, *Fire in the Minds of Men*, 41.

52. Billington, *Fire in the Minds of Men*, 522, n. 124.

Chapter 4. Nature and the Theory of Rights

1. Letter to Anonymous [Benjamin Rush], 16 Mar. 1789 [1790], *CW* 2:1286.

2. Richard Tuck, *Natural Rights Theories: Their Origin and Development* (Cambridge: Cambridge University Press, 1979), 1–2.

3. See also "Extracts from a Reply to the Bishop of Llandaff," published posthumously in *The Theophilanthropist* (1810), *CW* 2:769.

4. Robbins, "Lifelong Education of Paine," 140 and R. R. Palmer, "Thomas Paine— Victim of the Rights of Man," *Pennsylvania Magazine of History and Biography*, 66 (Apr. 1942): 172.

5. They shared the experience of being religious outcasts. Spinoza's Jewish congregation expelled him in 1656, and the faithful almost universally regarded Paine, after the publication of *The Age of Reason*, as an atheist. On Paine's death, even the Quakers thought it was not appropriate to inter the author of that infamous work in their graveyard.

6. Lewis Samuel Feuer, *Spinoza and the Rise of Liberalism* (Boston: Beacon Press, 1958), 101; see also 65–69, 179–82, 100–107. See Henry E. Allison, *Benedict de Spinoza*, (Boston: Twayne, 1975), 172–85, and Robert J. McShea, *The Political Philosophy of Spinoza* (New York: Columbia University Press, 1968), 57–59, 86–87.

7. Benedict de Spinoza to Henry Oldenburg, November or December, 1675, in *The Correspondence of Spinoza*, edited by A. Wolf (London: Frank Cass & Co., 1966), 343. See James Collins, *Spinoza on Nature* (Carbondale: Southern Illinois University Press, 1984).

8. Feuer, *Spinoza*, 49.

9. Benedict de Spinoza, *The Chief Works of Benedict de Spinoza*, translated by R.H.M. Elwes, proposition 36 (London: George Bell, 1900), 2 (pt. 4):211.

10. Feuer, *Spinoza*, 41. Preserved Smith, *The Age of Reformation* (New York: Henry

Holt, 1920), 154, calls them the "Bolsheviki of the sixteenth century."

11. Jacob, *Radical Enlightenment,* 46–47.

12. *Forester's Letters,* No. II (10 Apr. 1776), *CW* 2:68. See McWilliams, *Idea of Fraternity,* 174–77. For Smith, see Aldridge, *Paine's American Ideology,* 164–76.

13. See Hawke, *Paine,* 36; Foner, "Editor's Introduction," *CW* 2:15; Aldridge, *Paine's American Ideology,* 291.

14. "African Slavery in America," *Pennsylvania Journal* (8 Mar. 1775), *CW,* 2:16. Even if this piece is not authentically Paine's, we have evidence of his abhorrence of slavery. See letter, 16 Mar. 1790, in *The Letters of Benjamin Rush,* edited by Lyman H. Butterfield (Princeton: Princeton University Press, 1951), 1007–10, and Aldridge, *Paine's American Ideology,* 189–90.

15. Aldridge, *Paine's American Ideology,* 189–91, claims that the use of scripture in this passage was too orthodox to have come from Paine. The context of the piece (it was his first printed work in America), however, and the comparative similarity to his later views concerning the people's relationship to God through nature and creation suggest, as all previous Paine scholars believe, that it was Paine's work. See also McWilliams, *Fraternity in America,* 174–77.

16. Aldridge, *Paine's American Ideology,* 291, disputes Paine's authorship of this work also. As clerk of the Pennsylvania Assembly, Paine's duty was to provide drafts of legislation. If he drafted this preamble—and most scholars agree he did—he again emphasized the theme of rights given to men at their creation.

17. "Reflections on the Life and Death of Lord Clive," *Pennsylvania Magazine* (Mar. 1775), *CW* 2:27. Aldridge, *Paine's American Ideology,* 287, questions Paine's authorship of this piece as well.

18. [Thomas Paine], "An Occasional Letter on the Female Sex," *Pennsylvania Magazine* (Aug. 1776), *CW* 2:34. For more than fifty years, his authorship of this feminist piece has been debated. Frank Smith, "The Authorship of 'An Occasional Letter on the Female Sex," *American Literature* 2 (Nov. 1930): 277–80, suggested that a friend of Voltaire's had written it and had it translated into English and subsequently published in London, from where it made its way to America and to Paine, who, as editor of the *Pennsylvania Magazine,* printed it. Conway, *Life of Paine,* 1:45, noted that this piece was "unsigned, but certainly by Paine," and Foner included it in his edition of Paine's works. Foner, "Editor's Introduction," *CW* 2:34, notes that even if Paine did not write it, the very fact that it appeared in Paine's magazine "indicates his interest as editor of the magazine in the subject." Foner says some of the language is definitely Paine's but does not say why.

19. Emphasis added. For his French revolutionary audience Paine wrote in *Rights of Man* (173) that "it finally amounts to an accusation upon Providence, as if she had left to man no other choice with respect to government than between two evils." Few references to Providence in this period characterized it as female.

20. Letter to Nathanael Greene, 17 Oct. 1780, in the American Philosophical Society (photocopy only), the Thomas Paine Collection of Colonel Richard Gimbel, Philadelphia (emphasis added).

21. *To the Citizens of the United States,* "Letter III," *The National Intelligencer* (26 Nov. 1802), *CW* 2:920 (emphasis added).

22. Paine may have been a strong supporter of women's liberation, but he in no way

suggested that women be given the right to vote. His radical thought stopped at universal *manhood* suffrage.

23. F. P. Lock, *Burke's Reflections on the Revolution in France* (London: George Allen & Unwin, 1985), 64–99; Fennessy, *Burke, Paine and the Rights of Man*, 108–59; Michael Freeman, *Edmund Burke and the Critique of Political Radicalism* (Chicago: University of Chicago Press, 1980), 84–131; Frederick A. Dreyer, *Burke's Politics: A Study in Whig Orthodoxy* (Waterloo, Ont.: Wilfrid Laurier University Press, 1979), 54–67, 87–89; Pocock, *Politics, Language and Time*, 202–32, and in *Virtue, Commerce and History*, 193–212; Carl B. Cone, *Burke and the Nature of Politics* (Louisville: University of Kentucky Press, 1964), 2:314–69. For revisionist views, see Clark, *English Society, 1688–1832*, 247–58, and Isaac Kramnick, *The Rage of Edmund Burke: Portrait of an Ambivalent Conservative* (New York: Basic Books, 1977), 18–51 and *passim*. For a broad perspective, see Francis Canavan, S.J., "The Relevance of the Burke-Paine Controversy to American Political Thought," *Review of Politics* 49 (Spring 1987): 163–76.

24. "Speech on Reform of the Representation," in *The Works of the Right Honourable Edmund Burke* (London: Rivington, 1826), 10:99.

25. Fennessy, *Burke, Paine and the Rights of Man*, 132, says Burke purposely refused to return to man's origins, though he does not say why. Perhaps Burke thought it would lead him too close to Paine's position. See also Bruce James Smith, *Politics and Remembrance: Republican Themes in Machiavelli, Burke, and Tocqueville* (Princeton: Princeton University Press, 1985).

26. On the mythicization of history, see Martin Buber, *Moses* (Oxford: Oxford University Press, 1947), 17.

27. For the view that the use of natural rights after 1760 was not particularly radical, see Clark, *English Society*, 50: "Natural rights were an absolute survival in the Providential utilitarianism which could provide commonplace assumptions even for a conservative and theocratic universe."

28. Clark, *English Society*, 327–28, mentions, but makes little of, Paine's search for the origin of man's rights in his creation. See also Lock, *Burke's Reflections*, 160 for a view slightly different from mine. On the question whether Burke knew the facts of the French Revolution, see J. T. Boulton, "An Unpublished Letter from Paine to Burke," *Durham University Journal* 43 (Mar. 1951): 49–55.

29. On this point, see Mark Philp, *Paine*, Past Masters Series (Oxford: Oxford University Press, 1989), 56.

30. Richard K. Matthews, *The Radical Politics of Thomas Jefferson* (Lawrence: University of Kansas Press, 1984).

31. *Letter Addressed to the Addressers on the Later Proclamation* (1792), *CW* 2:484.

32. See also *Dissertation on the First Principles of Government* (1795), *CW*, 2:582–83; Fennessy, *Burke, Paine, and the Rights of Man*, 168–69. Chapter 5 is devoted to specific rights and duties in greater detail. See also Aldridge, *Paine's American Ideology*, 114–46.

33. As early as 1776, in a famous passage in *Common Sense* (66), he outlined how this happened. He also accepted the historical fiction of the Lockean social contract. See *Dissertation on First Principles of Government*, *CW*, 2:584–85.

34. Locke, *Second Treatise of Government*, 10, 66. In *Rights of Man*, Paine noted that a man's "natural rights are the foundation of all his civil rights" and that from those rights

which God granted to the people at Creation, civil rights would develop (68).

35. See McWilliams, *Fraternity in America,* 185.

Chapter 5. The Civil Rights of Man

1. Paine [and the Marquis de Condorcet], "Plan of a Declaration," (Oct. 1792), *CW* 2:558. For an example of how commentators have become confused over the issue of rights in Paine, see Moncure Daniel Conway, *Thomas Paine (1737–1809) et la révolution dans les deux mondes,* translated by Felix Rabbe (Paris: Plon-Nourrit, 1900), 157–89 and Aldridge, *Paine's American Ideology,* 126–27. See also Evelyn J. Hinz, "The 'Reasonable' Style of Tom Paine," *Queen's Quarterly* 79 (Summer 1972): 231–41. For the view that Paine did not distinguish between civil and political rights at all, which is not the position taken here, see Gunn, *Beyond Liberty and Property,* 256. For an excellent consideration of natural theory and its medieval and early-modern history, see Tuck, *Natural Rights Theories.*

2. John Stuart Mill, *On Liberty,* edited by Gertrude Himmelfarb (Harmondsworth: Penguin, 1974), 68.

3. Paine [and Condorcet], "Plan of a Declaration," *CW* 2:558.

4. See *RM* 125, 162, 169 and *Dissertation on the First Principles of Government, CW* 2:580, 584.

5. James Madison, *Federalist No. 10,* in Alexander Hamilton, James Madison, and John Jay, *The Federalist Papers,* edited by Clinton Rossiter (New York: New American Library, 1961), 83.

6. Letter to Jefferson, *CW* 2:1298.

7. Ibid.

8. Although Paine appeared to accept the Mosaic account of creation, he most likely did so for rhetorical reasons alone. For his rejection of this idea, see *The Age of Reason.* For the Antichrist, see Christopher Hill, *Antichrist in Seventeenth-Century England* (London: Oxford University Press, 1971). In "The Declaration of Rights of Man and Citizen," which Paine quoted in *Rights of Man,* the first three principles are clearly natural rights. These were not Paine's articulation, as Aldridge says, but were drawn directly from the declaration. See Aldridge, *Paine's American Ideology,* 131.

9. Locke, *Second Treatise of Government,* 9.

10. Ibid., 46–47. See Ian Shapiro, *The Evolution of Rights in Liberal Theory* (Cambridge: Cambridge University Press, 1986), 23–148.

11. Rousseau, *On the Social Contract,* 79.

12. Ibid., 27. See Asher Horowitz, *Rousseau, Nature and History* (Toronto: University of Toronto Press, 1986); Hilail Gildin, *Rousseau's "Social Contract": The Design of the Argument* (Chicago: University of Illinois Press, 1983); John B. Noone, *Rousseau's "Social Contract:" A Conceptual Analysis* (Athens: University of Georgia Press, 1980).

13. Rousseau, *On the Social Contract,* 24.

14. For an interesting assessment of the relationship of music to politics in matters unrelated to those considered here, see Ralph P. Locke, *Music, Musicians, and the Saint-Simonians* (Chicago: University of Chicago Press, 1986).

15. For a different view, see Aldridge, *Paine's American Ideology,* 126–28.

16. "Critical Remarks on Ludlow [Rush]," *CW* 2:274.

17. Letter to Thomas Walker, 14 Apr. 1790, in W.H.G. Armytage, "Thomas Paine

and the Walkers: An Early Episode in Anglo-American Co-operation," *Pennsylvania History* 18 (January 1951): 25.

18. Rousseau, *On the Social Contract*, 26.

19. Ibid., 29.

20. Paine [and Condorcet], "Plan of a Declaration," *CW* 2:559.

21. *Dissertation on the First Principles of Government*, *CW* 2:576–78 generally.

22. See Gunn, *Beyond Liberty and Property*, 242.

23. See Isaac Kramnick, *Republicanism and Bourgeois Radicalism;* "Republican Revisionism Revisited," *American Historical Review* 87 (June 1982): 629–64; and "Religion and Radicalism: English Political Theory in the Age of Revolution," *Political Theory* 5 (Nov. 1977): 505–34.

24. "The Constitution of 1795" (7 July 1795), *CW* 2:590.

25. See also "Serious Address to the People of Pennsylvania," *CW* 2:287–88; *Agrarian Justice, CW* 1:607; and J. P. Selsam, *The Pennsylvania Constitution of 1776* (Philadelphia: University of Pennsylvania Press, 1936).

26. See Kramnick, "Republican Revisionism Revisited" and *Republicanism and Bourgeois Radicalism;* Foner, *Paine and Revolutionary America*.

27. For Paine's enemies, see Aldridge, *Paine's American Ideology*, 95–97, 136 and Foner, *Paine and Revolutionary America*, 261–70.

28. But compare this statement to the one quoted from the *Dissertation on First Principles of Government* in note 33 above, where wealth is the presumptive evil of a dishonest person.

29. Emphasis added. See Fennessy, *Burke, Paine and the Rights of Man*, 173.

30. Locke, *Second Treatise of Government*, 21, 29. Thomas Jefferson to James Madison, 28 Oct. 1785, *The Portable Thomas Jefferson*, edited by Merrill D. Peterson (Harmondsworth: Penguin, 1975), 397.

31. Jefferson to Madison, 9 Sept. 1789, in *The Portable Thomas Jefferson*, 445. See Staughton Lynd, *Intellectual Origins of American Radicalism* (Cambridge: Harvard University Press, 1968), 67–99, and Matthews, *The Radical Politics of Thomas Jefferson*, 19–29.

32. See Staughton Lynd, *Intellectual Origins of American Radicalism*, 76–77, for an account of how Paine's ideas change from *Common Sense* to *Agrarian Justice*, a period of some thirty years.

Chapter 6. National Unity, Revolution, and the Debt

1. Istvan Hont and Michael Ignatieff, eds., *Wealth and Virtue: The Shaping of Political Economy in the Scottish Enlightenment* (Cambridge: Cambridge University Press, 1983), especially John Robertson, "The Scottish Enlightenment at the Limits of the Civic Tradition," pp. 137–78.

2. Hont and Ignatieff, *Wealth and Virtues*, 1–45, and in the same book, Nicholas Phillipson, "Adam Smith as Civic Moralist," 179–202, and Donald Winch, "Adam Smith's 'Enduring Particular Result:' A Political and Cosmopolitan Perspective," 253–71; also Winch, *Adam Smith's Politics: An Essay in Historiographic Revision* (Cambridge: Cambridge University Press, 1978), esp. 146–63.

3. Robertson, "The Scottish Enlightenment," 1–45; J.G.A. Pocock, *Machiavellian Moment*, 493–98, and *Virtue, Commerce and History*, 193–212.

4. Pocock, *Virtue, Commerce and History*, 194–95. See also Winch, *Adam Smith's Politics*, and for America, Drew R. McCoy, *The Elusive Republic: Political Economy in Jeffersonian America* (Chapel Hill: University of North Carolina Press, 1980).

5. Adam Smith, *The Wealth of Nations*, edited by Andrew Skinner (Harmondsworth: Penguin, 1980), 119. It is not clear when Paine first read Smith.

6. See chapter 9 for Paine's vision of how national unity might inaugurate a millennium.

7. Letter to Robert Morris, 20 Nov. 1782, *CW* 2:1215.

8. "Six Letters to Rhode Island," *Providence Gazette* (21 Dec. 1782–1 Feb. 1783), *CW* 2:350.

9. See McWilliams, *Fraternity in America*, 184–85.

10. See Aldridge, *Paine's American Ideology*, 74–75, for the first of these views, and Pocock, *Virtue, Commerce and History*, 289 for the second.

11. Paine was not, of course, a pacifist. War and violence were necessities that sometimes served a virtuous purpose. See Williamson, *Thomas Paine*, 80–81, 123–24; Aldridge, *Paine's American Ideology*, 87–91; Robert P. Falk, "Thomas Paine and the Attitude of the Quakers to the American Revolution," *Pennsylvania Magazine of History and Biography* 63 (1939): 302–10, and, "Thomas Paine: Deist or Quaker?" *Pennsylvania Magazine of History and Biography* 62 (1938): 52–63. For the Quaker view, see Isaac Sharpless, *Two Centuries of Pennsylvania History* (Philadelphia: J. B. Lippincott, 1900), 179–80.

12. See also *The Crisis Extraordinary*, *CW* 1:173–74.

13. Hawke, *Paine*, 318.

14. Pocock, *Machiavellian Moment*, 423–61, and see also Isaac Kramnick, *Bolingbroke and His Circle: The Politics of Nostalgia in the Age of Walpole* (Cambridge: Harvard University Press, 1968).

15. Smith, *Wealth of Nations*, 424.

16. See Foner, *Paine and Revolutionary America*, 145–82.

17. James Gibson, "Attack on Fort Wilson," *Pennsylvania Magazine of History and Biography* 5 (1881): 475–76; John K. Alexander, "The Fort Wilson Incident of 1779: A Case Study of the Revolutionary Crowd," *William and Mary Quarterly* 3d ser. 31 (Oct. 1974): 589–612; C. Page Smith, "The Attack on Fort Wilson," *Pennsylvania Magazine of History and Biography* 78 (Apr. 1954): 177–88. For the background, see Sharon V. Salinger, "Artisans, Journeymen, and the Transformation of Labor in Late Eighteenth-Century Philadelphia," *William and Mary Quarterly*, 3d ser., 40 (Jan. 1983): 62–84, and John K. Alexander, "The Philadelphia Numbers Game: An Analysis of Philadelphia's Eighteenth-Century Population," *Pennsylvania Magazine of History and Biography* 98 (July 1974): 314–24.

18. Foner, *Paine and Revolutionary America*, 166–74; Charles S. Olton, *Artisans for Independence: Philadelphia Mechanics and the American Revolution* (Syracuse: Syracuse University Press, 1975), 82–90; E. James Ferguson, *The Power of the Purse: A History of American Public Finance, 1776–1790* (Chapel Hill: University of North Carolina Press, 1961), 32–33, 122–24, 133–40; Sam Bass Warner, Jr., *The Private City: Philadelphia in Three Periods of Its Growth* (Philadelphia: University of Pennsylvania Press, 1968), 36–43.

19. Ferguson, *Power of the Purse*, 122–24; Olton, *Artisans for Independence*, 89–90; Bray Hammond, *Banks and Politics in America from the Revolution to the Civil War* (Princeton: Princeton University Press, 1957), 50–51.

20. Hawke, *Paine,* 157.

21. Given Paine's reputation as having an unusually high affection for alcohol, it is no wonder he would use such an obviously personal metaphor.

22. Paine's emphasis. Of course, Paine could very well be exaggerating.

23. Although Paine espoused ideas that can be said to be capitalist, he did not deal with the issue of competition. He seemed fairly well certain that capitalism with its internal emphasis on growth would be generally, or universally, beneficial to all citizens.

Chapter 7. Economic Democracy

1. Pocock, *Machiavellian Moment,* 462–67; "Virtue and Commerce in the Eighteenth Century," *Journal of Interdisciplinary History* 3 (1972): 119–34; and *Virtue, Commerce and History,* esp. 41–50.

2. See Anthony Arblaster, *The Rise and Decline of Western Liberalism* (Oxford: Basil Blackwell, 1984), 228–30.

3. Hawke, *Paine,* 10.

4. "The Case of the Officers of Excise," (1772), *CW* 2:5, 7.

5. One commentator describes *Common Sense* as embodying "a new literary tone and style . . . designed to reach a mass audience" (Foner, *Paine and Revolutionary America,* 80). Another has characterized the *Rights of Man* as an outright appeal to "the political have-nots against the ruling class" (Boulton, *Language of Politics,* 135). If sales are a barometer of Paine's appeal, certainly the mass distribution of both works was an eighteenth-century marketing phenomenon. Paine himself believed he was writing for a class of men who possessed the requisite sensibilities and innate virtue to understand his message. He was certainly not addressing any leading class. "Paine had not only to write a political vernacular prose, as he had already done [in *Common Sense*]," but to write in a manner that would refute the political implications of the literary skills represented by Edmund Burke" (Smith, *Politics of Language,* 41).

6. E. P. Thompson, *The Making of the English Working Class* (New York: Vintage, 1963), 79–88, 90, 94, 104, argues that Paine aimed at the workingmen to politicize them after the French Revolution for revolutionary democratic ends. He calls *Rights of Man* "a foundation text of the English working class movement." Foner, *Paine and Revolutionary America,* xvii, 96, 100 states that Paine's republicanism "struck its deepest chords among the artisans." America's commercial expansion would somehow mean that "all classes would share in economic abundance." For Foner, Paine was a bourgeois ideologist who thought that capitalism would strengthen everyone's economic condition. It makes little sense to try to push Paine forward, as Thompson does, to turn him into a proto-Marxist writer. For this reason, Foner is far closer to the true Paine. See also Kramnick, *Republicanism and Bourgeois Radicalism.*

7. Paine, *Address to the People of Pennsylvania,* in the *Pennsylvania Packet* (1 Dec. 1778), *CW* 2:283.

8. Richard Price, *Observations on the Importance of the American Revolution* (London, 1784), 60.

9. Letter to Henry Laurens, Spring 1778, *CW* 2:1142–43.

10. *Prospects on the Rubicon, CW* 2:632, and *RM* 228. Paine's full statement in *Prospects on the Rubicon* reads, "I defend the cause of the poor, of the manufacturers, of the trades-

men, of the farmers, and of all those on whom the real burden of taxes fall—but above all, I defend the cause of humanity."

11. Foner, *Paine and Revolutionary America,* 145–82.

12. In Madison's "Federalist No. 10," in Hamilton et al. *Federalist Papers,* 77–84.

13. It was also a distortion of sorts because Paine's support of the bank and economic progress often made him sound like a Federalist.

14. Paine thought the Federalists had moved far away from their original principles, that is, those of the 1780s, when he had agreed with them on the need for a Bank of the United States. He wrote in 1802, *To the Citizens,* "Letter II" (22 Nov. 1802), *CW* 2:915, that because undoubtedly many younger people did not understand the origins of the name Federalist, it was now "necessary, for their information, to go back and show the origin of the name, which is now no longer what it originally was." He also said, "Letter VIII" (5 June 1803), *CW* 2:955, that Adams and his allies only went "under the assumed and fraudulent name of *federalists.*"

15. See *To the Citizens,* "Letter III" (26 Nov. 1802), *CW* 2:921–23.

16. *To the Citizens,* "Letter VI" (12 Mar. 1803), *CW* 2:938.

17. *To the Citizens,* "Letter I" (15 Nov. 1802), *CW* 2:911.

18. *Constitutional Reform: To the Citizens of Pennsylvania on the Proposal for Calling a Convention,* distributed by the *Aurora,* Aug. 1805, *CW* 2:994.

19. *To the Citizens,* "Letter II" (22 Nov. 1802), *CW* 2:915–16.

20. "Letter III" (29 Nov. 1802), *CW* 2:919.

21. "Letter V" (29 Jan. 1803), *CW* 2:931.

22. "Letter II," *CW* 2:917.

23. "Letter VIII" (5 June 1805), *CW* 2:955. See also *Constitutional Reform, CW* 2:1000.

24. "Remarks on Gouverneur Morris' Funeral Oration," *Aurora,* 7 Aug. 1804, *CW* 2:962.

25. This was not really a classless society because there would be economic differentiation into various levels of the one class Paine referred to. Thus, he was in no way a pre- or proto-Marxist, as Thompson would have us believe. The class he defined included those whose humanity was manifested in their public-spiritedness, which included merchants and manufacturers as well as artisans and tradesmen.

26. Foner, *Paine and Revolutionary America,* 184.

27. "Letters on the Bank," *Pennsylvania Packet* (20 June 1786), *CW* 2:432.

28. Hawke, *Paine,* 121–30; Ferguson, *Power of the Purse,* 117–85; Foner, *Paine and Revolutionary America, passim;* A. Owen Aldridge, "Why Did Thomas Paine Write on the Bank?" *Proceedings of the American Philosophical Society* 93 (Sept. 1945): 309–15; Joseph Dorfman, "The Economic Philosophy of Thomas Paine," *Political Science Quarterly* 53 (Sept. 1953): 372–86; Janet Wilson, "The Bank of North America and Pennsylvania Politics, 1781–1787," *Pennsylvania Magazine of History and Biography* 66 (Jan. 1942): 3–28; E. James Ferguson, "The Nationalists of 1781–1783 and the Economic Interpretation of the Constitution," *Journal of American History* 61 (Sept. 1969): 241–61; M. L. Bradbury, "Legal Privilege and the Bank of North America," *Pennsylvania Magazine of History and Biography* 96 (Apr. 1972): 139–66.

29. Quoted in Clarence L. Ver Steeg, *Robert Morris, Revolutionary Financier* (Philadelphia: University of Pennsylvania Press, 1954), 38. See also Ferguson, *Power of the Purse,* 118–20.

30. "To the Public," *Freeman's Journal* (13 Mar. 1782), *CW* 2:187.

31. On this point, see John W. Seaman, "Thomas Paine: Ransom, Civil Peace, and the Natural Right to Welfare," *Political Theory* 16 (Feb., 1988): 120–42.

32. "Thus Paine's argument for welfare in *Rights of Man* rests on the doctrine of natural rights, not on utilitarian or other ethical grounds. Compensatory claims to welfare emerge when individual's property rights are dealt with in a way that violates their natural right of equal treatment" (Seaman, "Thomas Paine," 128).

Chapter 8. Constitutional Invention

1. Conway, *Life of Paine*, Appendix B, 2:468.

2. Hawke, *Paine*, 165.

3. Paine to Benjamin Franklin, 31 Mar. 1787, *CW* 2:1261.

4. Hawke, *Paine*, 161.

5. "Useful and Entertaining Hints" (1775), *CW* 2:1024–25.

6. Letter to Benjamin Franklin, 6 June 1786, *CW* 2:1027–28.

7. Letter to Sir George Staunton, Spring 1789, *CW* 2:1044–45.

8. Letter to Franklin, *CW* 2:1028.

9. "The Construction of Iron Bridges" (June 1803), *CW* 2:1051. Paine did, however, apply for a patent in England possibly because he wanted to reap a profit, possibly because he sought retribution from England for the failures of his first thirty-seven years or for England's mistreatment of America in the years before the Revolution.

10. "Thoughts on Defensive War," *Pennsylvania Magazine* (July 1775), *CW* 2:53, and "Shall Louis XVI Be Respited?" (19 Jan. 1793), *CW* 2:556. Aldridge, *Paine's American Ideology*, 87–89.

11. "Thoughts on Defensive War," *Pennsylvania Magazine* (July 1775), *CW* 2:52–53.

12. "Of the Comparative Powers and Expense of Ships of War, Gun-Boats, and Fortifications" (n.d.), *CW* 2:1075. See A. Owen Aldridge, "Thomas Paine and the New York *Public Advertiser*," *New York Historical Society Quarterly* 37 (Oct. 1953): 361–82. Of course, Paine turned out to be ludicrously and decisively wrong about the use of gunboats.

13. "Reasons for Preserving the Life of Louis Capet" (15 Jan. 1793), *CW* 2:555.

14. In *Common Sense*, however, Paine spoke of the English constitution as only being "flawed." See *CS* 68–71.

15. "Address to the People of Pennsylvania," *Pennsylvania Packet* (Dec. 1778), *CW* 2:281. Most commentators have suggested that Paine totally lacked a concern for history, that he had no historical consciousness. As proof, they cite passages such as the following: "Every age and generation must be as free to act for itself, in all cases, as the ages and generations which preceded it." He went on to say in this sentence, which echoes Jefferson, that "it is the living, not the dead, that are to be accommodated" (*RM* 41–42). The following analysis shows that this assessment is wrongheaded.

16. "Answer to Four Questions," *Chronique du mois* (June–July 1792), *CW* 2:528 (emphasis added).

17. *American Crisis, No. V* (21 Mar. 1778), *CW* 1:123. See Richard M. Gummere, "Thomas Paine: Was He Really Anticlassical?" *American Antiquarian Society, Proceedings* 75 (Oct. 1965): 253–69, and A. Owen Aldridge, "Thomas Paine and the Classics," *Eighteenth-Century Studies* 1 (June 1968): 370–80.

18. "Address to the People of Pennsylvania," *Pennsylvania Packet* (1 Dec. 1778), *CW* 2:280; *Letters on the Bank,* "Letter II," *Pennsylvania Packet* (7 Apr. 1786), *CW* 2:422; *Dissertation, CW* 2:585; and *RM* 199–200.

19. *Address and Declaration* (1791), *CW* 2:536.

20. *Address to the Addressers* (1792), *CW* 2:484.

21. "Answer to Four Questions," *Moniteur* (16 July 1791), *CW* 2:531–32.

22. Miller, *Rousseau,* 113–17.

23. Rousseau, *On the Social Contract,* bk. 3, 55.

24. Ibid., bk. 3, 74.

25. See Gunn, *Beyond Liberty and Property,* 242–59.

26. And the case of Northern Ireland in our own.

27. For a different view, see Aldridge, *Paine's American Ideology,* 263–64.

28. "Answer to Four Questions," *CW* 2:523–24.

29. See also *The Eighteenth Fructidor* (1797), *CW* 2:597.

30. "An Essay for the Use of New Republicans," *Le Patriote français* (20 Oct. 1792), *CW* 2:546.

31. "Answer to Four Questions," *CW* 2:524, 527.

32. Locke, *Second Treatise of Government,* 113. Richard Nixon, for one, experienced a taste of this effect when, through his prevarications and artifices, he tried to stonewall the true story of the Watergate break-in in 1972.

Chapter 9. The Vision of the Future

1. Letter to Anonymous, 12 May 1797, *CW* 2:1397. See Hole, *Pulpits,* 142–43.

2. This is generally accepted. See Ruth H. Bloch, *Visionary Republic: Millennial Themes in American Thought, 1756–1800* (Cambridge: Cambridge University Press, 1985), 194–201; Bernard Bailyn, *Pamphlets of the American Revolution, 1750–1776,* (Cambridge: Belknap Press of Harvard University Press, 1965); Fennessy, *Burke, Paine and the Rights of Man,* 180; Albert Goodwin, *The Friends of Liberty: The English Democratic Movement in the Age of the French Revolution* (Cambridge: Harvard University Press, 1979), 171–76; Thompson, *Making of the English Working Class,* 90–94; Foner, *Paine and Revolutionary America,* 71–106; Aldridge, *Paine's American Ideology,* 17–26.

3. See the following examples in *Rights of Man:* 145–47, 161, 213, 217–23. See also Jack Greene, "Paine, America, and the 'Modernization' of Political Consciousness," *Political Science Quarterly* 93 (Spring 1978): 73–92 and Stephen Newman, "A Note on *Common Sense* and Christian Eschatology," *Political Theory* 6 (Feb. 1978): 101–8.

4. The phrase *secular millennialism* is from Foner, *Paine and Revolutionary America,* 216. See also Eric Foner, "Tom Paine's Republic: Radical Ideology and Social Change," in *The American Revolution: Explorations in the History of American Radicalism* (DeKalb: Northern Illinois University Press, 1976), 205, and J.F.C. Harrison, *The Second Coming: Popular Millenarianism, 1780–1820* (New Brunswick: Rutgers University Press, 1979), 77, as well as "Thomas Paine and Millenarian Radicalism," in Dyck, *Citizen of the World,* 73–85. Newman, "A Note on *Common Sense,*" places Paine's "Lockean theory of republican government [at least in *Common Sense*] within an eschatological framework." For a different view, see Bloch, *Visionary Republic,* 194–201, which maintains that Paine was a utopian writer par excellence, adding that the *Rights of Man* was "the most important utopian Enlightenment text to appear in either England or America" (190).

5. Clarke Garrett, *Respectable Folly: Millenarians and the French Revolution in England and France* (Baltimore: Johns Hopkins University Press, 1975) and Jack Fruchtman, Jr., *The Apocalyptic Politics of Richard Price and Joseph Priestley: A Study in Late Eighteenth-Century English Republican Millennialism* (Philadelphia: American Philosophical Society, Transactions, 73, pt. 4, 1983).

6. Joseph Priestley to Theophilus Lindsey, May 17, 1795, in *The Theological and Miscellaneous Works of Joseph Priestley,* edited by John Towill Rutt, 25 vols. (Hackney, 1816–31), 1 (pt. 2): 302.

7. Priestley to Thomas Belsham, 14 Aug. 1796, *Works,* 1 (pt. 2): 351.

8. Priestley, *An Appeal to the Serious and Candid Professors of Christianity* (1770), *Works,* 2:384.

9. Priestley to Belsham, 5 June 1798, *Works,* 1 (pt. 2): 401. Priestley was referring to the great increase of knowledge that was to accompany the millennium. See Charles Webster, *The Great Instauration: Science, Medicine and Reform* (London: Duckworth, 1975).

10. See Harry Hayden Clark, "Historical Interpretation of Paine's Religion," and Robert Falk, "Paine: Deist or Quaker?" For a revisionist view, see Franklyn K. Prochaska, "Thomas Paine's *The Age of Reason* Revisited," *Journal of the History of Ideas* 33 (Oct.–Dec. 1972): 561–76.

11. "The Existence of God" (1797), *CW* 2:749.

12. *Prosecution of "The Age of Reason," CW* 2:737.

13. See Joseph Priestley, *A Continuation of the Letters to the Philosophers and Politicians of France* (Northumberland, 1794), in *Works,* 21:109ff.

14. The idea that a "good" religion teaches man to be "good" is fraught with ambiguity, especially since, perhaps intentionally, Paine never defined what he meant by *good.*

15. Joseph Priestley, *The Present State of Europe, Compared with Ancient Prophecies* (London, 1794), *Works,* 15:543, 548–49.

16. Priestley to Lindsey, 1 Nov. 1798, *Works,* 1 (pt. 2): 402.

17. Priestley to Belsham, 5 June 1798, *Works,* 1 (pt. 2): 402.

18. Thomas Belsham, *Memoirs of the Late Reverend Theophilus Lindsey* (London: Williams & Norgate, 1873), 243n. See also Joseph Priestley, *Notes on All Books of Scripture* (Northumberland, 1804), in *Works,* 12:329, and Priestley to Benjamin Rush, 8 Aug. 1799, in *The Scientific Correspondence of Joseph Priestley,* edited by Henry Carrington Bolton (New York: privately printed, 1892), 156.

19. Letter to John Inskeep, *Philadelphia Aurora* (10 Feb. 1806), *CW* 2:1480.

20. Ibid., *CW* 2:1480.

21. Letter to Anonymous, *CW* 2:1396.

22. Letter to Thomas Jefferson, 30 Jan. 1806, *CW* 2:1478.

23. Letter to Jefferson, 3 Sept. 1803, *CW* 2:1449.

24. Letter to George Washington, 1 May 1790, *CW* 2:1303.

25. "To the Citizens of the United States," *National Intelligencer* (5 June 1805), *CW* 2:956.

26. "The Will of Thomas Paine" (18 Jan. 1809), *CW* 2:1500.

27. Letter to Gilbert Wakefield, 19 Nov. 1795, *CW* 2:1383.

28. Letter to Kitty Nicholson Few, 6 Jan. 1789, *CW* 2:1276. Much of the analysis in this section is speculative, though solidly based on Paine's language.

29. See Newman, "A Note on *Common Sense*," 104–6 and Catherine L. Albanese, *Sons of the Fathers: The Civil Religion of the American Revolution* (Philadelphia: Temple University Press, 1976).

30. See a repeat of this traditionally Protestant millennialist notion in *Rights of Man*, 184.

31. See Hill, *Antichrist in Seventeenth-Century England*.

32. Price, *Observations on the American Revolution*. Like Priestley, Price held a millennialist faith that was Christ centered and prophetic. See Fruchtman, *Apocalyptic Politics*.

33. John Bunyan, *The Pilgrims's Progress* (New York: Rinehart, 1957), 117.

34. Richard Price, *The Evidence for a Future Period of Improvement in the State of Mankind* (London, 1787), 24, and Nathan O. Hatch, *The Sacred Cause of Liberty: Republican Thought and the Millennium in Revolutionary New England* (New Haven: Yale University Press, 1975), frontispiece.

35. Richard Price, *Observations on the Nature of Civil Liberty* (London, 1776), 8–9. See also Richard Price, *Discourse on the Love of Our Country* (London, 1790), 13.

36. Joseph Priestley, *A Sermon Preached at the Gravel-Pit Meeting* (London, 1793), *Works*, 15:513.

37. See also *RM* 160, 268–70, and *Letter to the Abbé Raynal, CW* 2:211–63; also Darrel Abel, "The Significance of the Letter to the Abbé Raynal in the Progress of Thomas Paine's Thought," *Pennsylvania Magazine of History and Biography* 66 (Apr. 1942): 176–90.

Chapter 10. Conclusion

1. For a study of those who would follow in Paine's pathway, see Michael Durey, "Thomas Paine's Apostles: Radical Emigres and the Triumph of Jeffersonian Republicanism," *William and Mary Quarterly*, 3d ser., 44 (Oct. 1987): 661–88.

2. *To the Citizens of the United States*, "Letter VIII," *Philadelphia Aurora*, 7 June 1805, *CW* 2:957.

3. For Rousseau, see Miller, *Rousseau*, esp. 6–8, 194–201.

4. "An Essay on Dream" (Paris, 1803; Philadelphia, 1807), *CW* 2:845 (emphasis added).

BIBLIOGRAPHY

Manuscript Sources

Richard Gimbel Collection of Thomas Paine Manuscripts, American Philosophical Society, Philadelphia.

Original Printed Sources

Belsham, Thomas. *Memoirs of the Late Theophilus Lindsey*. London and Edinburgh: Williams & Norgate, 1873.

Bunyan, John. *Pilgrim's Progress*. New York: Rinehart, 1957.

Burke, Edmund. *The Correspondence of Edmund Burke*, edited by Thomas W. Copeland. Cambridge: Cambridge University Press, 1960.

————. *Reflections on the Revolution in France*, edited by Conor Cruise O'Brien. Harmondsworth: Penguin, 1969.

————. *The Works of the Right Honourable Edmund Burke*. London: Rivington, 1826.

De Crèvecoeur, J. Hector St. John. *Letters from an American Farmer and Sketches of Eighteenth-Century America*, edited by Albert E. Stone. Harmondsworth: Penguin, 1981.

Hamilton, Alexander, James Madison, and John Jay. *The Federalist Papers*, edited by Clinton Rossiter. New York: New American Library, 1961.

Hobbes, Thomas. *Leviathan*, edited by Michael Oakeshott. London: Collier, 1962.

Jefferson, Thomas. *The Portable Jefferson*, edited by Merrill D. Peterson. Harmondsworth: Penguin, 1975.

Locke, John. *Second Treatise of Government*, edited by C. B. MacPherson. Indianapolis: Hackett, 1980.

Machiavelli, Niccolo. *The Discourses*, edited by Bernard Crick. Harmondsworth: Penguin, 1970.

Mill, John Stuart. *On Liberty*, edited by Gertrude Himmelfarb. Harmondsworth: Penguin, 1974.

Paine, Thomas. *Common Sense,* edited by Isaac Kramnick. Harmondsworth: Penguin, 1976.
———. *The Complete Writings of Thomas Paine,* edited by Philip S. Foner. 2 vols. New York: Citadel, 1945.
———. *Rights of Man,* edited by Henry Collins, with an introduction by Eric Foner. Harmondsworth: Penguin, 1984.
———. *The Thomas Paine Reader,* edited by Michael Foot and Isaac Kramnick. Harmondsworth: Penguin, 1987.
Price, Richard. *Discourse on the Love of Our Country.* London, 1790.
———. *The Evidence for a Future Period of Improvement in the State of Mankind.* London, 1787.
———. *Observations on the Importance of the American Revolution.* London, 1784.
———. *Observations on the Nature of Civil Liberty.* London, 1776. Reprinted in *Two Tracts on Civil Liberty,* London, 1778.
———. *Observations on Reversionary Payments,* 2d ed. London, 1772.
Priestley, Joseph. *The Scientific Correspondence of Joseph Priestley,* edited by Henry Carrington Bolton. New York: privately printed, 1892.
———. *The Theological and Miscellaneous Works of Joseph Priestley,* edited by J. T. Rutt. 25 vols. Hackney, 1816–31.
Reid, Thomas. *An Inquiry into the Human Mind,* edited by Timothy Duggan. Chicago: University of Chicago Press, 1970.
Rousseau, Jean-Jacques. *The Confessions,* edited by J. M. Cohen. Harmondsworth: Penguin, 1979.
———. "Discourse on the Origin and Foundations of Inequality among Men," edited by Roger D. Masters. New York: St. Martin's Press, 1964.
———. *Emile, or On Education,* edited by Allan Bloom. New York: Basic Books, 1979.
———. "Letter to M. D'Alembert on the Theatre," in *Politics and the Arts,* edited by Allan Bloom. Ithaca: Cornell University Press, 1968.
Rush, Benjamin. *The Autobiography of Benjamin Rush,* edited by George Corner. Princeton, N.J.: Princeton University Press, 1948.
Smith, Adam. *The Wealth of Nations,* edited by Andrew Skinner. Harmondsworth: Penguin, 1980.
Spinoza, Benedict de. *The Chief Works of Benedict de Spinoza,* translated by R.H.M. Elwes. London: George Ball, 1900.
———. *The Correspondence of Spinoza,* edited by A. Wolf. London: Frank Cass & Co., 1966.
Walpole, Horace. *Horace Walpole's Correspondence,* edited by W. S. Lewis. New Haven: Yale University Press, 1961.

Secondary Sources: Books

Albanese, Catherine L. *Sons of the Fathers: The Civil Religion of the American Revolution.* Philadelphia: Temple University Press, 1976.
Aldridge, Alfred Owen. *Man of Reason: The Life of Thomas Paine.* Philadelphia: Lippincott, 1959.
——— *Benjamin Franklin and Nature's God.* Durham: Duke University Press, 1967.

————. *Shaftesbury and the Deist Manifesto.* Philadelphia: American Philosophical Society, Transactions, vol. 41, pt. 2, 1951.

————. *Thomas Paine's American Ideology.* Newark: University of Delaware Press, 1985.

Alexander, John K. *Render Them Submissive: Responses to Poverty in Philadelphia, 1760–1800.* Amherst: University of Massachusetts Press, 1980.

Allison, Henry E. *Benedict de Spinoza.* Boston: Twayne, 1975.

Alston, William P. *Philosophy of Language.* Englewood Cliffs, N.J.: Prentice Hall, 1964.

Arblaster, Anthony. *The Rise and Decline of Western Liberalism.* Oxford: Basil Blackwell, 1984.

Ayer, Alfred J. *Thomas Paine.* London: Secker & Warburg, 1988.

Backo, Bronislaw. *Lumière de l'utopie.* Paris: Payot, 1978.

Bailyn, Bernard. *Pamphlets of the American Revolution, 1750–1776.* Cambridge: Belknap Press of Harvard University Press, 1965.

————. *The Ideological Origins of the American Revolution.* Cambridge: Harvard University Press, 1967.

Bellah, Robert N. *The Broken Covenant: American Civil Religion in the Time of Trial.* New York: Seabury Press, 1975.

Berens, John F. *Providence and Patriotism in Early America, 1640–1815.* Charlottesville: University Press of Virginia, 1978.

Billington, James H. *Fire in the Minds of Men: Origins of the Revolutionary Faith.* New York: Basic Books, 1980.

Black, Max. *Models and Metaphors.* Ithaca: Cornell University Press, 1962.

Bloch, Ruth H. *Visionary Republic: Millennial Themes in American Thought, 1756–1800.* Cambridge: Cambridge University Press, 1985.

Blum, Carol. *Rousseau and the Republic of Virtue: The Language of Politics in the French Revolution.* Ithaca: Cornell University Press, 1986.

Boulton, James T. *The Language of Politics in the Age of Wilkes and Burke.* Westport, Conn.: Greenwood Press, 1975.

Bridenbaugh, Carl. *Mitre and Sceptre: Transatlantic Faiths, Ideas, Personalities, and Politics, 1689–1775.* New York: Oxford University Press, 1962

Buber, Martin. *Moses.* Oxford: Oxford University Press, 1947.

Claeys, Gregory. *Thomas Paine: Social and Political Thought.* Winchester: Unwin Hyman, 1989.

Clark, J.C.D. *English Society, 1688–1820: Ideology, Social Structure and Political Practice.* Cambridge: Cambridge University Press, 1985.

Collins, James. *Spinoza on Nature.* Carbondale: Southern Illinois University Press, 1984.

Cone, Carl B. *Burke and the Nature of Politics,* vol. 2. Louisville: University of Kentucky Press, 1964.

Conway, Moncure D. *The Life of Thomas Paine.* 2 vols. New York: Putnam, 1892.

————. *Thomas Paine 1737–1809 et la révolution dans les deux mondes,* translated by Felix Rabb. Paris: Plon-Nourrit, 1900.

Dickinson, H. T. *Liberty and Property: Liberal Political Thought in Eighteenth-Century Britain.* New York: Holmes & Meier, 1977.

Dreyer, Frederick A. *Burke's Politics: A Study in Whig Orthodoxy.* Waterloo, Ont.: Wilfrid Laurier University Press, 1979.

Dunn, John. *The Political Thought of John Locke: An Historical Account of the "Two Treatises of Government."* Cambridge: Cambridge University Press, 1969.

——. *Rethinking Modern Political Theory.* Cambridge: Cambridge University Press, 1985.

Dyck, Ian. *Citizen of the World: Essays on Thomas Paine.* London: Christopher Helm, 1987.

Ellenburg, Stephen. *Rousseau's Political Philosophy: An Interpretation from Within.* Ithaca: Cornell University Press, 1976.

Feingold, Richard. *Nature and Society: Later Eighteenth Century Uses of the Pastoral and Georgic.* New Brunswick, N.J.: Rutgers University Press, 1978.

Fennessy, R. R. *Burke, Paine and the Rights of Man: A Difference of Political Opinion.* The Hague: Martinus Nijhoff, 1963.

Ferguson, E. James. *The Power of the Purse: A History of American Public Finance, 1776–1790.* Chapel Hill: University of North Carolina Press, 1961.

Feuer, Lewis Samuel. *Spinoza and the Rise of Liberalism.* Boston: Beacon Press, 1958.

Fink, Zera S. *The Classical Republicans: An Essay on the Recovery of a Pattern of Thought in Seventeeth Century England.* Evanston: Northwestern University Press, 1945.

Fliegelman, Jay. *Prodigals and Pilgrims: The American Revolution against Patriarchal Authority, 1750–1800.* Cambridge: Cambridge University Press, 1982.

Foner, Eric. *Tom Paine and Revolutionary America.* New York: Oxford University Press, 1976.

Freeman, Michael. *Edmund Burke and the Critique of Political Radicalism.* Chicago: University of Chicago Press, 1980.

Fruchtman, Jack, Jr. *The Apocalyptic Politics of Richard Price and Joseph Priestley: A Study in Late Eighteenth-Century English Republican Millennialism.* Philadelphia: American Philosophical Society. Transactions, vol. 73, pt. 4, 1983.

Garrett, Clarke. *Respectable Folly: Millenarians and the French Revolution in England and France.* Baltimore: Johns Hopkins Univeristy Press, 1975.

Gildin, Hilail. *Rousseau's "Social Contract:" The Design of the Argument.* Chicago: University of Chicago Press, 1983.

Goodwin, Albert. *The Friends of Liberty: The English Democratic Movement in the Age of the French Revolution.* Cambridge: Harvard University Press, 1979.

Gunn, J.A.W. *Beyond Liberty and Property: The Process of Self-Recognition in Eighteenth-Century Political Thought.* Montreal: McGill-Queen's University Press, 1983.

Hammond, Bray. *Banks and Politics in America from the Revolution to the Civil War.* Princeton, N.J.: Princeton University Press, 1957.

Hare, R. M. *The Language of Morals.* Oxford: Clarendon Press, 1952.

Harrison, J.F.C. *The Second Coming: Popular Millenarianism, 1780–1820.* New Brunswick, N.J.: Rutgers University Press, 1979.

Hatch, Nathan. *The Democratization of American Christianity.* New Haven: Yale University Press, 1989.

——. *The Sacred Cause of Liberty: Republican Thought and the Millennium in Revolutionary New England.* New Haven: Yale University Press, 1975.

Hawke, David Freeman. *Paine.* New York: Harper & Row, 1974.

Heimert, Alan. *Religion and the American Mind.* Cambridge: Harvard University Press, 1966.

Henderson, Ernest F. *Symbol and Satire in the French Revolution*. New York: G. P. Putnam's, 1912.

Hill, Christopher. *Antichrist in Seventeenth-Century England*. London: Oxford University Press, 1971.

———. *The World Turned Upside Down: Radical Ideas during the English Revolution*. New York: Viking, 1972.

Hole, Robert. *Pulpits, Politics and Public Order in England, 1760–1832*. Cambridge: Cambridge University Press, 1989.

Hont, Istvan, and Michael Ignatieff, eds. *Wealth and Virtue: The Shaping of Political Economy in the Scottish Enlightenment*. Cambridge: Cambridge University Press, 1983.

Horowitz, Asher. *Rousseau, Nature and History*. Toronto: University of Toronto Press, 1986.

Hudson, Winthrop S., ed. *Nationalism and Religion in America: Concepts of American Identity and Mission*. New York: Harper & Row, 1970.

Jacob, Margaret C. *The Radical Enlightenment: Pantheists, Freemasons and Republicans*. London: George Allen & Unwin, 1981.

Jehlen, Myra. *American Incarnation: The Individual, the Nation, and the Continent*. Cambridge: Harvard University Press, 1986.

Kates, Gary. *The Cercle Social, the Girondins and the French Revolution*. Princeton: Princeton University Press, 1985.

Kramnick, Isaac. *Bolingbroke and His Circle: The Politics of Nostalgia in the Age of Walpole*. Cambridge: Harvard University Press, 1968.

———. *Republicanism and Bourgeois Radicalism: Political Ideology in Late Eighteenth-Century England and America*. Ithaca: Cornell University Press, 1990.

———. *The Rage of Edmund Burke: Portrait of an Ambivalent Conservative*. New York: Basic Books, 1977.

Lewis, R.W.B. *The American Adam: Innocence, Tragedy, and Tradition in the Nineteenth Century*. Chicago: University of Chicago Press, 1955.

Lincoln, Anthony. *Some Political and Social Ideas of English Dissent*. New York: Octagon, 1971.

Lock, F. P. *Burke's Reflections on the Revolution in France*. London: George Allen & Unwin, 1985.

Locke, Ralph P. *Music, Musicians, and the Saint-Simonians*. Chicago: University of Chicago Press, 1986.

Lynd, Staughton. *Intellectual Origins of American Radicalism*. Cambridge: Harvard University Press, 1968.

McCoy, Drew R. *The Elusive Republic: Political Economy in Jeffersonian America*. Chapel Hill: University of North Carolina Press, 1980.

McShea, Robert J. *The Political Philosophy of Spinoza*. New York: Columbia University Press, 1968.

McWilliams, Wilson Carey. *The Idea of Fraternity in America*. Berkeley: University of California Press, 1973.

Marx, Leo. *The Machine in the Garden: Technology and the Pastoral Ideal in America*. New York: Oxford University Press, 1964.

Matthews, Richard K. *The Radical Politics of Thomas Jefferson*. Lawrence: University of Kansas Press, 1984.

Meek, Ronald L. *Social Science and the Ignoble Savage.* Cambridge: Cambridge University Press, 1976.

Miller, Charles A. *Jefferson and Nature: An Interpretation.* Baltimore: Johns Hopkins University Press, 1988.

Miller, James. *Rousseau: Dreamer of Democracy.* New Haven: Yale University Press, 1984.

Miller, Perry. *The New England Mind: From Colony to Province.* Cambridge: Belknap Press of Harvard University Press, 1953.

Morgan, Edmund S. *Visible Saints: The History of a Puritan Idea.* New York: New York University Press, 1963.

Noone, John B. *Rousseau's "Social Contract:" A Conceptual Analysis.* Athens: University of Georgia, 1980.

Olton, Charles S. *Artisans for Independence: Philadelphia Mechanics and the American Revolution.* Syracuse, N.Y.: Syracuse University Press, 1975.

Onuf, Peter S. *The Origins of the Federal Republic: Jurisdictional Controversies in the United States, 1775–1787.* Philadelphia: University of Pennsylvania Press, 1983.

Ozouf, Mona. *Festivals and the French Revolution,* translated by Alan Sheridan. Cambridge: Harvard University Press, 1988.

Paulson, Ronald. *Representations of Revolution 1789–1820.* New Haven: Yale University Press, 1983.

Philp, Mark. *Paine.* London: Oxford University Press, Past Masters Series, 1988.

Plattner, Marc F. *Rousseau's State of Nature.* DeKalb: Northern Illinois University Press, 1979.

Poggioli, Renato. *The Oaten Flute: Essays on Pastoral Poetry and the Pastoral Ideal.* Cambridge: Cambridge University Press, 1975.

Powell, David. *Tom Paine: The Greatest Exile.* New York: St. Martin's Press, 1985.

Pocock, J.G.A. *The Machiavellian Moment: Florentine Political Thought and the Atlantic Republican Tradition.* Princeton: Princeton University Press, 1975.

———. *Politics, Language and Time: Essays in Political Thought and History.* New York: Atheneum, 1973.

———. *Virtue, Commerce and History: Essays in Political Thought and History, Chiefly in the Eighteenth Century.* Cambridge: Cambridge University Press, 1985.

Rapaczynski, Andrzej. *Nature and Politics: Liberalism in the Philosophies of Hobbes, Locke, and Rousseau.* Ithaca: Cornell University Press, 1987.

Robbins, Caroline. *The Eighteenth-Century Commonwealthman: Studies in the Transmission, Development and Circumstances of English Liberal Thought from the Restoration of Charles II until the War with the Thirteen Colonies.* Cambridge: Harvard University Press, 1959.

Ryerson, Richard A. *The Revolution Is Now Begun: The Radical Committees of Philadelphia, 1765–1776.* Philadelphia: University of Pennsylvania Press, 1978.

Sanford, Charles L. *The Quest for Paradise: Europe and the American Moral Imagination.* Urbana: University of Illinois Press, 1961.

Selsam, J.P. *The Pennsylvania Constitution of 1776.* Philadelphia: University of Pennsylvania Press, 1936.

Shapiro, Ian. *The Evolution of Rights in Liberal Theory.* Cambridge: Cambridge University Press, 1986.

Sharpless, Isaac. *Two Centuries of Pennsylvania History.* Philadelphia: J. B. Lippincott, 1900.

Shklar, Judith N. *Men and Citizens: A Study of Rousseau's Social Theory.* Cambridge: Cambridge University Press, 1969.

Skinner, Quentin. *The Foundations of Modern Political Thought.* 2 vols. Cambridge: Cambridge University Press, 1978.

Smith, Bruce James. *Politics and Remembrance: Republican Themes in Machiavelli, Burke, and Tocqueville.* Princeton: Princeton University Press, 1985.

Smith, Henry Nash. *Virgin Land: The American West as Symbol and Myth.* Cambridge: Harvard University Press, 1950.

Smith, Olivia. *The Politics of Language, 1791–1819.* Oxford: Clarendon Press, 1984.

Smith, Preserved. *The Age of Reformation.* New York: Henry Holt, 1920.

Stearns, Raymond Phineas. *Science in the British Colonies of America.* Urbana: University of Illinois Press, 1970.

Strout, Cushing. *The New Heavens and the New Earth: Political Religion in America.* New York: Harper & Row, 1974.

Talmon, J. L. *The Origins of Totalitarian Democracy.* New York: W.W. Norton, 1970.

Thompson, E. P. *The Making of the English Working Class.* New York: Vintage, 1963.

Tiersot, J. *Les Fêtes et les chants de la révolution française.* Paris: Hachette, 1908.

Tuck, Richard. *Natural Rights Theories: Their Origin and Development.* Cambridge: Cambridge University Press, 1979.

Ver Steeg, Clarence L. *Robert Morris, Revolutionary Financier,* Philadelphia: University of Pennsylvania Press, 1954.

Voitle, Robert. *The Third Earl of Shaftesbury, 1671–1713.* Baton Rouge: Louisiana State University Press, 1984.

Warner, Sam Bass, Jr. *The Private City: Philadelphia in Three Periods of Its Growth.* Princeton: Princeton University Press, 1957.

Webster, Charles. *The Great Instauration: Science, Medicine and Reform.* London: Duckworth, 1975.

Whitney, Lois. *Primitivism and the Idea of Progress in English Popular Literature in the Eighteenth Century.* Baltimore: Johns Hopkins University Press, 1934.

Williamson, Audrey. *Thomas Paine: His Life, Work and Times.* London: George Allen & Unwin, 1973.

Wilson, David A. *Paine and Cobbett: The Transatlantic Connection.* Montreal: McGill-Queen's University Press, 1988.

Wilson, David Schofield. *In the Presence of Nature.* Amherst: University of Massachusetts Press, 1978.

Winch, Donald. *Adam Smith's Politics: An Essay in Historiographic Revision.* Cambridge: Cambridge University Press, 1978.

Wood, Gordon S. *The Creation of the American Republic, 1776–1787.* Chapel Hill: University of North Carolina Press, 1969.

Secondary Sources: Articles

Abel, Darrel. "The Significance of the Letter to the Abbé Raynal in the Progress of Thomas Paine's Thought." *Pennsylvania Magazine of History and Biography* 66 (Apr. 1942): 176–90.

Aldridge, Alfred Owen. "The Apex of American Literary Nationalism." In *Early American Literature: A Comparative Approach*. Princeton: Princeton University Press, 1982, 186–208.

————. "The Poetry of Thomas Paine." *Pennsylvania Magazine of History and Biography* 79 (Jan. 1951): 89–93.

————. "Thomas Paine and the Classics." *Eighteenth-Century Studies* 1 (June 1968): 370–80.

————. "Thomas Paine and the New York *Public Advertiser*." *New York Historical Society Quarterly* 37 (Oct. 1953): 361–82.

————. "Why Did Thomas Paine Write on the Bank?" *Proceedings of the American Philosophical Society* 93 (Sept. 1945): 309–15.

Alexander, John K. "The Fort Wilson Incident of 1779: A Case Study of the Revolutionary Crowd." *William and Mary Quarterly*, 3d series, 31 (Oct. 1974): 589–612.

————. "The Philadelphia Numbers Game: An Analysis of Philadelphia's Eighteenth-Century Population." *Pennsylvania Magazine of History and Biography* 98 (July 1974): 314–24.

Armytage, W.H.G. "Thomas Paine and the Walkers: An Early Episode in Anglo-American Co-operation." *Pennsylvania History* 18 (Jan. 1951): 16–30.

Barry, Alyce. "Thomas Paine: Privateersman." *Pennsylvania Magazine of History and Biography* 101 (Oct. 1977): 451–61.

Boulton, J. T. "An Unpublished Letter from Paine to Burke." *Durham University Journal* 63 (Mar. 1951): 49–55.

Bradbury, M. L. "Legal Privilege and the Bank of North America." *Pennsylvania Magazine of History and Biography* 96 (Apr. 1972): 139–66.

Buchanan, Michelle. "Savages, Noble and Otherwise, and the French Enlightenment." *Studies in Eighteenth-Century Culture*, vol. 15. Madison: University of Wisconsin Press, 1986, 97–109.

Burrows, Edwin G., and Michael Wallace. "The American Revolution: The Ideology and Psychology of National Liberation." *Perspectives in American History* 6 (1972): 167–306.

Canavan, Francis, S.J. "The Relevance of the Burke-Paine Controversy to American Political Thought." *Review of Politics* 49 (Spring, 1987): 163–76.

Clark, Harry Hayden. "An Historical Interpretation of Thomas Paine's Religion." *University of California Chronicle* 35 (1933): 56–87.

————. "Toward a Reinterpretation of Thomas Paine." *American Literature* 5 (May 1933): 133–45.

Daniels, Stephen. "The Political Iconography of Woodland in Later Georgian England." In Denis Cosgrove and Stephen Daniels, eds., *The Iconography of Landscape: Essays on the Symbolic Representation and Use of Past Environments*. Cambridge: Cambridge University Press, 1988, 43–82.

De Prospo, R. C. "Paine and Sieyès." *Thought* 65 (June 1990): 190–202.

Dorfman, Joseph. "The Economic Philosophy of Thomas Paine." *Political Science Quarterly* 53 (Sept. 1938): 372–86.

Dunn, John. "The Identity of the History of Ideas." *Philosophy* 43 (Apr. 1968): 85–104.

Durey, Michael. "Thomas Paine's Apostles: Radical Emigres and the Triumph of Jeffersonian Republicanism." *William and Mary Quarterly*, 3d ser., 44 (Oct. 1987): 661–88.

Essick, Robert N. "William Blake, Thomas Paine, and Biblical Revelation." *Studies in Romanticism* 30 (Summer 1991): 189–212.

Falk, Robert P. "Thomas Paine and the Attitude of the Quakers to the American Revolution." *Pennsylvania Magazine of History and Biography* 63 (1939): 302–10.

———. "Thomas Paine: Deist or Quaker?" *Pennsylvania Magazine of History and Biography* 62 1938): 52–63.

Ferguson, E. James. "The Nationalists of 1781–1783 and the Economic Interpretation of the Constitution." *Journal of American History* 61 (Sept. 1969): 241–61.

Foner, Eric. "Tom Paine's Republic: Radical Ideology and Social Change." In *The American Revolution: Explorations in the History of American Radicalism.* DeKalb: Northern Illinois University Press, 1976.

Frayling, Christopher, and Robert Wokler. "From the Orang-Utan to the Vampire: Towards an Anthropology of Rousseau." In R. A. Leigh, ed., *Rousseau after Two Hundred Years: Proceedings of the Cambridge Bicentennial Colloquium.* Cambridge: Cambridge University Press, 1982, 109–29.

Fruchtman, Jack, Jr. "Nature and Revolution in Paine's *Common Sense,*" *History of Political Thought* 10 (Autumn 1989): 421–38.

———. "The Revolutionary Millennialism of Thomas Paine." In O. M. Brack, Jr., ed., *Studies in Eighteenth-Century Culture,* vol. 13. Madison: University of Wisconsin Press, 1984, 65–77.

Gibson, James. "Attack on Fort Wilson." *Pennsylvania Magazine of History and Biography* 5 (1881): 475–76.

Godwin-Jones, Robert. "The Rural Socrates Revisited: Kleinjogg, Rousseau, and the Concept of Natural Man." *Eighteenth-Century Life* 7 (Oct. 1981): 86–104.

Greene, Jack P. "Paine, America, and the 'Modernization' of Political Consciousness." *Political Science Quarterly* 93 (Spring 1978): 73–92.

Gummere, Richard M. "Thomas Paine: Was He Really Anticlassical?" *American Antiquarian Society, Proceedings* 75 (Oct. 1965): 253–69.

Harlan, David. "Intellectual History and the Return of Literature." *American Historical Review* 94 (June 1989): 581–609.

———. "Reply to David Hollinger." *American Historical Review* 94 (June 1989): 622–26.

Hinz, Evelyn J. "The 'Reasonable' Style of Tom Paine." *Queen's Quarterly* 79 (Summer 1972): 231–41.

Hollinger, David. "The Return of the Prodigal: The Persistence of Historical Knowing." *American Historical Review* 94 (June 1989): 610–21.

Jehlen, Myra. "J. Hector St. John De Crèvecoeur: A Monarcho-Anarchist in America." *American Quarterly* 31 (Summer 1979): 204–22.

Jordan, Winthrop D. "Familial Politics: Thomas Paine and the Killing of the King." *Journal of American History* 60 (Sept. 1973): 294–308.

Kramnick, Isaac. "Religion and Radicalism: English Political Theory in the Age of Revolution." *Political Theory* 5 (Nov. 1977): 505–34.

———. "Republican Revisionism Revisited." *American Historical Review* 87 (June 1982): 629–64.

McWilliams, Wilson Carey. "Civil Religion in the Age of Reason: Thomas Paine on Liberalism, Redemption, and Revolution." *Social Research* 54 (Autumn 1987): 447–90.

Meng, John J. "The Constitutional Theories of Thomas Paine." *Review of Politics* 8 (July 1946): 283–306.

Newman, Stephen. "A Note on *Common Sense* and Christian Eschatology." *Political Theory* 6 (Feb. 1978): 101–8.

Palmer, R. R. "Thomas Paine—Victim of the Rights of Man." *Pennsylvania Magazine of History and Biography* 66 (Apr. 1942): 161–75.

Paulson, Ronald. "Revolution in the Visual Arts." In Roy Porter and Mikulas Teich, eds., *Revolution in History*. Cambridge: Cambridge University Press, 1986.

Penniman, Howard. "Thomas Paine—Democrat." *American Political Science Review* 37 (Apr. 1943): 244–62.

Pocock, J.G.A. "The History of Political Thought: A Methodological Enquiry." In P. Laslett and W. G. Runciman, eds., *Philosophy, Politics, and Society*, 2d ser. London: Basil Blackwell, 1962, 183–202.

———. "Virtue and Commerce in the Eighteenth Century." *Journal of Interdisciplinary History* 3 (1972): 119–34.

Prochaska, Franklyn K. "Thomas Paine's *The Age of Reason* Revisited." *Journal of the History of Ideas* 33 (Oct.–Dec. 1972): 561–76.

Robbins, Caroline. "The Lifelong Education of Thomas Paine 1737–1809: Some Reflections upon His Acquaintance among Books." *Proceedings of the American Philosophical Society* 127 (June 1983): 135–42.

Salinger, Sharon V. "Artisans, Journeymen, and the Transformation of Labor in Late Eighteenth-Century Philadelphia." *William and Mary Quarterly* 3d ser. 60 (Jan. 1983): 62–84.

Schlessinger, Arthur. "Liberty Tree: A Genealogy." *New England Quarterly* 25 (Dec. 1952): 435–48.

Seaman, John W. "Thomas Paine: Ransom, Civil Peace, and the Natural Right to Welfare." *Political Theory* 16 (Feb. 1988): 20–42.

Skinner, Quentin. "Hermeneutics and the Role of History." *New Literary History* 7 (Autumn 1975): 209–32.

———. "Hobbes' *Leviathan*." *Historical Journal* 7 (1964): 321–33.

———. "Introduction: the Return of Grand Theory." In *The Return of Grand Theory in the Human Sciences*. Cambridge: Cambridge University Press, 1985, 1–20.

———. "The Ideological Context of Hobbes's Political Thought." *Historical Journal* 9 (1966): 286–317.

———. "The Limits of Historical Explanation." *Philosophy* 41 (July 1966): 199–215.

———. "Meaning and Understanding in the History of Ideas." *History and Theory* 8 (1969): 3–53.

Smith, C. Page. "The Attack on Fort Wilson." *Pennsylvania Magazine of History and Biography* 78 (Apr. 1954): 177–88.

Smith, Frank. "The Authorship of 'An Occasional Letter on the Female Sex,'" *American Literature* 2 (Nov. 1930): 277–80.

Tarcov, Nathan. "Locke's 'Second Treatise' and 'The Best Defence against Rebellion,'" *Review of Politics* 43 (Apr. 1981): 198–217.

Wilson, Janet. "The Bank of North America and Pennsylvania Politics, 1781–1787." *Pennsylvania Magazine of History and Biography* 66 (Jan. 1942): 3–28.

INDEX

Adam, 70, 171
Adams, John, 127–29, 164, 194n.14
Adams, Samuel, 181n.6
Affective sensibility and common sense, 20–21, 24–25, 34–35
Agrarian law, 97
Aldridge, A. Owen, 11, 183n.36, 186n.41, 188nn.14–17, 190n.8
Alien and Sedition Acts, 127–28
American national unity, 102–8
American Philosophical Society, 9, 179n.13
Ames, William, 60
Amos, ix
Anabaptists, 60
Ancient constitution, myth of, 13
Antichrist, 83–84, 159, 168; Paine as, 162; pope as, 166; monarchy as, 170
Anticonstitutionalists, the, 32–33
Apocalyptic language, 6, 157–71, 197n.28, 198n.30
Aristotle, 147
Armies, professional standing, 101, 129
Arnold, Benedict, 64
Articles of Confederation, 104, 112, 139
Artifice, 40–58
Artisans, craftsmen, tradesmen, 39, 124–35, 137–38
Audience, Paine's use of, 2, 4–6, 11, 12, 20, 23, 24–25, 39, 41, 44, 72–73, 77–78, 80, 97–98, 106, 130, 147, 157, 172–74, 186n.29, 188n.19, 193nn.5, 6

Babeuf, Gracchus Noël, 123
Bank of England, 111–13
Bank of North America, 15, 113, 116, 131–35, 186n.29; of U.S., 194n.14
Bastille, the, 46–48, 50, 167, 170, 186n.26; and Champ de Mars, 47–48
Bell, Robert, 178n.4
Belsham, Thomas, 158, 161
Berens, John F., x
Bevis, Dr. John, 42
Bible, the, 2–3, 25, 28–29, 59, 70–71, 133, 156–64, 165, 180n.26, 183n.32, 188n.15; Acts, 180n.26; Daniel and Revelation, 158, 167; Isaiah, 168; language of, 4, 157–71; prophecy, 158–64; Sodom and Gemorrah, 142
Bill of Rights (1689), 151
Billington, James H., 55
Blake, William, 184n.7
Bloch, Ruth H., 196n.4
Bonaparte, Napoleon, 15, 161
Bonneville, Benjamin, 187n.45
Bonneville, Marguerite de, 55, 171, 187n.46
Bonneville, Nicholas de, 41, 55–56, 58, 169, 187n.46
Boulton, James T., 185n.18, 193n.5
Bourgeois ideology, 13, 91, 94
Bucolic, 38–42, 184n.8
Bunyan, John, 167
Burke, Edmund, 12, 13, 31, 39, 40, 44, 49–51, 65–73, 78, 83, 87, 93, 94, 101, 117, 122, 143, 144, 145, 166, 172, 174, 175, 189n.25; and concept of

Burke, Edmund, *(cont.)*
  prescription, 65–67, 166; concept of rights, 68–69; Paine's attack on, 67–73; *Reflections on the Revolution in France*, 65–69, 101
Calvinist Elect, 93
Capitalism, 101–3, 122–23, 193n.23
Cato, 61–62
Cercle Social, 41
Cheetham, James, 187n.46
Christ, 157, 159–71
Christianity, as fabulous religion, 2, 38–39, 44, 157, 161–62
Church of England, x–xi, 2, 8, 83–84
Civic humanism. *See* Country ideology
Civil religion, x, 180n.26
Clark, J.C.D., 189nn. 27, 28
Class consciousness, 122–30; and the bank, 130–35; useful classes of citizens, 126–27, 150
Classical antiquity, paradigms of, 144–49
Classical republicanism. *See* Country ideology
Clive, Lord, 63–64
Collegiants, Dutch, 60
Commerce, 105, 109–10, 115, 117–18, 121, 125, 133–34; incompatible with war economies, 110–13
Common sense, concept of, 20–37, 40, 44–45; as reason and sensibility, 21–25, 29, 53, 71; as sensibility, 32; as virtuous, 35
Commonwealthman ideology. *See* Country ideology
Condorcet, Marie-Jean-Antoine-Nicolas de Caritat, marquis de, 169
Congress, U.S., 103–4, 141, 150
Conscience, right of. *See* Toleration, religious
Constitution, American, 81, 144, 147, 155, 170
Constitution, British, 150, 152, 170, 195n.14; Priestley's admiration for, 169–70
Constitution, French: of 1793, 91, 144; of 1795, 91–92, 144
Constitution making, 11, 13, 65, 142–52; as alternative to revolution, 154–55
Constitution of 1776, Pennsylvania, 144, 146, 147
Constitutional amendments, theory of, 11, 146–47, 153–55
Constitutionalists, 33
Conway, Moncure Daniel, 11, 42, 188n.18
Country ideology, 1, 12, 13, 80–81, 90, 114, 117, 121–22, 149, 151, 169
Creation, 10, 44–45, 52–53, 69–72, 78–79, 156,

159, 161, 164, 175, 190n.8; and plurality of worlds, 42–43
Crèvecoeur, J. Hector St. John, 185n.9

Danton, Georges-Jacques, 23
d'Artois, comte de (brother of Louis XVI), 167
David, Jacques-Louis, 46–47
Deane, Silas, 14, 133
"Declaration of Rights of Man and Citizen," 6, 90–91, 167, 190n.8
Deism, 3, 7, 52–53, 157, 160–61
Democracy, as anarchy, 147–48
Democratic republic, xi, 6, 10, 13, 44, 62, 79–80, 86–87, 92, 94, 97–98, 124–25, 138, 155, 170, 175; and economic development, 94–99, 121–24; formation of, 143–52; and millennium, 157–64; and rights, 77–94
Depression (1929), 98
Devil. *See* Satan
Dissenters, 39, 83, 146
Dormancy, idea of, 19
Dutch Collegiants and Quakers (inner light philosophy), 60–61; East Indies, 109. *See also* United Provinces

Economic democracy, 10, 121–38
Economic justice, 97–99, 104
Economics, and finance, 100–118, 130
Economy, natural, 114–18; hard species (gold and silver), 114–17
Elizabeth I, 62
Emlen, George, 132–33, 134, 135
English finance, 111–18, 130–31
Enlightenment, the, 13, 61, 146–47, 162, 196n.4; radical, 52–53
Equality, 57–58, 61–65, 71, 77, 130–35, 149; and rights of man, 89–94
Erskine, Thomas, 52–53

Farmers and cultivators, and backcounty, 133–35; as men of first necessity, 126–27, 131
Federalist Papers, 81
Federalists, 64–65, 124, 126, 155, 162, 163, 164, 172, 173, 194nn.13, 14; Paine's difficulties with, 127–30
Fennessy, R. R., 189n.25
Fêtes révolutionnaires, 46–48, 54, 185n.21
Feuer, Lewis, 60
Findley, William, 132
Fitch, John, 139

Fliegelman, Jay, 181n.5
Foner, Eric, 11–12, 132, 193nn.5, 6, 196n.4
Foner, Philip, 183n.31, 188n.18
Fort Wilson riot, 115
Franklin, Benjamin, 40, 139, 181n.33, 181n.6
Friends, Society of (Quakers), 15, 43, 60–61, 84, 141–42, 187n.5, 192n.11
Frontiersmen, 133–35

Genesis, 159, 170
George III, 23, 24, 127
Georgic, 2. *See also* Bucolic
God, x, xi, xii, 30–32, 36, 50, 51, 83, 92, 97, 99, 139, 171–72; and civil rights, 78–79; as creator, 26–29; as indwelling in nature, 38–42, 58–61, 160, 188n.15; millennial themes and, 155–67; and natural law, 150–51; nature and light in, 52–54; and origins of natural rights, 68–73; and religion of nature, 7–10, 24; and Spinoza, 58–61. *See also* Homiletics; Nature's God; Religion of nature
Gordon riots, 50
Government: as necessary evil, 30–33, 181n.1; and Burke, 66–68
Great Britain: and credit, 131–35; and temperament, 34–37, 51–52, 63; and war economy, 100, 106–7, 117–18
Greene, Gen. Nathanael, 64
Grotius, 60
Gunboats, 42, 142, 195n.12

Hamilton, Alexander, 129
Harrington, James, 12
Hart, Levi, 168
Hatch, Nathan O., 5
Hawke, David Freeman, 11, 112, 186n.41
Hebrews. *See* Jews
Hill, Christopher, 180n.26
History, mythicizing of, 67–73, 145
Homiletics, ix–xi, 1–2, 20–21, 26, 30, 36–39, 44, 46, 49, 59 61, 70, 72, 89, 91, 100; Paine's use of, 4–12, 171–76. *See also* Nature's God; Paine, Thomas; Religion of nature
Homo faber, 10–11, 140–55. *See also* Invention and nature; Paine, Thomas, themes in, invention
Hosea, ix
Howe, Lord, 25
Hudson, Winthrop S., x
Hume, David, 7, 21, 101, 117

Illuminism, 41, 55–56
India, 63–64
Influence, problem of, 13–14
Inheritance tax, 97–99
Innovation, 14, 144 164–66, 171
Inskeep, John, 162
Invention and nature, 2–4, 7, 10–11, 22, 39–40, 43–48, 126, 139–52, 175; and artifice, 70–71; and rights, 77–79, 88–89, 90; and property, 95–99. *See also Homo faber;* Paine, Thomas, themes in, invention
Isaiah, 168

Jacob, Margaret C., 60, 186n.41
Jacobinism, 13
Jefferson, Thomas, 5, 69, 78, 81, 87, 97, 127, 129, 139, 155, 163, 173, 195n.15
Jehlen, Myra, 7
Jeremiah, ix–xi, 163
Jews, 29, 58, 60, 165–66, 183n.33; Restoration of (at the millennium), 159. *See also* Paine, Thomas, themes in, millennium
Jordan, Winthrop S., 25
Judaism, as fabulous theology, 162
Just price, theory of, 116–17

King of Prussia (ship), 42
Kings, lords, commons, 3, 19, 23, 24, 38–39, 51, 71, 108, 124, 150; corruptions of, 25–29
Kramnick, Isaac, 183n.31

Labor, idea of, 95; and theory of value, 96–97, 109–10, 136. *See also* Locke, John
Lafayette, marquis de (Marie Joseph Paul Yves Roch Gilbert Motier), 127, 167
Landscape theme, images of, 38–42, 184nn.8, 9
Language: Paine's use of, 1–15; of country ideology, 13, 148–49; of Georgic, 38–43; of Lockean rights and liberties, 2–3, 33–34; of Madison, 81; of political economy, 100–103; millennial, 156–71; of religion of nature, 4, 7–11, 42–56
Lanthénas, François-Xavier, 169
Laurens, Henry, 126–27
Law/lawmaking, 89–94
Legislative veto, 150
Levellers, 94
Liberty, 1, 19–20, 21, 25–37, 38, 43–48, 49, 51–52, 57, 61, 163; and slavery, 62–65

Liberty, religious, 59. *See* Religious liberty; Toleration
Liberty tree, 49, 51
Lilburne, John, 94
Lincoln, Anthony, 183n.38
Lindsey, Theophilus, 158
Livingstone, Robert, 131
Lock, F. P., 189n.28
Locke, John, 12, 21, 27, 31, 32, 33, 41, 97, 136, 177n.14, 178n.13, 180n.29, 189n.33, 196n.4; and government and society, 30–31; and labor theory of value, 109–10, 136; and natural and civil rights, 58, 71, 85–86; and property rights, 95; and right to revolution, 154; social contract, 1, 24, 81, 84–86. *See also* Rights, civil; Social contract; State of nature
Louis XVI, 23, 29, 141, 182n.18
Luxembourg Prison, 91, 154, 177n.8

Machiavelli, Niccoló, 12
McWilliams, Wilson Carey, 9, 183n.33, 184n.2
Madison, James, 1, 81, 127
Magna Carta, 151
Mandeville, Bernard, 118
Manufacturers and mechanics: and Manichean imagery, 167, 170; as men of second necessity, 126–27, 135
Marat, Jean-Paul, 141
Marxism, 123, 194n.25
Masonry, 41; French, 52, 53–54, 186n.41
Matlock, Timothy, 20, 124
Mayhew, Jonathan, x
Mennonites, and Quakers (inner light philosophy), 60–61
Merchants and shopkeepers, 124–27, 131, 137–38
Meredith, William, 170
Mill, John Stuart, 79
Millennialism, secular, 1–2, 12, 156–71, 197n.9
Miller, Perry, x
Modernization, 130–35
Monied interests, 114
Monroe, James, 163
Montesquieu, Charles de Secondat, 183n.30
Morgan, Edward S., x, 177n.2
Morris, Robert, 15, 20, 104, 116, 124, 127, 131–33
Moses, 64, 190n.8
Music, analogy to politics, 86–89, 190n.14

National Convention (France), 155
National debt, 101–2, 104–13

Natural law, 30–32
Nature, 2–4, 7–11, 41–43, 95, 156, 185n.14; and affection, 20–25, 182n.10; and democracy, 41–42, 44–46, 62, 144; and freedom, 45–48, 49–50, 61–65, and God, 7–8; human, stifled, 19, 20–21, 23–24, 25–29, 38; images of, 19–29, 185n.14; and paper money, 114–17; physical, 19, 38–42; and reason, 20–25; state of, 86–87, 96, 184n.9
Nature's God, 3–4, 8–12, 42, 52–56, 64. *See also* Paine, Thomas, life of, as preacher; Pantheism; Preaching; Religion of nature
Navy, 101, 107, 109, 115
New Deal, 98
Newman, Stephen, 196n.4
New World, 9, 40–41
Nixon, Richard, 196n.32
Nonconformists. *See* Dissenters
Northern Ireland, 196n.26

Old Whig ideology. *See* Country ideology
One, few, many, 13, 148, 175

Paine, Thomas
—*life of*, 14–15, 42–43, 54–56, 125, 139–41, 177n.8, 178n.9, 180n.29, 188n.16, 193nn.21, 23, 195n.9; appeal to various audiences, 2, 4–6, 11–12, 20, 23, 34–35, 39, 41, 72–73, 77–78, 80, 97–98, 106, 130, 147, 157, 172–74, 188n.19, 193nn.5, 6; as atheist, 1, 160–61; and bridge, paradigm of, 13, 140–41, 152, 185n.15, 195n.9; as Cromwellian, 180n.26; as deist, 3, 7, 9–10; and historical consciousness, 144–46, 195n.15; as nonphilosophical, xi, 3; as preacher, ix–xi, 4–12, 36–37; use of various languages, xiii, 1–2, 6–7, 13, 54, 100–106, 157–71; will of, 164–65
—*images in*:, Bastille (*see* Bastille, the); butterflies, 45–46; cattle, 50; denatured man, 3–4, 20, 23, 24, 25–29, 30, 36–37, 142, 153, 156–57, 173; dreams, 176; illumination and light, 22, 47–48, 52–56, 60–61, 62, 167; kings as worms, parasites, 27, 46; Manichean imagery, 167, 170; nature, 44–45, 156; nature's God, 3–4, 8–12, 52–56; oak, 19, 48–52, 186n.34; parasites, 126–27; Saturn devouring his children, 27–28; seasons, 45–46; somnolence, 19–20, 22, 34–35, 151, 153, 172–73, 175–76; spiders, 33, 140, 144, 185n.15
—*themes in*: America, 14–15; the Bible, xi, 2, 4,

160; bridge building, 13, 22, 140–41, 195n.9; common sense, 19–23, 40, 41, 44–45, 56, 71; constitutional amendments, 146, 153–55; economic democracy, 102, 121–38; equality, 59, 61–65, 70, 89–99; exchange of rights, 82–89; experimentation, 139–40, 144, 146–47; free expression, 59, 84–85; government and society, 30–32; human temperament, 32–37; invention, 4, 39–40, 88–89, 95–96, 139–55, 156, 175; millennium, 157–71; mythicization of history, 67–71, 92, 145; national unity, 103–8, 110; natural/unnatural, 22–23, 25–30; novelty, 144–45; paper money, 101, 113–17; poverty, 96–99; private property, 94–99, 124, 136–38; religious liberty, 83–84; representation, 91–94, 148–52; revolution (*see* Revolution); right to work, 95; rights, civil, 2–3, 77–99, 152; rights, natural, 57–73, 80–81; rooting out, 49–50, 186n.34; slavery, 61–65, 94; sociability, 24–25, 30–32, 89, 100; social class, 70–71, 100, 122–37, 150, 194n.25; social welfare, 97–99, 100, 125–26, 135–38, 175, 195n.32; sustenance, 100–101; temperament, 32–35; toleration, 82–83; universal civilization, 156–57, 165–71; use of imagery, 9; voting, 89–94, 152, 175; voting as alternative to revolution, 153; women's liberation, 64–65

—works of: *Age of Reason*, 9, 10, 21–22, 28–29, 38, 42, 45–46, 53 54, 59, 158–63, 165; *Agrarian Justice*, 39, 92–93, 97–99, 136; *American Crisis, The*, 5, 64, 107–8, 110, 171; *Common Sense*, ix, 5, 7, 19–29, 34, 39, 78, 96, 106–7, 115, 117, 127, 164, 165, 167, 170, 173, 195n.14; *Decline and Fall of the English System of Finance, The*, 106, 111–18, 130–31; *Dissertations on Government*, 90–93; *Forester Letters*, 61–63; "Letters on the Bank," 132–35; "Liberty Tree" (poem), 51; "Public Good," 103; *Rights of Man*, xi, 2, 5, 6, 7, 22, 39–40, 41, 45, 54, 58, 65, 67, 69, 77–78, 80, 84, 89, 100, 136, 153, 155, 162–63, 165, 167, 170, 171, 173 188n.19, 189n.34., 196n.4, 198n.30; "Six Letters to the Citizens of Rhode Island," 104–6; "To the Citizens of the United States," 127–29

Palmer, R. R., 59

Pantheism, in Paine's thought, 3, 52–53, 58–61, 160–61

Paper money and credit, debate over, 101, 113–17

Parliament, 64, 150, 152

Pastoral, 2, 38–42. *See* Bucolic; Georgic

Paulson, Ronald, 27

Peale, Charles Willson, 20, 25, 124

Pitt, William, the Younger, 37

Pocock, J.G.A., 101, 107, 114, 121–22, 180n.30, 181n.4

Political argument, structure of, 12

Political economy, 1–2, 12, 100–102, 117. *See* Language

Poor, the, 97–99, 100, 135–38

Poverty, 96, 122, 136; and wealth, 130, 191n.28

Preaching, Paine's style of, ix–xii, 4–8, 36–37, 44, 172–76, 178n.3. *See also* Homiletics; Nature's God; Religion of nature

Prescriptive rights, 65–67, 145. *See also* Burke, Edmund

Price, Richard, 39, 50, 65, 68–69, 126, 166, 168–71, 198n.32; *Discourse on the Love of Our Country*, 65; and millennium, 168–71

Priestley, Joseph, 66, 68–69, 158–64, 165, 197n.9, 198n.32; and millennium, 168–71; and republican government, 169–70

Primogeniture, English system of, 28

Private property, right to, 94–99, 124, 150; and poverty, 136–38; and voting rights, 93–94

Progress, 2–3, 8–12, 13, 15, 40–42, 125–26, 129, 146–47, 156–71; economic, and wilderness, 133–35

Progressive era, 98

Prophets/prophecy, ix–x, 158–63

Providence, as a woman, 64. *See also* Nature's God

Public credit, debate over, 101, 113

Public finance, 11–18, 130–35

Public good, 102–3, 118, 121–22

Puritan, Paine as, 180n.26; and Puritan Revolution, x

Quakers. *See* Friends, Society of

Radicalism, of Paine, 12–15, 125, 153–54, 175–76

Raynal, Abbé Guillaume, 43, 84

Reason, faculty of, 21–23, 68–71, 139, 156–62, 168; Burke's condemnation of, 68–69

Reid, Thomas, 21

Religion, revealed and natural, 7–8

Religion of nature, 1–4, 7–11, 43, 59–60

Religious liberty, 59, 83–84. *See also* Toleration, religious

Renewal, idea of, 44–47

Representation, 148–49

Republic, 13, 80, 122, 151; and apocalypse, 157, 170; with or without king, 169–70

Revolution, advocacy of, 35–36, 77–78, 80–81, 152; distaste for, 91–92, 94, 97–99; worldwide effects of, 169. *See also* Paine, themes in

Revolution, American, ix–x, 20, 29, 32, 33–36, 41, 100–118, 122, 125–26, 141, 152–55; and millennium, 157, 165

Revolution, French, ix–x, 5–6, 15, 30, 32, 35, 36–37, 40–41, 44, 45, 58, 77–80, 89, 90–92, 101, 104, 111, 122–25, 137, 141, 142, 148, 153–55; and millennium, 156–71

Revolutions, general, 35–36, 72–73; and common sense, 22–37

Rhode Island, Paine's letters to, 104–6

Richmond, Duke of (Charles Lennox), 49

Rights, civil, 2–3, 72–73, 77–99, 142, 150–52; of defective power, 78, 87–88; of personal competency, 77, 78, 84–86; of personal protection, 88–89; trial by jury, 152; voting, 89–94, 152, 175

Rights, natural, 56, 57–61, 77–80, 86–88, 142, 189n.27; divine origins of, 67–73, 189n.28; and economic goods, 100–101; exchanged for civil rights, 82–89, 189n.34, 190n.1; and social welfare, 136–38, 175, 195n.32

Rittenhouse, David, 20, 25, 181n.6

Robbins, Caroline, 13–14, 59, 184n.6

Robespierre, Maximilien-Marie-Isidore de, 64, 153, 162, 163

Rousseau, Jean-Jacques, 9, 11, 41, 42, 47–48, 50, 80, 84–86, 88, 89, 103, 147–49, 155, 175, 176, 182n.9, 184n.6, 184n.9; and general will, 85–86, 149

Royal Society of London, 9, 42

Rush, Benjamin, 139, 181n.6

St. Just, Louis-Antoine de, 153, 183n.29

Satan, 10, 26–29, 37, 38, 84, 127–28, 142, 163, 168, 172, 183n.32

Science of politics, 144–45

Scripture. *See* Bible, the

Seaman, John W., 194n.32

Shaftesbury, third earl (Anthony Ashley Cooper), 21, 30

Shklar, Judith N., 178n.15

Sieyès, Abbé Emmanuel-Joseph, 14, 26

Slavery/slave trade, 61–63

Smilie, John, 132–33, 134, 135

Smith, Adam, 101, 102–4, 111, 112–13, 114, 117, 130, 192n.5; *The Wealth of Nations*, 101–3

Smith, Frank, 188n.18

Smith, Olivia, 193n.5

Social contract, 31–32, 50, 71–72, 81–82, 85, 92, 189n.33

Spence, Thomas, 93, 97, 175

Spinoza, Benedict de, 58–61, 187n.5

State of nature, 81, 85–87, 96, 184n.9

Stiles, Ezra, x

Talmon, Jacob, 14, 181n.32

Tempers, passive, 33–39

Terror, the (French revolutionary), 28, 64, 81, 91, 127, 153, 155, 164, 174, 177n.8, 183n.29

Theocritus, 38

Theophilanthropists, 41, 53–56

Thetford, 42–43, 54–55

Thompson, E. P., 193n.6, 194n.25

Toleration, religious, 82–84

Tuck, Richard, 57

Turkish empire, fall of (at millennium), 159. *See also* Paine, Thomas, themes in, millennium

Tyranny, x, 34, 50, 86, 146, 149–50, 162, 166–71, 173–74; financial and economic, 100

United Provinces, 23–24

Universal civilization, 118, 167–71

Universal manhood suffrage, 90–92

Vergniaud, Pierre Victurien, 28

Virgil, 38

Virtue and corruption, language of, 6, 13, 30, 35, 107, 143, 146, 155, 175; and millennium, 167–68; and political economy, 121–24

Wakefield, Gilbert, 165

Walpole, Horace, 47

War: economy, criticisms of, 106–9, 110, 168–69; paradigm of, 141–42

Washington, George, 127

Watergate break-in, 196n.32

Welfare, social, 12, 97–99, 195n.32

Whig government, 100–104

Whig ideology, Old. *See* Country ideology

Whitehill, Robert, 132

Will, general, 85–86, 90, 149, 151, 155

William, Prince of Orange, 62
William the Conqueror, 128, 129, 151
Williamson, Audrey, 42, 186n.41
Wilson, James, 116, 124

Winthrop, John, xi
Wollaston, William, 7
Women: and liberation, 64–65, 188nn.18, 22;
    Providence as a woman, 64, 188n.19

Thomas Paine and the Religion of Nature

Designed by Ann Walston

Composed by Agnew's Electronic Manuscript Processing Service
in Adobe Caslon text and display

Printed by The Maple Press Company
on 50-lb. MV Eggshell Cream